ARIZONA'S OFFICIAL
FISHING GUIDE

181 Top Fishing Spots, Directions & Tips
BY RORY AIKENS

ARIZONA
HIGHWAYS

In Partnership with **ARIZONA GAME & FISH DEPARTMENT**

This book was created as a collaboration between *Arizona Highways* magazine and the Arizona Game and Fish Department.

Text: RORY AIKENS
Photographs: ALL BY RORY AIKENS EXCEPT AS OTHERWISE CREDITED
Book Editor: RANDY SUMMERLIN
Copy Editors: DEBORAH PADDISON AND BETH DEVENY
Designer: MARY WINKELMAN VELGOS
Production Assistant: ANNETTE PHARES
Creative Director: BARBARA GLYNN DENNEY
Photography Editor: JEFF KIDA
Maps: KEVIN KIBSEY

Library of Congress Control Number: 2011934470
ISBN 978-0-9845709-4-2
First printing, 2011. Printed in China.

Published by the Book Division of *Arizona Highways* magazine,
a monthly publication of the Arizona Department of Transportation,
2039 W. Lewis Avenue, Phoenix, Arizona 85009.
Telephone: 602-712-2200
Website: www.arizonahighways.com

Publisher: WIN HOLDEN
Editor: ROBERT STIEVE
Senior Editor/Books: RANDY SUMMERLIN
Managing Editor: KELLY KRAMER
Associate Editor: KATHIE RITCHIE
Creative Director: BARBARA GLYNN DENNEY
Photography Editor: JEFF KIDA
Design Production Assistant: DIANA BENZEL-RICE
Production Director: MICHAEL BIANCHI

Front Cover: Evening and nighttime fishing is popular at Lake Pleasant during the summer. | PAUL MARKOW

Back Cover: A fly fisherman casts into the Little Colorado River near Greer. | RICHARD MAACK

LET'S GO FISHIN'...6

WHITE MOUNTAINS
Region Map...10
1 Becker Lake...12
2 Big Lake...14
3 Carnero Lake ...18
4 Concho Lake...20
5 Crescent Lake...21
6 Fool Hollow Lake...23

Greer Lakes Recreation Area...25
7 Bunch Reservoir...26
8 River Reservoir...28
9 Tunnel Reservoir...28
10 Little Colorado River...29
11 Lee Valley Lake...30
12 Luna Lake...32
13 Lyman Lake...34
14 Nelson Reservoir...36
15 Rainbow Lake...38
16 Scott Reservoir...40
17 Show Low Lake...42
18 Woodland Lake...44

Streams...45
19 West Fork of Little Colorado
   River at Sheeps Crossing...45
20 East Fork of Black River...47
21 West Fork of Black River...48
22 Silver Creek...50

NORTH-CENTRAL ARIZONA
Region Map...54

Flagstaff-Area Lakes...56
1 Ashurst Lake...56
2 Upper Lake Mary...58
3 Lower Lake Mary...58
4 Kinnikinick Lake...60
5 Long Lake...62

Williams-Area Lakes...64
6 Cataract Lake...64
7 Dogtown Reservoir...66
8 JD Dam Lake...68
9 Elk Tank...68
10 Middle Tank...68
11 Perkins Tank...68
12 Kaibab Lake...70
13 Whitehorse Lake...72

Verde Valley-Area Fisheries...74
14 Beaver Creek...74
15 Dead Horse Ranch State
   Park...76
16 Fossil Creek...77
17 Oak Creek...80
18 Verde River (Verde Valley)...82
19 West Clear Creek...84

Prescott-Area Lakes...86
20 Fain Lake...86
21 Goldwater Lake...87
22 Lynx Lake...89

COLORADO RIVER NORTHWEST

Region Map...158
1 Lake Powell...161
2 Wahweap Marina...170
3 Antelope Point Marina...170
4 Halls Crossing Marina...170
5 Bullfrog Marina...171
6 Dangling Rope Marina...171
7 Hite...171
8 Lees Ferry...172
9 Lake Mead...177
10 Boulder Basin...182
11 Overton Arm...182
12 Temple Basin...183
13 Gregg Basin...183
14 Willow Beach...184
15 Lake Mohave...188
16 Cottonwood Cove...191
17 Katherine's Landing...191
18 Below Davis Dam (Casino Row and Beyond)...192
19 Davis Camp...195
20 Fisherman's Access...195
21 Laughlin Bay...195
22 Big Bend State Recreation Area...195
23 Topock Marsh/Havasu National Wildlife Refuge...196
24 Topock Marina/Levee Road...197
25 Topock Marsh...197
26 Lake Havasu...198
27 Windsor Beach State Park...203
28 Cattail Cove State Park...203
29 Chemehuevi Indian Tribe...203

MOGOLLON RIM

Region Map...92
1 Bear Canyon Lake...94
2 Black Canyon Lake...96
3 C.C. Cragin Reservoir (formerly Blue Ridge Reservoir)...98
4 Chevelon Canyon Lake...100
5 Knoll Lake...102
6 Willow Springs Lake...104
7 Woods Canyon Lake...106
Mogollon Rim Streams...109
8 Canyon Creek...109
9 Christopher Creek...111
10 Haigler Creek...113
11 Horton Creek...115
12 Tonto Creek...116
13 East Verde River...119

CENTRAL ARIZONA

Region Map...122
1 Lake Pleasant...124
Salt River Watershed...130
2 Theodore Roosevelt Lake...130
3 Apache Lake...136
4 Canyon Lake...140
5 Saguaro Lake...143
6 Lower Salt River...146
7 Tempe Town Lake...149
Verde River Watershed...152
8 Bartlett Lake...152
9 Horseshoe Lake...152

COLORADO RIVER SOUTHWEST

Region Map...206
1 Parker Strip...208
2 Buckskin Mountain State Park...210
3 River Island State Park...210
4 La Paz County Park...210
5 Colorado River (between Palo Verde Diversion Dam and Walter's Camp)...211
6 Mayflower County Park, Riverside County, California...213
7 Riviera Blythe Marina Park...213
8 McIntyre Park...213
9 Palo Verde Park...213
10 Cibola National Wildlife Refuge...213
11 Colorado River (between Walter's Camp and Picacho State Park)...214
12 Walter's Camp...215
13 Colorado River (between Picacho State Recreation Area and Imperial Dam)...216
14 Picacho State Park...218
15 Martinez Lake...218
16 Fishers Landing...218
17 Meer's Point (Imperial National Wildlife Refuge)...219
18 Hidden Shores...219
19 Squaw Lake Area...219
20 Mittry Lake...220
21 Colorado River (between Laguna Dam and Morelos Dam)...222
22 Morelos Dredge Launch...222
23 Mode II...222
24 Yuma West Wetlands Park...223
25 Backwater No. 33 (Colorado River)...223
26 Gila River Confluence...223
Yuma Area Ponds...224
27 Fortuna Pond...224
28 Redondo Pond...224
29 Yuma West Wetlands Pond...224
30 Alamo Lake...226

SOUTHEAST ARIZONA

Region Map...230
1 Arivaca Lake...232
2 Peña Blanca Lake...234
3 Patagonia Lake...236
4 Parker Canyon Lake...238
5 Roper Lake...240
6 Riggs Flat Lake...242
7 Rose Canyon Lake...244

INDIAN LANDS

White Mountain Apache Indian Reservation...250
Region Map...250
1 A-1 Lake...252
2 Big Bear Lake (Shush Be Tou)...253
3 Bog Tank...254
4 Bootleg Tank...254
5 Christmas Tree Lake...254
6 Cooley Lake...255
7 Cyclone Lake...255
8 Diamond Creek...255
9 Drift Fence Lake...256
10 Earl Park...256
11 Hawley Lake...257
12 Horseshoe Cienega Lake...257
13 Hurricane Lake...258
14 Little Bear (Shush Be Zahze)...258
15 Pacheta Lake...258
16 Reservation Lake...259
17 Sunrise Lake...260
San Carlos Apache Indian Reservation...262
Region Map...262
1 San Carlos Lake...265
2 Talkalai Lake...267
3 Point of Pines Lake...267
4 Seneca Lake...268
5 Black River...269
6 Salt River...269
Navajo Indian Reservation...270
Region Map...270
1 Cow Springs Lake...272
2 Ganado (Lók aahnteel) Lake...272
3 Many Farms (Dá ák eh Haláni) Lake...275
4 Tsaile (Tséhílí)...276
5 Wheatfields Lake...276

URBAN FISHING PROGRAM...278

ARIZONA'S SPORT FISH...296

FISHING 101: BASIC HOW-TO GUIDE...304

GLOSSARY...310

RESOURCES...330

INDEX...334

Let's Go Fishin'

Despite being an arid state, or maybe because of it, Arizona is blessed with abundant and diverse fishing opportunities, from the enormous impoundments along the Colorado River to the intimate trout lakes in the cool mountains, and plenty of low-elevation fishing holes in between.

Those new to Arizona (and sometimes those who have been here awhile) are often surprised to find this state is a veritable fishing paradise amid diverse and intriguing landscapes.

Lake Mead and Lake Powell are not only the two largest man-made lakes in North America, they are larger than many states. You could spend years fishing these giant bodies of water and probably not fish every part of them (many of us are valiantly still trying).

Arizona Highways and the Arizona Game and Fish Department put their expertise together to make this guidebook an enjoyable and interesting read for you — and a practical fishing resource to help you catch fish and enjoy our incredible outdoors. You'll find basic information and interesting details for the majority of Arizona's lakes, streams, and rivers. Where appropriate, we also provided seasonal fishing tips, especially for the more popular or prolific waters.

Each fishery has its own personality, and we did our best to capture those in an easy-to-read, conversational style of writing. Many of these waters have colorful pasts, so the book is liberally spiced with brief historical notes and anecdotes.

The 21st Century Digital Age

With the proliferation of 21st century technology, from computers and cell phones to GPS devices and Internet sites, along with blogs and social-media sites, we did our best to make this book compatible with the digital age. You'll find Internet addresses, where possible, for contacts and fishing resources. There are GPS coordinates for each lake or fishing spot, and also the applicable telephone numbers so you can call and get more information, make campground reservations where possible, or just talk to a live person who can answer your questions.

How to Use This Book

This guidebook is organized by the same geographical regions you will find on the Arizona Game and Fish Department's weekly Internet fishing report or in the department's *Arizona Fishin' Holes* pamphlet. We organized it this way so you could read about a particular lake, river, or stream, and then go to www.azgfd.gov or visit one of the social-media sites and get the latest fishing reports.

In addition, we've included sections on three of Arizona's major Indian reservations that provide fascinating fishing opportunities. They are each unique, but somewhat similar as well (see *Indian Lands*, page 246). Putting them together seemed to make sense if you want the adventure of fishing the reservation lands.

If you're a beginner, or just need some technical help, you might benefit from our *Glossary*, on page 310. We also offer help to those who need to learn knots and rigging — see page 304.

We hope you'll find this book an easy-to-use guide to a lifetime of fishing excursions in Arizona. So get outdoors often and go catch some memories. Maybe I'll see you out there.

— Rory Aikens

WHITE MOUNTAINS

Fishing amid fall color at Aspen Point on Big Lake.

Little Colorado River

77

Snowflake

Taylor

St. Johns

Concho

4
Concho Lake

191

61

White Mountain Lake

22

Silver Creek

Lyman Lake

13

Fool Hollow Lake

6

Linden

60

Show Low

17
Show Low Lake

APACHE-SITGREAVES NATIONAL FORESTS

Springerville

60

16
Scott Reservoir

Lakeside

Carnero Lake

1

Becker Lake

15
Rainbow Lake

18

Pinetop

3

Eagar

60

FR 117

FR 117A

14
Nelson Reservoir

Woodland Lake

To Globe

McNary

260

7

8

9

261

WHITE MOUNTAIN APACHE INDIAN RESERVATION

73

Hawley Lake

273

Greer

10

Nutrioso

191

North Fork White River

Sheeps Crossing

19

FR 113

Baldy Peak ▲

11

5
Crescent Lake

Alpine

Luna Lake

Lee Valley Lake

2
Big Lake

12

Three Forks

FR 249

180

East Fork White River

Whiteriver

Y55

FR 24

FR 276

Fort Apache

21

20
Buffalo Crossing

White River

FR 68

W H I T E

Big Bonita Creek

Y70

FR 24

Black River

Black River

M O U N T A I N S

FR 25

Hannagan Meadow

Blue River

1500

SAN CARLOS APACHE INDIAN RESERVATION

Eagle Creek

APACHE-SITGREAVES NATIONAL FORESTS

1000

Point of Pines

191

Arsenic Tubs

To Clifton

Many first-time visitors have called the White Mountains the most surprising Montana-like experience to be found in the arid Southwest.

This mountainous region where conservationist Aldo Leopold and John Wayne loved to roam is certainly not the visual image most people have of Arizona. Your frame of mind about the state will be forever altered once you trek through the long, high alpine meadows that meander through vast forests of mixed conifer and spruce, and visit the area's dazzling mountain reservoirs or rushing trout streams.

The stunning high-elevation landscape enjoys some of the most abundant precipitation in the state, especially from the snow in winter and wild afternoon thunderstorms in summer. The profusion of wildlife here may astound you; this region is widely renowned for huge bull elk with magnificent racks.

The White Mountains will entice you with diverse trout-fishing experiences at some of the largest, highest, and most spectacular mountain reservoirs in the state. Yet it will also draw you with small, intimate lakes, creeks, and beaver ponds where elk, deer, and wild turkey come to drink cold, clear water. You can satisfy your appetite for catching abundant rainbow trout, experience the thrill of large cutthroat trout dancing across the water, or excitedly reel in some energetic brook trout. There are opportunities to battle wits with bruiser browns or feel the frenetic energy of feisty arctic grayling testing your drag.

The Apache trout is Arizona's state fish. This native salmonid is making a historic and heroic comeback from the brink of extinction. Come experience some of this ongoing eco-history on the end of your fishing line.

You can find places to camp where the sound of gurgling trout streams accompanies your dreams, or possibly even thrill to the plaintive howls of reintroduced Mexican gray wolves wandering wild habitats. Yet you can also luxuriate at a five-star resort where fly-fishing tutorials are part of the daily routine.

At some of the lower-elevation lakes, there are chances to also fish for warm-water species such as bass, catfish, and sunfish. Enjoy gambling for delectable walleye? State-record walleye have been caught in two reservoirs within the city limits of Show Low, named for a famous poker showdown between two pioneers.

The White Mountains offers an intriguing mix of high-mountain extremes and living eco-history you'll want to explore and experience.

① Becker Lake

This trophy-trout lake is so close to Springerville that you can purchase a hot sandwich in town and still have it warm while unloading your angling gear at this year-round fishery. Becker is renowned for producing nice-quality trout dancing on the end of the line.

Becker Lake has 107 surface acres with a maximum depth of 21 feet and an average depth of 10 feet. It is located on a diversion of the Little Colorado River in the broad, verdant valley encompassing Springerville and Eagar. The Arizona Game and Fish Department owns water rights in the lake, so water levels can be maintained.

The lake is stocked with sub-catchable rainbow trout twice a year, and many of these fish survive the winter, reaching a good size the following spring. The lake also contains native Little Colorado suckers and illegally introduced green sunfish.

This productive fishery in the 622-acre Becker Wildlife Area is also a popular birding and waterfowl area where wintering bald eagles can be spotted most years in nearby cottonwood trees. Ospreys routinely dive into the water and catch fish at Becker. You can even experience formations of honking geese stopping for a visit during autumn and late-winter migrations.

In summer, be sure to bring insect repellent; the abundant insects that help fatten the trout might choose to dine on you if you aren't prepared.

HISTORICAL NOTE

Built around 1880, Becker Lake is one of the oldest reservoirs in the White Mountains. The Arizona Game and Fish Department acquired the lake and property around it in 1973.

Pontoon boats are popular on Becker Lake.

Fishing Tips: This is a year-round fishing lake that is typically ice-free in winter. It is a favorite lake with fly fishers, but is also popular with spin anglers as well. In spring, rainbow trout spawn in gravel beds near the boat ramp. Big fish also lurk along the weed beds. Trout activity at this lake can slow down in summer, but monsoon storms often prompt the fish into increased activity levels. This is a viable winter trout fishery as well; although the lake rarely freezes over, there can be ice around the edges of the lake in the early mornings on colder days.

➤ Try lures such as Super Dupers, spinners (Panther Martins and Rooster Tails), rainbow-colored Z-Rays, and Kastmasters. Try these flies: peacock ladies, brown nymphs, semi-seal leeches, prince nymphs, Zug Bugs,

Relaxing on the fishing pier.

pheasant tails, hare's ears, small scuds, zebra midges, and wooly worms and wooly buggers in brown, black, or gray.

Special Notes: Becker Lake is catch-and-release only for trout, using artificial lures and flies with single barbless hooks. All trout must be immediately released unharmed.

1 | FISHERY FACTS

LOCATION AND DIRECTIONS: GPS — 34°9'12.55"N; 109°18'22.32"W
The lake is located at an elevation of 6,910 feet. Easily accessible, it is a mere 2 miles from the center of Springerville, off the west side of U.S. Route 60.

AMENITIES: There is a new fishing pier installed here. The lake has a boat ramp, dirt parking, and barrier-free restroom. The Game and Fish Department has developed two hiking trails through the Becker Wildlife Area. No camping is allowed at the lake, but there is a private RV campground nearby. Restaurants and lodging options ranging from hotels to bed-and-breakfast inns can be found in the nearby towns of Springerville and Eagar.

2 Big Lake

With 532 surface acres, Big Lake is the trout-fishing giant of Arizona's high country, though not just because of its impressive size.

Unlike many other trout waters, Big Lake offers diversity. The primary fish species here include rainbow, brook, and cutthroat trout, with an occasional Apache trout, Arizona's official state fish.

Don't expect to catch a creel full of recently stocked trout here. Big Lake is different.

Each year, the Game and Fish Department stocks an average of 300,000 fingerling and sub-catchable trout, which are 2- to 6-inch fish. Most of these are rainbows. Because the trout are stocked small, they grow up strong in this vast mountain reservoir. For anglers, this means the trout they catch at Big Lake are as wild and woolly as any wild-spawned trout.

That isn't all.

When midsummer fishing doldrums settle in at other White Mountain lakes and streams because of increased water temperatures and lower levels of dissolved oxygen, Big Lake typically continues to produce decent

Big Lake is one of Arizona's few high-mountain reservoirs with boats available for rent.

fishing action, although the active fish are often found in deeper waters away from the shorelines and are best fished from a boat, canoe, kayak, or float tube. At 9,000 feet in elevation, it is one of the higher trout lakes in the state.

Because of its size, productivity, wild-like trout, trout diversity, summer efficacy, and visitor amenities, Big Lake is considered one of Arizona's finest trout fisheries. In fact, on any given day it might well be the state's premier mountain fishery. By the way, Big Lake also receives the most fishing pressure, but it's easy to understand why.

This area is also wildlife-viewing heaven.

Anglers at Big Lake are often treated to the sight of elk, deer, or wild turkey coming down to water. North American pronghorn spend their summers in the long, verdant meadows near Big Lake, where bluebirds also often congregate.

Big Lake is also in the Mexican gray wolf recovery area, and campers are sometimes treated to the sounds of wolves howling at night. Ospreys and bald eagles routinely ply the skies over Big Lake searching for trout dinners.

You'll also find energetic swallows nesting around the Big Lake store and zipping through the air to feed on insects from late spring through early autumn. They are part of the experience.

So be sure to bring your camera, binoculars, and wildlife-identification guides.

Young anglers enjoy fishing at Big Lake.

Fishing Tips: There is plenty of shoreline access here, so bring camp chairs and your favorite book to read. Boat and shore anglers can try all the trout-fishing baits, such as Power Bait, worms, corn, and salmon eggs, or lures such as spinners, Z-Rays, Rapalas, and Super Dupers, especially in the spring and fall.

➤ This is a superb lake to exercise your two-pole stamp. Fish the bottom using a slip sinker and your preferred bait. Use your second pole to work spinners or other lures along the top of the water column, especially at first and last light, or when monsoon thunderstorms are building and the barometer is dropping almost as fast as a sinker heading for the lake bottom.

➤ During summer, shore anglers don't do as well because trout typically hold deeper. However, boaters still succeed trolling spinners and flies. Many anglers also catch trout trolling Ford Fenders and cowbells. However, the trout can get very active when thunderstorms visit the area, typically in the summer afternoons.

➤ An often-ignored summer technique for trout is fishing at night. A good hint is that lights attract insects, and trout love to gobble up insects struggling in the water. Also watch for the summer Perseid meteor showers, usually late in July to early August. Night fishing is spectacular when meteors streaking across the sky are reflected in the mirror-like lake surface. It's an experience you'll never forget.

➤ Big Lake provides some of the best fishing for cutthroat trout in Arizona. Hard-fighting cutthroats can typically be caught using lures that resemble crayfish.

➤ Brook trout will hit flies, but also try night crawlers on the bottom. When brook trout spawn during the fall, catch them with roe or salmon eggs. Big Lake is well known for producing large brookies in October and November just before the snow flies.

Special Notes: Boat motors are restricted to electric or 10-hp-and-under gas motors. Big Lake is not accessible to motor vehicles during the winter due to deep snowdrifts across the roads; some use cross-country skis or snowmobiles to ice fish here. However, this large lake can have unstable ice during mild winters.

2 | FISHERY FACTS

LOCATION AND DIRECTIONS: GPS — 33°53'04.80"N; 109°24'54.88"W
Big Lake is located in the Apache-Sitgreaves National Forests, about 30 miles south of Springerville and Eagar, accessed by paved road via state routes 260 and 261, and is approximately one hour's drive from Pinetop using SR 260 and 273 (Forest Road 113). Vehicle access is restricted in the winter when roads are closed due to snow, generally December to early April.

AMENITIES: There are several visitor amenities here that the Forest Service maintains, including more than 200 fee-camping sites, three boat ramps, fish-cleaning stations, picnic tables, restrooms with flush toilets, showers, drinking water, a dump station, and a visitors center open during the summer.

Tucked among the aspens and conifers is a new campground, the Apache Trout Campground, with 124 spaces, 42 of which have full hookups, along with a modern dump station. There are even hot showers at this campground. Make reservations at www.reserveusa.com, or by calling 877-444-6777.

A concessionaire operates a small country store where you can purchase fishing licenses, food, gas, and fishing supplies, or rent a boat. They also have a certified scale to weigh your catch-of-a-lifetime. The store typically opens in early spring and stays open until Thanksgiving, or until the snow flies, whichever comes first.

It's always a good idea to stop by the store and find out the fish-feeding patterns and what top baits or techniques are working for trout. Believe it or not, one of the top-selling items anglers and campers buy at this store is ice cream.

③ Carnero Lake

What Carnero lacks in amenities, it more than makes up for in quality fish, and this lake can grow *big* fish. But don't come expecting to fish from shore; you'll likely be disappointed.

Carnero Lake is a shallow 65-acre headwater impoundment of Carnero Creek near the imposing heights of Greens Peak in Apache County. This is also prime elk country.

The lake has a maximum depth of 10 feet and has a lot of weeds, making it productive, with corresponding rapid growth rates for fish. But those weeds also pose a challenge for anglers; this is not an easy lake to fish from shore.

Carnero is better suited for anglers with pontoon boats, kayaks, or canoes who care more about catching big fish than enjoying amenities. Keep in mind that the weeds often make this lake unsuitable for electric motors.

Carnero is stocked with sub-catchable and catchable rainbow trout in the spring. Because it sits at 9,033 feet in elevation and is shallow, it's

Fishing at Carnero Lake is often challenged by weeds and little open water.

subject to periodic winterkills. But this altitude also means its waters can stay nice and cold well into late spring.

The best time to fish at Carnero is in the spring or fall. Once the weeds begin growing, it's hard to get a boat or float tube from the shore out to open water, and, at times, it can be difficult to find much open water at all. When water temperatures drop in autumn, the weed beds slowly die back and the fish feed more aggressively.

Because this lake is somewhat off the beaten path, anglers are routinely treated to the sight of an elk herd coming down to drink. North American pronghorn can often be seen racing across the high grasslands leading into this small trout lake. Be sure to be "bear aware."

Fishing Tips: Carnero is best fished with flies or other surface-type lures from a float tube, canoe, or kayak. Fly-fish with wooly buggers, prince nymphs, or light-colored nymphs in open areas. During summer, cicada and grasshopper patterns can work well.

Special Notes: Special fishing regulations apply at Carnero. Anglers may use artificial lures and flies only with barbless hooks. The daily bag limit is two trout for licensed adults or one for unlicensed anglers under the age of 14. Boat motors are restricted to electric only. Due to snow and ice, the roads are typically inaccessible from mid-November to mid-April.

Be prepared with a variety of trout lures, flies, and hooks.

3 | FISHERY FACTS

LOCATION AND DIRECTIONS: GPS — 34°07'0.15"N; 109°31'41.21"W
Carnero Lake is located in the Apache-Sitgreaves National Forests. To get there, drive east on State Route 260 from Pinetop-Lakeside. About 3 miles past the SR 273 junction to Sunrise Park, make a left onto Forest Road 117. Follow this road for 2.5 miles, then turn right onto FR 117A. Drive 3 miles, and look for the Carnero Lake sign and turnoff on the right side of the road. Follow this two-track road a couple hundred yards to the parking area adjacent to the lake.

AMENITIES: There's a cindered parking area, but no boat ramp or restroom. You'll find a shallow dirt area suitable for launching your small boat or other device. Some dispersed camping is allowed in the area. The nearest developed campgrounds and amenities such as food, gas, and lodging are 15 miles away in the Greer Valley.

(4) Concho Lake

Concho Lake is located in the high grasslands of Apache County not far from St. Johns, the county seat. This shallow, weedy lake sits immediately adjacent to the golf course belonging to the private Concho Valley Country Club.

It has 80 surface acres with a maximum depth of 16 feet and an average depth of 8 feet. A small watershed and nearby spring feed this lake.

The Game and Fish Department routinely stocks catchable rainbow trout each spring. You can catch green sunfish and an occasional largemouth bass here. The water level is drawn down considerably in the summer for irrigation.

This lake can freeze over in winter, but often has open water that attracts waterfowl and even bald eagles. The nearby high grasslands are home to herds of North American pronghorn, the fastest quadruped on the continent.

Much of the surrounding land is privately owned; the rest is owned by the Bureau of Land Management, but is managed for sport fishing and wildlife resources by the Game and Fish Department.

Fishing Tips: There is plenty of shoreline access at this small lake; however, increasing development is beginning to impact that access.
➤ Concho is best fished in spring when the water levels are highest and after it is stocked with trout. It often has low water levels and high water temperatures during summer and fall, and can be subject to summer fishkills.
➤ To try your luck at trout, float a night crawler a couple of feet from the bottom or suspend it under a bobber. Also try trolling flies or small lures from a boat. When the weeds start to take over, surface fishing can become necessary. Spin anglers should try casting floats and larger flies, such as wooly buggers.

Special Notes: Boat motors are restricted to either electric or 10-hp-and-under gas motors.

4 | FISHERY FACTS

LOCATION AND DIRECTIONS: GPS — 34°26'35.37"N; 109°37'40.57"W
Concho Lake is located in the Eastern Arizona grasslands at 6,299 feet in elevation. It's an irrigation reservoir situated in the town of Concho, on the east side of State Route 61, about 16 miles west of St. Johns.

AMENITIES: There is a boat ramp, dirt parking, picnic benches, and a portable toilet. Overnight camping is not allowed. The nearest lodging and dining is in St. Johns.

(5) Crescent Lake

If you love catching brook trout, Crescent Lake can be sheer bliss, but weeds can make it frustrating to fish. This productive brook and rainbow trout fishery in the high alpine grasslands at 9,040 feet in elevation can often rival the action of its mighty neighbor to the south, Big Lake, especially during the spring and fall. Summer weeds can become a challenge.

This moderately sized lake, which is shaped like its name, sits within view of 11,420-foot-tall Mount Baldy, in the second highest mountain range in Arizona. Crescent has 100 surface acres with an average depth of 10 feet. To say it is visually appealing is like saying the *Mona Lisa* has an OK smile. Bring your camera.

Crescent allows trout to gain size quickly; however, its shallow waters encourage weed growth and algae blooms, subjecting the fish to periodic late-summer and winter kills. The Game and Fish Department stocks the lake with large numbers of sub-catchable and catchable fish in spring.

Although the area is renowned for its vast elk population, the high grasslands adjacent to Crescent Lake also attract herds of North American pronghorn once the deep winter snows have melted. There are also nesting bald eagles close by that routinely fish this lake and Big Lake. Please do not disturb the nest. You can also expect to find lots of waterfowl attracted to this lake, especially in autumn.

Fishing Tips: This fishery is shore-angler-friendly but is also favored by float-tube fly anglers. Spring and fall are the most productive times to fish Crescent. During the summer, fish at first and last light, or even at night.

Shore fishing at Crescent Lake.

➤ Bait and shore anglers can try night crawlers and Power Bait. Rocky points on the west side can be the best spots for shore anglers when the lake is weedy.

➤ Try worms, Power Bait, corn, salmon eggs, and lures such as small Z-Rays, Super Dupers, Kastmasters, and spinners (Mepps, Panther Martins, and Rooster Tails). Fly anglers should try wooly worms, wooly buggers, leech patterns, peacock ladies, Warden's worrys, prince nymphs, and Zug Bugs. Also try small nymphs in brown, black, or green.

The sun rises over the fishing pier and dock at Crescent Lake.

➤ Those trolling from boats might want to try cowbells or Ford Fenders. Slow-trolling flies can also be very effective.

Special Notes: Boat motors are restricted to electric or 10-hp-and-under gas motors. This lake is not accessible by vehicle during winter when roads are closed due to snow, generally December through May.

5 | FISHERY FACTS

LOCATION AND DIRECTIONS: GPS — 33°54'32"N; 109°25'9.71"W
Crescent Lake is located approximately 2 miles north of Big Lake, at the junction of State Route 261 and Forest Road 113 (SR 273). It is less than 30 miles southwest of Springerville and Eagar by paved road, or less than an hour's drive from Pinetop using state routes 260 and 273.

AMENITIES: There are three boat ramps, only one of which, located on the west side, is usable in low-water conditions. There are three sets of barrier-free toilets. There is no camping in the immediate vicinity of the lake; the nearest campground is at Big Lake. A small seasonal store rents boats and sells bait, tackle, snacks, and drinks. Two new fishing piers have been constructed on the south end of the lake.

⑥ Fool Hollow Lake

If you want fishing variety from bass to trout, along with plenty of amenities including camping and picnic areas, give Fool Hollow a try; this fishery has a veritable piscatorial smorgasbord to offer everyone from first-time anglers to seasoned veterans.

At 6,260 feet in elevation, Fool Hollow Lake contains self-sustaining populations of largemouth and smallmouth bass, sunfish, walleye, carp, and black crappie. The Game and Fish Department stocks the lake with catchable rainbow trout throughout the spring and summer. The fishery is popular with walleye anglers in the autumn.

The lake consists of 150 surface acres, with an average depth of 23 feet. It is located within the Fool Hollow Recreation Area and is cooperatively managed by Arizona State Parks, the Forest Service, the Arizona Game and Fish Department, and the City of Show Low.

Craggy banks lined with tall pines give Fool Hollow Lake a feeling of seclusion.

Even though Fool Hollow has first-rate visitor amenities and is minutes from Show Low, its craggy banks and beautiful vistas give visitors a feeling of forested seclusion.

Fishing Tips: Fool Hollow Lake provides a great opportunity for novices and youngsters to catch anything that bites, or for veteran anglers to catch multiple species in the same day.

➤ Night crawlers fished along the bottom or under a bobber are a good way to go. More experienced anglers can try spinnerbaits, jigs, and night crawler rigs around underwater rocky structures, where large bass and walleye lurk. By the way, this is a great lake to catch trophy-sized walleye.

➤ You can also catch catfish in summer and early fall with night crawlers or chicken livers on the bottom.

➤ When other lakes are suffering from the summer doldrums, the warm-water fish in this versatile lake, such as largemouth bass and smallmouth bass, can provide anglers lots of interesting action. Try for smallmouth along the rocky areas and largemouth along the large muddy flats using small spinners or crayfish-like lures.

➤ The lake is open year-round, rarely icing over and never for long.

Special Notes: There is no bag limit on crappie, sunfish, or carp. Fool Hollow Lake has produced catch-and-release state records for channel catfish (32 inches) and walleye (33 inches). Boat motors are restricted to electric or 10-hp-and-under gas motors.

6 | FISHERY FACTS

LOCATION AND DIRECTIONS: GPS — 34°16'41.6"N; 110°04'26.2"W
Fool Hollow Lake is located less than 2 miles from downtown Show Low, off Old Linden Road. Access Old Linden Road either from U.S. Route 60 in town or at its western end from State Route 260.

AMENITIES: Arizona State Parks maintains visitor amenities that include 31 tent-camping sites, 92 RV sites with water and electric hookups, two boat ramps, two fish-cleaning stations, picnic tables, barrier-free restrooms, showers, drinking water, and a dump station. There are four barrier-free fishing piers, 10 single-family picnic ramadas, and five large-group ramadas that can each accommodate up to 150 people. For more information, call the park at 928-537-3680 or visit their website at www.azstateparks.com.

GREER LAKES RECREATION AREA

The picturesque Greer Valley is a trout-fishing and outdoor-recreation paradise just off the beaten path between Pinetop and Springerville in the Apache-Sitgreaves National Forests. It is truly a four-season outdoor wonderland.

Fishing is just one of the popular outdoor activities in the Greer Lakes Recreation Area. | GEORGE ANDREJKO

This high mountain valley includes what is commonly known as the Greer Lakes: Bunch, River, and Tunnel reservoirs. However, life in this well-appointed mountain hamlet is tied together and often defined by the Little Colorado River.

Although called a river, here the Little Colorado is really a picturesque gurgling stream winding its way through the verdant valley, where elk herds routinely graze. Traveling along the creek, you'll discover private fishing ponds; fly-fishing instruction is available at some of the top-notch mountain resorts dotting the landscape. Some lodges and restaurants offer trout fishing and fine dining on their bill of fare.

The Greer Valley is also a short drive away from Big Lake, Crescent Lake, Lee Valley Lake, Sheeps Crossing of the Little Colorado River, and Sunrise Lake.

Special Notes: Boat motors are restricted to electric-only at Bunch and Tunnel, and to either electric or 10-hp-and-under gas motors at River.

(7) Bunch Reservoir

Bunch Reservoir is 20 acres in size and has an average depth of 10 feet. The Game and Fish Department stocks the lake with catchable rainbow trout in the spring and summer. Like its two neighboring reservoirs, Bunch gets a few brown and Apache trout from the Little Colorado River diversion that refills it in the winter, but browns are not stocked here.

With plenty of shoreline spots, the Greer Lakes appeal to fishing families. | GEORGE ANDREJKO

The Little Colorado River traverses the Greer Valley, drawing fly anglers and spin anglers alike. | GEORGE ANDREJKO

8 River Reservoir

Originally built in 1896 on the Little Colorado River, River Reservoir is the largest and deepest of the Greer Lakes. Even though it's been around for more than 100 years, it's now like a new lake. The reservoir was drained in 2004 because of safety issues, and the dam was repaired in 2005. Like the other two Greer Lakes, it also has new amenities.

River Reservoir has 50 surface acres with a maximum depth of 45 feet and an average depth of 20 feet. The Arizona Game and Fish Department stocks it with catchable rainbow trout in the spring and summer.

Like its two neighboring reservoirs, River gets a few brown trout from the Little Colorado, which flows directly into the lake, but browns are not stocked here. Wild brown trout can get quite big in River.

River Reservoir. | GEORGE ANDREJKO

9 Tunnel Reservoir

The smallest of the three Greer Lakes, Tunnel Reservoir is 15 acres in size, with an average depth of 10 feet.

The lake is filled in the winter through a diversion off the Little Colorado River. The Arizona Game and Fish Department stocks catchable rainbow trout in the spring and summer. Occasionally, a few brown trout make it into the lake from the diversion. As it is an irrigation reservoir, the lake is drawn down considerably by late summer, which can impact water oxygen levels.

Fishing Tips: These three reservoirs offer plenty of shoreline-fishing opportunities. Power Bait and night crawlers are by far the most popular techniques, but corn and salmon eggs can work at times. Also try Z-Rays, Super Dupers, Rapalas, and in-line spinners (such as Mepps or Rooster Tails). Trolling cowbells or Ford Fenders can also work for boaters at the larger reservoirs. Brown trout spawn in the late fall, which is an excellent time to fish for these bruisers, if the water levels are sufficiently high after a summer of irrigating crops.

(10) Little Colorado River

This picturesque stream winds through the lush meadows and woodlands in the Greer Valley. The Arizona Game and Fish Department stocks the stream with native Apache trout from late spring through the end of summer, and will sometimes stock rainbow trout as well.

Simply follow State Route 373 through Greer to its end and you will find parking areas. Or find public access to the stream as it winds through the valley.

Fishing Tips: Try drifting worms, Power Bait, corn, and salmon eggs through pools. Cast small lures such as spinners (Mepps, Rooster Tails, and Panther Martins); spoons such as Super Dupers, Z-Rays, and Kastmasters; flies such as wooly worms, and small nymphs in black, brown, or green colors.

➤ Knowledgeable anglers say the best fishing can be found upstream past where the bait fishermen usually tread.

7 | 8 | 9 | 10 | FISHERY FACTS

LOCATION AND DIRECTIONS: GPS — 34°01'50.98"N; 109°26'33.46"W for the Greer Lakes.

Surrounded by the Apache-Sitgreaves National Forests, the Greer Valley is a 45-minute drive from Pinetop-Lakeside across the scenic White Mountain Apache Reservation via state routes 260 and 373. At the junction of the two highways, take SR 373 south into the valley. Greer aficionados affectionately call 373 the "Road to Nowhere."

To reach Bunch, Tunnel, and River reservoirs, turn left onto Forest Road 87B. Bunch is the first lake on the left. Just follow the signs.

GREER VALLEY AMENITIES: In this picturesque mountain valley, you can discover quaint cabins to rent on a weekly basis or even spend quality time in high-end resorts, all within easy access to fishing, hiking, wildlife-watching, and other outdoor-recreation opportunities. This is also a popular winter retreat, although few anglers are typically seen wetting a line. But on milder winter days, the fish have been known to bite along the Little Colorado, though you might have to wear snow boots and ski bibs.

There is camping at nearby Benny Creek and Rolfe Hoyer campgrounds, both operated by the Forest Service. Hoyer has 100 individual sites with top-of-the-line amenities, including barrier-free flush toilets and showers. Both campgrounds charge a fee. Make reservations by going to www.reserveusa.com or by calling 877-444-6777. The nearby mountain town of Greer provides everything in the way of gas, lodging, food, and tackle.

The Little Colorado River in Greer can still be fishable in winter.

⑪ Lee Valley Lake

At 9,418 feet in elevation, Lee Valley holds the distinction of being Arizona's highest-elevation lake. Beloved by fly anglers and breathtaking in its setting, this shimmering lake nudges the flanks of Mount Baldy, in Arizona's second highest mountain range.

Lee Valley offers anglers the opportunity to catch golden-colored Apache trout, Arizona's state fish, but is also one of only two lakes in Arizona with arctic grayling. The lake is stocked with catchable and sub-catchable Apache trout in the spring. Some of these fish overwinter, reaching a good size the following spring. The Game and Fish Department owns the water rights, so water levels can be maintained.

Lee Valley is especially glorious in the fall when quaking aspen are changing color and elk can be heard bugling at dawn and dusk. You might even hear a wolf howl. Ospreys and bald eagles routinely catch fish at this classic mountain lake.

Lee Valley Lake has 35 surface acres with a maximum depth of 20 feet and an average depth of 9.5 feet. It is located on Lee Valley Creek, an Apache trout recovery stream. The creek naturally flows into the East Fork of the Little Colorado River; however, the spillway directs overflow to the West Fork of the Little Colorado River. Both streams are also designated for Apache trout recovery, thus Lee Valley finds itself at the heart of three Apache trout recovery streams and is managed accordingly.

This lake is also within the Mexican gray wolf recovery area, and some anglers have reported seeing these shy predators ghosting in and out of the adjacent woodlands of the Mount Baldy Wilderness.

Fishing Tips: Float tubes are popular and easy to use at this lake; however, fishing success from shore is comparable to fishing from a float tube or a boat.

➤ Lee Valley holds the state record for arctic grayling. Either end of the dam provides good places to fish from shore.

➤ Fly-fishing is probably the most productive technique at this lake. Wet flies to try are hare's ear nymphs, small peacock ladies, and prince nymphs in sizes 14 to 16. Just before dark, surface action can be quite good with dry flies, such as small Adams, mosquito or midge larvae, and light Cahills in sizes 16 to 20.

➤ Spinning lures to try are small Panther Martins, small Z-Rays, or very small Kastmasters fished from the dam.

Special Notes: Lee Valley Lake can only be fished with artificial lures and flies. The daily bag limit is two trout, which includes grayling, and each must be a minimum of 12 inches long. For unlicensed anglers under the age of 14, the limit is one trout. Boat motors are restricted to electric motors only.

11 | FISHERY FACTS

LOCATION AND DIRECTIONS: GPS — 33°56'28.40"N; 109°30'3.24"W
Located in the Apache-Sitgreaves National Forests, Lee Valley Lake is a one-hour drive from Pinetop using state routes 260 and 273 (Forest Road 113). Vehicle access is restricted in the winter when roads are closed due to snow, generally December to early April.

AMENITIES: There is a boat ramp, paved parking, and a barrier-free restroom. No camping is allowed around the lake, but overnight visitors can camp at nearby Winn Campground. This fee campground includes 63 sites plus a group site and has water, vault toilets, picnic tables, and fire rings. Firewood is available and there is a host. Reserve a site at Winn Campground by visiting www.reserveusa.com or by calling 877-444-6777.

(12) Luna Lake

This productive 154-acre trout lake along the upper San Francisco River is the last chance to fish in Eastern Arizona before crossing the New Mexico state line a short distance away. The imposing mass of Escudilla Mountain dominates the northern horizon.

Large, scenic, with lots of visitor amenities and close to the town of Alpine, Luna Lake sits at 7,890 feet in elevation and offers good spring and early summer fishing for locals and visitors alike.

Luna is stocked annually with fingerling and sub-catchable rainbow and cutthroat trout, which rapidly grow to catchable size due to the high productivity of the lake. This lake holds the current state record for cut-throat trout at 6 pounds, 5 ounces.

Luna Lake has a maximum depth of 21 feet and an average depth of 8 feet. Because it is a shallow, nutrient-rich lake, it is subject to excessive weed growth, especially during summer. The Game and Fish Department annually harvests weeds to alleviate some of the water-quality problems.

Luna Lake Wildlife Area, which encompasses the upper end of the lake, is also a superb place to observe waterfowl. Nesting bald eagles can often be seen swooping down and catching fish in the lake.

Fishing Tips: Trolling flies works well in spring and early summer at Luna. Try night crawlers, worms, corn, salmon eggs, and Power Bait; lures such as Panther Martins, Rooster Tails, and Mepps spinners; small spoons like Kastmasters, Z-Rays, and Super Dupers; and flies such as wooly worms and wooly buggers, peacock ladies, Zug Bugs, prince nymphs, and black, brown, or green nymphs.

➤ As water temperatures increase during the summer, fish in deeper, cooler water. During winter, ice fishing is possible, but always check ice conditions before setting out. Milder winter days can render ice unstable.

Special Notes: Luna Lake Wildlife Area is closed to public entry annually from April 1 through July 31 for nesting waterfowl and bald eagles. Boat motors are restricted to either electric or 10-hp-and-under gas motors.

A rocky perch at Luna Lake.

Escudilla Mountain dominates Luna Lake's northern horizon.

12 | FISHERY FACTS

LOCATION AND DIRECTIONS: GPS — 33°49′44.92″N; 109°05′22.56″W
Luna Lake is located about 3 miles east of Alpine, just north of U.S. Route 180, on the Apache-Sitgreaves National Forests. It's accessible year-round but ices over in winter months.

AMENITIES: A concessionaire operates a small store near the dam where you can purchase tackle, bait, drinks, and snacks or rent a boat during the prime fishing season, typically from late spring through early autumn. There is one boat ramp, barrier-free toilets, picnic tables, and dirt parking at the lake.

The Luna Lake Campground, which includes 40 individual fee-camping sites, three group sites, picnic tables, restrooms, and drinking water, is located on Forest Service land about a quarter-mile north of the lake. Reserve a site by visiting www.reserveusa.com or by calling 877-444-6777.

13 Lyman Lake

The largest lake in the region, with 1,500 surface acres, great amenities, and no boat-motor restrictions, Lyman Lake in the high grasslands along the Little Colorado River attracts anglers as well as campers and water-skiers year-round.

An irrigation impoundment, Lyman Lake sits at 5,978 feet with the sole access through Lyman Lake State Park. Water levels fluctuate, but when full, the average depth is 22 feet, with a maximum depth of 57 feet. Lyman Lake is a warm-water reservoir containing largemouth bass, channel catfish, green sunfish, carp, and a few walleye.

HISTORICAL NOTE

Lyman Lake became Arizona's first recreational state park and the fourth in the system, behind Tubac Presidio, Tombstone Courthouse, and Yuma Territorial Prison. The official dedication of Lyman Lake State Park was held on July 1, 1961.

Anglers can land bass, sunfish, and walleye along rocky areas of Lyman Lake. | GEORGE ANDREJKO

The west end of the lake is buoyed off and restricted as a no-wake area (5 mph limit). This allows anglers the opportunity to fish without being disturbed by speedboats and water-skiers.

Fishing Tips: This lake is a catfish-lover's special; channel catfish are plentiful. Try using night crawlers or chicken livers, particularly at the upper end of the lake. Bass anglers at this lake are often surprised to catch channel catfish on lures.

➤ Also try fishing for bass, walleye, and sunfish along rocky or weedy areas of the lake. Walleye are light sensitive, so the

Bass boats are welcome at Lyman Lake, which has no motor restrictions. | GEORGE ANDREJKO

best time to fish for them is at first and last light, or even at night. You can catch carp with corn or dough baits.

Special Notes: There are no motor restrictions here. There is a fish-con-sumption advisory at Lyman Lake; for more information concerning the advisory, call the Game and Fish Department at 928-367-4281. Access to the lake can be restricted by state park closures.

13 | FISHERY FACTS

LOCATION AND DIRECTIONS: GPS — 34°21'30.96"N; 109°21'55.04"W
Lyman Lake is located adjacent to U.S. Route 180/191, 11 miles south of St. Johns and 17 miles north of Springerville.

AMENITIES: Arizona State Parks maintains year-round visitor amenities that include 23 tent-camping sites; 38 RV sites with water, sewer, and electric hook-ups; four cabins; and four yurts (tent-like structures).

There is a boat ramp, fish-cleaning station, picnic tables, shade ramadas, handicapped-accessible restrooms, showers, drinking water, and a dump station. A well-stocked convenience store, which sells bait, tackle, ice, and firewood, is open from early April until the end of September. In the summer, Lyman Lake State Park conducts interpretive tours of nearby petroglyphs.

(14) Nelson Reservoir

Anyone who has driven from Springerville to Alpine has experienced this long, narrow reservoir along Nutrioso Creek near Escudilla Mountain.

Nelson sits in a grassland valley and is not your typical pine-tree-lined reservoir, so it is sometimes overlooked. However, Nelson often has larger holdover trout that can be caught year-round, making it popular with local anglers. Its barrier-free fishing platforms also make it popular with those experiencing mobility problems.

At an elevation of 7,412 feet and with 90 surface acres, Nelson has a maximum depth of 24 feet and an average depth of 8 feet. When the lake stops spilling in the spring, it is stocked with up to 20,000 catchable rainbow trout.

This reservoir typically experiences water-quality issues in summer that preclude the possibility of stocking. It is subject to algae blooms and excessive weed growth as summer progresses, although such aquatic plant growth makes it a popular stopover for waterfowl and migrating shore birds. A large marshy area on the southern edge of the lake attracts geese and snowy egrets occasionally.

The lake contains native bluehead suckers and illegally introduced black crappie and green sunfish. It also once contained brown, cutthroat, and brook trout, but none remain today.

Fishing Tips: When the lake is first stocked in late spring, just about anything works. This lake often has larger holdover trout, but they are often difficult to catch.

➤ Try worms, Power Bait, lures such as spinners (Panther Martins, Rooster Tails, and Mepps), small spoons (Kastmasters, Z-Rays, and Super Dupers), jigs, and flies such as wooly worms, wooly buggers, peacock ladies, prince nymphs, and Zug Bugs. Also try nymphs in black, brown, or green colors.

➤ As the weather warms, fish deeper with bait rigs. In the fall and spring,

Nelson Reservoir, near Springerville, is often overlooked by anglers. | GEORGE ANDREJKO

try trolling with wooly bugger flies or Panther Martin spinners, or try suspending a night crawler below a bobber. The south end of the lake can become difficult to fish in late summer because of weed growth, but it becomes a superb area to watch waterfowl. During these times, fishing is best closer to the dam.

➤ The lake sometimes freezes for short periods during the winter, but typically is open to fishing year-round.

Special Notes: Special regulations apply at Nelson Reservoir. There is no bag limit on rainbow and brown trout from September 1 through March 31. Boat motors are restricted to either electric or 10-hp-and-under gas motors.

14 | FISHERY FACTS

LOCATION AND DIRECTIONS: GPS — 34°03′21.86″N; 109°11′25.63″W
Nelson Reservoir is on the Apache-Sitgreaves National Forests and is easily accessed by driving south on U.S. Route 180/191 about 7 miles south from Eagar.

AMENITIES: At the dam on the north end of the lake, there is a small boat ramp, paved parking, a barrier-free fishing platform, and barrier-free restroom. Two additional barrier-free fishing platforms can be accessed from this parking area by way of a newly constructed, handicapped-accessible trail.

There is also a paved parking lot and barrier-free toilet at the upper, south end of the lake. The boat ramp at this location is usable only when the water level is high. There is no camping near the lake; the nearest camping is at the Alpine Divide campground approximately 11 miles south of the lake, just off U.S. 180/191.

(15) Rainbow Lake

Located in Pinetop-Lakeside, this in-town lake gets most of its fishing pressure from local anglers (especially youngsters), including those with second homes along the shoreline.

Rainbow Lake sits at 6,760 feet in elevation and has 116 surface acres, with a maximum depth of 14 feet and an average depth of 7 feet. The Arizona Game and Fish Department stocks catchable rainbow trout here during the spring and early summer.

Most of the land surrounding Rainbow Lake is privately owned, but a public-access parcel is maintained for recreation.

Naturally propagating warm-water species include largemouth bass, channel catfish, black bullhead, bluegill, and green sunfish. The lake also contains illegally introduced northern pike. Because it is shallow and weedy, Rainbow Lake is subject to water-quality problems.

The land surrounding the lake is privately owned and inaccessible to the public; however, the Arizona Game and Fish Department owns a small parcel of land adjacent to the dam and maintains it for public fishing and recreational boating.

HISTORICAL NOTE

By damming Walnut Creek in 1903, Mormon settlers created Rainbow Lake. Eventually, the settlement grew into the town of Lakeside, now incorporated as Pinetop-Lakeside.

Fishing Tips: Because so much shoreline is privately owned, Rainbow Lake is best fished from a boat, canoe, kayak, or float tube. Spring and early summer are the best times to fish for trout because that's when water quality is at its best, the weeds are down, and Game and Fish is stocking fish.

➤ Troll for trout with Panther Martin and Rooster Tail spinners, small Kastmasters, or wooly bugger flies. You may also have some luck fishing from shore with worms or Power Bait.

➤ Casting near structure with spinners can work well for largemouth bass and northern pike. Fish on the bottom with night crawlers or stink baits to catch black bullheads and channel catfish.

Special Notes: Boat motors are restricted to electric or 10-hp-and-under gas motors.

15 | FISHERY FACTS

LOCATION AND DIRECTIONS: GPS — 34°09′44.0″N; 109°58′9.89″W
Rainbow Lake is located near the heart of Lakeside. To reach the public parcel, turn south on Rainbow Lake Road or Lakeview Lane from State Route 260.

AMENITIES: On the Game and Fish parcel, there's a boat ramp for public use, a barrier-free fishing pier, paved parking, and a portable toilet.

The nearby Lakeside Campground, while not on the banks of the lake, is just a few hundred yards from the dam. Lakeside Campground is on SR 260, about a quarter-mile west of Porter Mountain Road. This campground has 82 sites, vault toilets, potable water, and firewood for sale. You can make reservations for a campsite by visiting www.reserveusa.com or by calling 877-444-6777.

Additional amenities, in the form of boat rentals, are available from Rainbow's End Resort, a private business adjacent to the public-access area. Cabin rentals are available at Lazy Oaks, where guests can use one of two private fishing piers or rent a boat.

(16) Scott Reservoir

Scott Reservoir is an unheralded fishery just off the beaten path that is often overlooked by those visiting the mountains. Built in 1928, this irrigation impoundment on Porter Creek near Pinetop-Lakeside is the least developed of the "in-town" lakes and is surrounded by trees, giving it a secluded feel. Local anglers know a secret: You can catch big catfish here in the fall.

Scott Reservoir has 80 surface acres with an average depth of 10 feet, and lies at 6,720 feet in elevation. It is usually somewhat turbid, which helps control algae blooms and aquatic weeds. This, coupled with a good perennial stream flowing in, means there are no real water-quality problems.

This lake is stocked with catchable rainbow trout in spring, early summer, and fall, and occasionally stocked with channel catfish. There are a few largemouth bass. Area school children also know a secret: Raccoons visit Scott Reservoir after sunset to dine on the abundant crayfish here.

Even though Scott is on the fringe of town, anglers are often treated to the site of elk coming to water. In autumn, anglers can hear the clacking of antlers as elk spar in the forest during the rut.

Fishing Tips: Fish for trout in spring and early summer using a boat or float tube at the upper end of the lake, where overwintering fish tend to congregate. Troll spinners or fish with night crawlers off the bottom. For stocked trout, try night crawlers or Power Bait.

➤ For catfish in the summer, try chicken liver or water dogs. Larger cat-

fish in the fall are typically caught using water dogs. There are some bass in this lake, but catch rates are low. Small spinners can work for bass and trout as well.

Special Notes: Only electric boat motors are allowed on this lake.

16 | FISHERY FACTS

LOCATION AND DIRECTIONS: GPS — 34°10'47.1"N; 109°57'66.3"W
Scott Reservoir lies just outside the Pinetop-Lakeside town limits on the Apache-Sitgreaves National Forests. To get there, drive 1.4 miles north on Porter Mountain Road from State Route 260, then make a right turn across from the Chuck Wagon Steak House. The lake is 0.7 miles from Porter Mountain Road.

AMENITIES: There is a boat ramp with barrier-free restrooms nearby. Along the road into the lake is a 15-site campground. Each site has a fire ring and picnic table, but there are no other amenities. A campground host is present during summer months. Camping is free, but there is a five-day stay limit.

Additional camping is available nearby at the Lakeside Campground, located on SR 260 about a quarter-mile west of Porter Mountain Road. This campground has 82 sites, vault toilets, potable water, and firewood for sale. You can make reservations for a campsite by visiting www.reserveusa.com or by calling 877-444-6777.

Fall is prime time for larger catfish at scenic Scott Reservoir.

(17) Show Low Lake

Many knowledgeable anglers consider Show Low Lake to be Arizona's premier walleye fishery.

This remarkable lake inside the city limits of Show Low has yielded the last five state-record walleye, and numerous "Big Fish-of-the-Year Program" catches as well. Local resident Gregg Munck caught the existing state-record walleye here in November 2002. It weighed in at a whopping 16 pounds, 2 ounces.

This lake maintains good water quality year-round, and is stocked with rainbow trout from April through September. Anglers in the springtime are often treated to larger holdover trout.

It may look a bit unpretentious, but Show Low Lake is home to big fish, especially walleye and catfish.

The Game and Fish Department occasionally stocks channel catfish. The lake also contains reproducing populations of walleye, largemouth and smallmouth bass, bluegill, and green sunfish.

Show Low Lake has 100 surface acres with an average depth of 33 feet and a maximum depth of 50 feet. It's situated at an elevation of 6,500 feet.

Fishing Tips: Show Low Lake is open year-round. Trout fishing from the shore is always possible because the lake doesn't get weedy. Many trout survive the winter here and can get quite large by early spring. Try trolling spinners in early spring to catch one of these fat trout. For stocked trout, try Power Bait or night crawlers.

➤ Walleye fishing is best in spring and fall. Try fishing rocky bottom structures or by the dam with crankbaits or jigs. Walleye love night crawlers, so even while using jigs, put on a small piece of worm. Stay in the shallows and fish at dawn or dusk to improve catching odds. For the lunkers, try large crankbaits in the shallows or along the shoreline, or bounce a night crawler rig slowly on the bottom.

➤ Catfishing can be exciting here. A 32-pound channel catfish caught in 2009 threatened the state record. Try fishing for catfish on summer or fall nights using chicken liver, night crawlers, or water dogs. In spring, channel catfish and walleye congregate at the upper end, where Show Low Creek flows into the lake.

➤ Small bass and sunfish can be caught with night crawlers in the rocks along the dam.

➤ Spring runoff can sometimes make this lake turbid and slow down the bite, but those inflows also add to the productivity of this fishery.

➤ The lake can have ice around its rim during winter, but during milder winter months it has open water to fish.

Special Notes: There is no bag limit on bluegill or green sunfish. Boat motors are restricted to electric or 10-hp-and-under gas motors.

17 | FISHERY FACTS

LOCATION AND DIRECTIONS: GPS — 34°11'6.15"N; 110°00'3.47"W
Show Low Lake is adjacent to Show Low Lake Road, about 1 mile from State Route 260. You can access Show Low Lake Road from the traffic light between Wal-Mart and Summit Healthcare Regional Medical Center in Show Low.

AMENITIES: The lake has a boat ramp with a restroom nearby. A new boat dock is located along the boat ramp, and two fishing piers have been installed. There's a year-round concession with a campground that has 75 sites, seven of which have electric hookups. There are two group sites that can accommodate up to 75 and 150 people, respectively.

There is drinking water, a dump station, a playground, and a shower building. Picnic ramadas are available for day use with a fee, and a small store rents boats and sells fishing licenses, bait, tackle, drinks, and snacks. There are several barrier-free restrooms in the campground. Reserve a site at 888-537-7762.

(18) Woodland Lake

Located in the heart of Pinetop-Lakeside, Woodland Lake and the park surrounding it have been called this area's "crown jewel."

In addition to trout fishing, the lake provides other outdoor-recreation opportunities and is vigorously used by residents and visitors alike. A path around the lake is routinely utilized by joggers and power-walkers.

Woodland Lake is situated at 6,893 feet in elevation. At full capacity, it has a surface area of 18 acres with a maximum depth of 20 feet. Because the lake is part of the local irrigation district, at drawdown it averages 10 surface acres.

It is shallow and nutrient rich, making it subject to water-quality problems in the summer. For this reason, the lake is stocked primarily with catchable rainbow trout in the spring and early summer. The lake also contains a few largemouth bass and channel catfish.

Fishing Tips: Woodland Lake is a great shore-fishing destination for kids and adults alike. Cast a spinning lure from the dam, fishing pier, or the shoreline to try your luck. Also try fishing with a night crawler off the bottom or with a bobber for trout, bass, or sunfish. Trolling can be productive, but only early in the season before the lake weeds begin growing.

Special Notes: Boat motors are restricted to electric only.

18 | FISHERY FACTS

LOCATION AND DIRECTIONS: GPS — 34°07'35.96"N; 109°57'6.69"W
Woodland Lake resides on an island of Apache-Sitgreaves National Forests property just west of White Mountain Boulevard in Pinetop. It is surrounded by residential areas. To get there, turn south on Woodland Lake Road and drive a quarter-mile to one of two entrances to the park. The park is closed daily after 8 p.m.

AMENITIES: The Town of Pinetop-Lakeside maintains Woodland Park, which includes hiking trails, picnic tables and ramadas, barrier-free restrooms, a sand volleyball court, a tennis court, two children's playgrounds, multiple softball fields, a boat ramp, and a barrier-free floating fishing dock. There is no overnight camping at the park, but many lodging options are available in town.

The nearest campground is Lakeside Campground on State Route 260 about a quarter-mile west of Porter Mountain Road. This campground has 82 sites, vault toilets, potable water, and firewood for sale. You can make reservations for a campsite by visiting www.reserveusa.com or by calling 877-444-6777.

STREAMS

19 West Fork of Little Colorado River at Sheeps Crossing

This is the headwater fishery of the Little Colorado River, where cold, clear water tumbles down the heavily forested flanks of Mount Baldy, an extinct volcano at 11,403 feet in elevation.

Sheeps Crossing sits at 9,230 feet in elevation and is one of the trailheads for the popular West Baldy Trail up this imposing mountain, a 14-mile round-trip. Even in mid-July, backpackers on Mount Baldy can awaken to discover a thin covering of ice on water left out overnight. So bring cold-weather gear.

The West Baldy Trail follows the stream for 2 miles or so from the trail-head parking lot up on the ridge, offering anglers ready-made access to a series of beaver ponds, quick gurgling runs, and small energetic waterfalls in a classic mountain valley.

Heading downstream, there are abundant stream-fishing opportunities along the secluded 7 miles to the Greer Valley, although most anglers never venture far. Nor do they have to.

The Game and Fish Department routinely stocks native Apache trout from late spring to the end of summer. Many a youngster or Arizona angler is first introduced to the pleasures of catching one of these golden-colored native trout while fishing this rambunctious stretch of wild stream.

The West Fork is being managed as a recovery stream for Apache trout. Work on the stream to remove competing non-native trout resulted in low densities of trout. Apache trout have been reintroduced in several locations along the stream, but it will take time for natural spawning events to expand the Apache trout population into all available stream habitats.

Fishing Tips: This is stream fishing at its finest. Use stealth; stream fish can be spooky. Don't let your shadow scare fish in the pools and runs. You'll find lots of vegetation along the creek, but there are beaver dams creating open pools interspersed with quick gurgling runs. Waders aren't necessary, but sometimes wading is best for casting to the prime hiding holes.

➤ This small stream is perfect for using cane or alder poles to delicately drop natural baits such as garden worms, meadow grasshoppers, or tree cicadas into fast runs or deep pools.

➤ The best fishing times are at dawn and dusk, or any other time fish are rising to the surface to feed, such as when billowing clouds are piling up before summer's afternoon thundershowers.

➤ Generally, bait will work to catch Apache trout if it looks natural. Some prepared baits can work at times for Apache trout, but they are not usually as effective.

Small pools like this one make fishing Sheeps Crossing popular with novice and experienced anglers.

➤ For lures, think small. Smaller spinners work best, such as Panther Martins, Super Dupers, or Rooster Tails. Quarter-ounce gold Kastmasters can work well occasionally.

➤ Fly anglers should use small hooks, in sizes 14 through 18, which are usually better for Apache trout, especially throughout the day. Use patterns that have olive green, brown, or black coloring. Popular patterns include peacock ladies, pheasant-tail nymphs, hare's ear nymphs, Zug Bugs, scuds, or stonefly, mayfly, or caddis fly nymph imitations. Larger wet flies, using size 6 to 8 hooks, that work well include wooly buggers, wooly worms, streamers, and muddler minnows. Colors in purple, black, brown, and green work best.

➤ During summer, fly anglers should consider using grasshopper, ant, or beetle imitations, and summer cicadas when present. Pay attention to size when fishing hopper patterns.

Special Notes: The road to Sheeps Crossing is closed in winter due to deep snow.

19 | FISHERY FACTS

LOCATION AND DIRECTIONS: GPS — 33°57'34.94"N; 109°30'28.07"W
Access is via Forest Road 273 from the Sunrise turnoff at State Route 260. Sheeps Crossing is 8 miles from Sunrise Lake; or, from the other direction, 12 miles from Big Lake along FR 273.

AMENITIES: There is a gravel parking area, but no facilities. Plan to be self-reliant; it's pack-it-in, pack-it-out.

There is camping at the Wynn Campground a few miles down the road and dispersed camping opportunities nearby. There is a country store with gas pumps a half-hour drive away at Big Lake and another seasonal store at nearby Sunrise Lake.

20 East Fork of Black River

If you desire to camp with the rhythmic sounds of a fast-running trout stream close by, the East Fork of Black River is made to order. In fact, there are camping spots where you can catch trout within sight of your campfire or hammock.

This energetic trout stream flows down a deep canyon, providing almost 6 miles of angling opportunities, including plenty of fast runs and lazy pools along an alder-rich mountain riparian area that is a wildlife magnet.

The upper end of the canyon is approximately 8,100 feet in elevation, while Buffalo Crossing at the lower end is at 7,540 feet. Forest Road 276 follows along this creek, and there are numerous pullouts and small campgrounds.

The Arizona Game and Fish Department stocks this stream with native Apache trout from late spring through the end of summer. This stream also has abundant wild brown trout, which are often sought by anglers during the fall spawn.

Anglers are routinely treated to the site of deer, elk, and turkey coming down to water, with an occasional visit from Rocky Mountain bighorn sheep. But you may have to share the better fishing pools with great blue herons or belted kingfishers. Youngsters often delight in the occasional small garter snakes and skater bugs darting across the chilly pools.

Farther downstream, past the confluence with the West Fork, you can hunt for secretive browns or feisty smallmouth bass hiding in seldom-visited pools along a wild rock-walled canyon that looks relatively untouched by man.

Fishing Tips: This is a fun stream to fish, where you'll see youngsters dangling night crawlers in the water not far from serious fly anglers catching stocked Apache trout or wild, secretive browns.

➤ During summer, kids can also catch plentiful grasshoppers, and in some years, there are cicadas to use as bait. Cane or alder poles can add to the fishing adventure for kids. Prepared trout baits, such as Power Bait, don't work as well for these native salmonids.

➤ Spin anglers should think small; spinners work best, such as Panther Martins, Super Dupers, or Rooster Tails. Quarter-ounce gold Kastmasters can work well at times.

➤ For fly anglers, small hooks, in sizes 14 through 18, are usually better for Apache trout, especially throughout the day. Use patterns that have olive green, brown, or black coloring. Popular patterns include peacock ladies, pheasant-tail nymphs, hare's ear nymphs, Zug Bugs, scuds, or stonefly, mayfly, or caddis fly nymph imitations. Larger wet flies (size 6 to 8 hooks) that work well include wooly buggers, wooly worms, streamers, and muddler minnows.

Special Notes: This stream becomes inaccessible in winter due to snow. The season is typically from May to early November, depending on snow-melt in the spring and snowstorms in early winter.

20 | FISHERY FACTS

LOCATION AND DIRECTIONS: Buffalo Crossing GPS — 33°45'40.38"N; 109°21'24.55"W

From the Big Lake entrance, head south toward Three Forks and turn right at Forest Road 249E (there are signs along the way). Travel about a mile and turn left onto FR 24, then travel about 12 miles to the East Fork of Black River, and turn left on FR 276.

You can also access this area from Alpine, approximately 13 miles to the east. From Alpine, drive 2 miles north on U.S. Route 191 to FR 249. Turn west for 5 miles to FR 276. Turn south and follow FR 276 for 6 miles to the upper end of the East Fork developed camping area.

AMENITIES: There are six small campgrounds: Diamond Rock, Deer Creek, Horse Springs, Aspen, Raccoon, and Buffalo Crossing (the largest campground, with 18 sites). These Forest Service campgrounds have just the basic amenities, with vault toilets, picnic tables, and grills. Most have potable water available. The closest stores are at Big Lake and Alpine. There are no RV hookups.

(21) West Fork of Black River

The West Fork of Black River starts its life as a quick, cold trickle plum-meting down the steep slopes of Mount Baldy and turns into an intimate, narrow creek meandering across high meadows and verdant mountain valleys just a short drive from Big Lake.

The upper stretch of the West Fork receives the most attention from anglers and hikers alike, since there is a trailhead with parking along for-est roads 68 and 116. The appealing stretch of the creek and some of its tributaries provide anglers catch-and-release fishing opportunities for wild and stream-wise Apache trout, Arizona's state fish. This segment of the West Fork is a recovery stream for Apache trout, which were on the brink of extinction just a few decades ago. The Game and Fish Depart-ment stocks them during the spring and summer.

At the trailhead, there are some choices. You can work upstream along the meadow, where it is often possible to step across the narrow, meandering creek. You can also work downstream, which is where you will encounter stream-improvement structures. There are some nice pools to fish behind these structures, which also create picturesque waterfalls. You can also fish the lower end of this stream, where it passes through the West Fork Campground but where there are no special regulations to observe.

Once past the campground, the West Fork ambles across wide, lush meadows full of summer wildflowers and the promise of trout to catch until it finally joins up with the East Fork to become the Black River proper.

Fishing Tips: Spin anglers should think small; spinners work best, such as Panther Martins, Super Dupers, or Rooster Tails. Quarter-ounce gold Kastmasters can work well at times.

➤ For fly anglers, small hooks, in sizes 14 through 18, are usually better for Apache trout, especially throughout the day. Use patterns that have olive green, brown, or black coloring. Popular patterns include peacock ladies, pheasant-tail nymphs, hare's ear nymphs, Zug Bugs, scuds, or stonefly, mayfly, or caddis fly nymph imitations.

Fishing on the West Fork of Black River.

Special Notes: The West Fork from Hayground Creek upstream to the White Mountain Apache Indian Reservation, including tributaries, is catch-and-release only, with artificial lures and flies with single barbless hooks.

21 | FISHERY FACTS

LOCATION AND DIRECTIONS: The trailhead for the West Fork trail (GPS — 33°53'4.78"N; 109°28'10.92"W), which follows the drainage, is 4 miles south of State Route 273 on Forest Road 68, which is also the route to Reservation Lake. It is within a few miles of Big Lake.

For the West Fork Campground, drive 2 miles north of Alpine on U.S. Route 191 to FR 249. Turn west and follow this wide, graveled forest road 5 miles to FR 276. Turn south and follow FR 276 for 13 miles to FR 25 at Buffalo Crossing. Continue on FR 25 about 3 miles to FR 68, then turn and drive 3 miles to FR 68A just after the stream crossing. Follow FR 68A a short distance to the campground. You can also access this campground from Big Lake via FR 68.

AMENITIES: The upper segment of the West Fork offers no amenities, although Big Lake is a 10-minute drive away, where there are plenty of camping opportunities, a store, and even boat rentals.

The West Fork Campground along the lower stretch of stream has 70 "undefined" campsites, and there are vaulted toilets and fire rings. Plan to bring your own water, although there is a bubbling spring. Three-sided Adirondack shelters give this campground a rustic atmosphere. This campground is a 30- to 40-minute drive from Big Lake.

22 Silver Creek

This meandering creek adjacent to the Arizona Game and Fish Department's Silver Creek Fish Hatchery may be short in physical length, but it still ranks high in fishing stature, especially in winter.

HISTORICAL NOTE

Early settlers who built homes along the creek came up with the name it because it was "clear and silvery."

When other mountain creeks and streams are challenged with deep snow and ice, Silver Creek remains accessible and easily fishable. Sitting at 6,500 feet in elevation, Silver Creek is a spring creek. It rises mostly from a single main spring at a constant 61 to 63 degrees and a rate of 2.4 cubic feet per second. Therefore, it does not ice over in the winter, even during a hard freeze.

But there are two faces to this marvelous year-round stream fishery. From April 1 to the end of September, you can use barbed hooks and bait to catch and keep trout if you desire. However, that all changes on October 1, when trout must be immediately released unharmed and you must use single barbless hooks.

On October 1 every year, the Silver Creek Hatchery stocks this stream with native Apache trout and some rainbow trout as well. But what makes

Silver Creek is liberally stocked with trout annually on October 1.

lots of anglers smile is the fish planted here aren't the run-of-the-mill stockers; there are often some huge Apaches and rainbows mixed into this single, beginning-of-the-season stocking.

In fact, the opening day for this seasonal catch-and-release fishery has taken on an informal festival-like quality, with fly anglers from across the state vying to be the first ones to catch and release these quality trout.

This fishery is special for another reason: It is located in an 840-acre wildlife area that is a pop-

Anglers compete to catch prize Apache trout at Silver Creek.

ular destination for wildlife viewing. Be sure to bring binoculars along with your fly rod. There is a worn trail along the stream for those who would like an easy walk to explore the various runs and pools, but this trail can become extremely muddy immediately following storms.

Another distinction of this fishery is its close relationship to the Silver Creek Fish Hatchery, which is the primary facility for growing and stocking Apache trout in state waters. This small hatchery produces about 90,000 catchable Apache trout each year.

Fishing Tips: Spin anglers should think small — spinners work best, such as Panther Martins, Super Dupers, or Rooster Tails. Quarter-ounce gold Kastmasters can work well at times.

➤ For fly anglers, small hooks, in sizes 14 through 18, are usually better for Apache trout, especially throughout the day. Use patterns that have olive green, brown, or black coloring. Popular patterns include peacock ladies, pheasant-tail nymphs, hare's ear nymphs, Zug Bugs, scuds, or stonefly, mayfly, or caddis fly nymph imitations.

➤ Larger wet flies (size 6 to 8 hooks) that work well include wooly buggers, wooly worms, streamers, and muddler minnows. Colors in purple, black, brown, and green work well.

22 | FISHERY FACTS

LOCATION AND DIRECTIONS: GPS — 34°23'37.46"N; 110°02'53.69"W
Silver Creek is located about 5 miles east of Show Low on U.S. Route 60. Turn north off U.S. 60 onto Bourdon Ranch Road for 5 miles to Hatchery Way Road. Turn east on Hatchery Way Road for 1 mile to the Silver Creek Hatchery, then park in the parking lot and follow the signs to the creek.

AMENITIES: There are public restrooms available at the hatchery. Show Low is just 15 to 20 minutes away for everything else, including lodging, restaurants, and stores.

NORTH-CENTRAL ARIZONA

Oak Creek provides a scenic landscape for trout anglers and offers everything from put-and-take fishing for stocked rainbows to a catch-and-release section where elusive brown trout hide

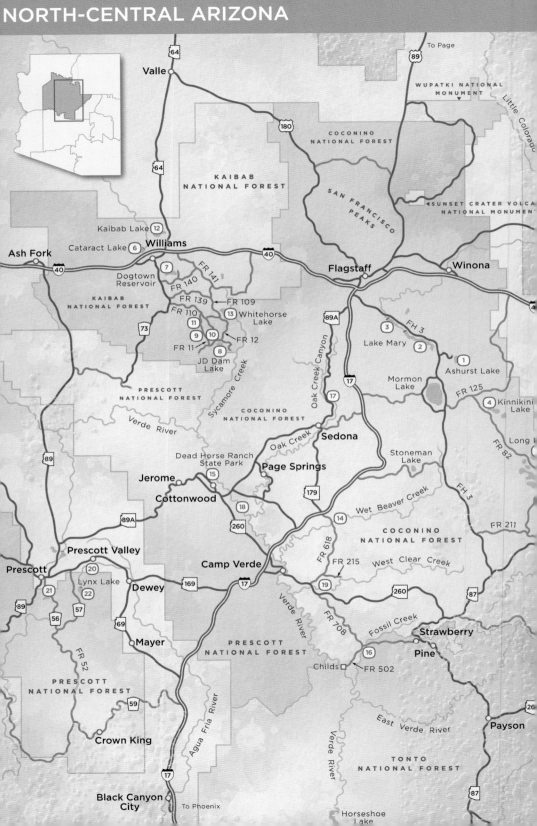

North-Central Arizona is an interesting contrast of habitats and diverse fisheries spread across a spectacular landscape encompassing some of this country's largest and oldest national forests. This vast area is dominated by the Colorado Plateau and boasts pine forests, montane chaparral, mixed conifers, piñon-juniper woodlands, alpine meadows, vast stands of quaking aspen, and even surviving patches of alpine tundra, all within about a two-hour drive from the Phoenix area.

You will discover a myriad of nearby fishing adventures while experiencing one of the world's most intriguing landscapes. This region will also fascinate you with its geological and archaeological wonders, including the Grand Canyon, Oak Creek Canyon, and Sunset Crater, as well as Walnut Canyon, Wupatki, Montezuma Castle, and Tuzigoot national monuments. There are lava tubes full of ice to visit, extinct volcanoes to scale, petrified forests to prowl, a colorful ancient desert to paint, and even an intriguing meteor crater to investigate. North-Central Arizona is also home to Arizona's tallest mountain range, the San Francisco Peaks, as well as the largest Indian reservation in North America, home to the Navajo Nation.

You can experience sparkling high-mountain lakes stocked with feisty trout and reel in some cool-water specimens, such as northern pike and walleye. You can fish and explore quick-running creeks flowing through remote and rugged wilderness areas, or ease your spirit along more docile waters in red-rock canyons. If you really feel adventuresome, slip on a backpack and hike down to fish lonely stretches of majestic streams hiding near the bottom of the Grand Canyon, where millions of years of Earth's history are dramatically exposed. While you have trout-fishing opportunities galore, you can also angle for bass, sunfish, catfish, and crappie as well.

Fishing in this region doesn't end when snowfall begins. The Verde Valley and Prescott areas offer popular prospects for winter trout fishing, along with many year-round fishing opportunities for warm-water species. Oak Creek also provides the state's only year-round fishing for both rainbow and brown trout in one of the most spectacular landscapes in a region full of such natural treasures. Some waters, such as Upper Lake Mary near Flagstaff, offer anglers the chance to catch multiple species of fish, from northern pike and walleye to yellow bass and perch. North-Central Arizona is also home to Arizona's two natural lakes: Mormon Lake and Stoneman Lake. Ironically, these two lakes are often dry, which is a testament to the arid and variable nature of our wondrously rugged landscapes.

FLAGSTAFF-AREA LAKES

1 Ashurst Lake

Ashurst Lake is a steadfast fishery on the Coconino National Forest that does not suffer as much during the periodic dry times in the arid South-west, nor is it as affected by the summer doldrums. Ashurst is routinely stocked with rainbow trout by the Arizona Game and Fish Department from spring through the end of summer, but it also contains illegally intro-

Along with trout and pike, anglers catch superb views of the San Francisco Peaks at Ashurst Lake.

duced northern pike. In fact, the state-record pike, weighing 32 pounds, 5.6 ounces, was caught here by Ronald Needs of Flagstaff on November 5, 2004.

This 229-acre fishery sits at 7,113 feet in elevation and is tucked among the piñon-juniper woodlands and high grasslands of Anderson Mesa, which is renowned for its speeding herds of pronghorns, North America's fastest land mammal. This is a relatively shallow lake, with an average depth of 12 feet. Anglers are treated to superb views of the San Francisco Peaks not far away. Bald and golden eagles often ply the skies over a rugged landscape renowned for its majestic elk.

Fishing Tips: Ashurst remains a viable fishing hole even during the dog days of summer. However, when weather fronts are moving through the state, the winds roaring across Anderson Mesa can whip this lake into whitecaps, making it a challenge to fish.

➤ Ashurst affords easy access for shore anglers, but is also popular with boat anglers. In early spring after snowdrifts on the road have melted, anglers are often treated to larger holdover rainbow and brook trout. This is primarily a rainbow trout fishery, but huge pike are often caught by anglers fishing for trout. There are also channel catfish in this lake.

➤ A good strategy to catch both pike and trout is to use in-line spinners such as Mepps and Rooster Tails. Some anglers use trout-looking swim baits to target pike, but the catch rates are typically low.

➤ During fall, this fishery is often a favorite with local anglers out of Flagstaff. Each year is different, but sometimes this lake is fishable in winter when snowdrifts don't block the road. However, this is definitely not a place for safe ice fishing.

➤ Ashurst is also full of crayfish, which is good to keep in mind if you are bottom fishing. If fishing deep, try using baits that will float up off the bottom. Youngsters often enjoy catching crayfish — all you need is some line on a stick and a small piece of meat, such as a hot dog or bacon.

Special Notes: Boat motors are limited to 10 hp or less. Drinking water is not available during winter.

1 | FISHERY FACTS

LOCATION AND DIRECTIONS: GPS — 35°1'16.0674"N; 111°24'27.072"W
Take Forest Highway 3 (Lake Mary Road) and then turn east on Forest Road 82. You will reach Ashurst Lake in 4 miles. This road can be closed during winter due to snowdrifts.

AMENITIES: There is a boat ramp and 50 single-unit campsites (25 at each of two campgrounds) with tables, fire rings, and cooking grills, plus drinking water and vault toilets. There is also a seasonal store operated out of a trailer from late spring to early September.

pper Lake Mary

③ Lower Lake Mary

Upper and Lower Lake Mary are Flagstaff's sister lakes, but the lower lake alternates from being a huge elk pasture in some years to becoming one of the state's most productive trout fisheries following a good winter's snowpack.

At 600 surface acres and 5 miles long when full, Upper Lake Mary on Walnut Creek is the long, rambling queen of the high-country fisheries. This elongated, narrow lake is renowned for its plentiful northern pike and delectable walleye, which are both considered cool-water fishes.

Upper Lake Mary is more like a warm-water fishery in the high country; it has crappie, sunfish, and channel catfish. Largemouth bass, yellow bass, and yellow perch are sometimes caught. Bass anglers especially favor this lake because they can use their bass boats — there are no boat-motor restrictions here. This large lake is also popular with water-skiers. Sometimes anglers are treated to the site of elk swimming in this cool, refreshing mountain lake not far from the San Francisco Peaks.

Fishing Tips: Northern pike are plentiful at these lakes, so you might want to consider using steel leaders for these toothy predators. Although no baitfish are allowed, you can use such things as water dogs and frozen anchovies. Small in-line spinners like Mepps or Rooster Tails can work well.
➤ One species that has become more plentiful in recent years is the yellow bass. Try gold Kastmasters and spinners for these delightful small fighters. These lakes can also be the state's most productive yellow perch fishery at times.

➤ The best fishing is in the spring and fall, although like most mountain waters, the lakes get their most intense use during summer. The lakes can be frozen over in winter, but they aren't considered safe for ice fishing. However, they draw lots of bald eagles in winter, providing superb wildlife-watching possibilities.

➤ When Lower Lake Mary is full, it can be the most productive trout fishery in the state. Stocked trout often grow so fast that

Water levels at Lower Lake Mary fluctuate from year to year.

Upper Lake Mary is ideal for kayak and canoe fishing.

their body length cannot keep up with their increasing size, making them look like fat footballs rather than streamlined salmonids.

Special Notes: There is no limit on boat-motor size. In the winter, the picnic areas and boat launches will not have daily maintenance performed. The upper lake is a Forest Service special-fee area.

2 | 3 | FISHERY FACTS

LOCATION AND DIRECTIONS: GPS — 35°4'52.644"N; 111°31'53.3994"W
These lakes are just 12 miles from Flagstaff on Lake Mary Road. On the way, you will first see Lower Lake Mary, which may or may not have any water in any given year or season.

AMENITIES: There are three boat ramps, a picnic area, a handicapped-accessible fishing ramp at the narrows, 76 single-unit campsites with tables, fire rings, and cooking grills, plus drinking water and toilets at the campgrounds. In addition, Flagstaff is just minutes away. There are also other campgrounds in the area.

(4) Kinnikinick Lake

A spring-fed, 126-acre lake with an unusual name, Kinnikinick is an out-of-the-way trout fishery on the rocky high prairies of Anderson Mesa, where pronghorns, elk, and bald eagles roam freely. From the air, it is shaped like an ice cream scoop. Kinnikinick has an average depth of 22 feet and sits at an elevation of 7,000 feet. It also affords nice views of the iconic San Francisco Peaks near Flagstaff. Knowledgeable anglers visit this fishery not for high catch rates, but for quality fish — it has nice-sized rainbows and some good-sized browns. However, this lake typically gets only nominal fishing pressure, so it can be a place to escape the crowds. Some have described this lake in the wind-blown grasslands and woodlands as being "aesthetically challenged." Kinnikinick is best suited for self-reliant visitors with self-contained rigs suitable for bumpy roads, or those who just want to day fish. Be sure to pack it in and pack it out.

HISTORICAL NOTE

The name "Kinnikinick" comes from the bearberry plant. Kinnikinick is also a mixture of tobacco, dried sumac leaves, and bark that was smoked instead of tobacco by some American Indians and pioneers. The term can refer to any of the plants used for such a mixture.

Fishing Tips: Kinnikinick Lake is amenable to shore angling but is best fished from a float tube, pontoon, canoe, or kayak.

➤ It is an especially good place for beginning fly anglers — there isn't a lot of tall vegetation to get in the way of back casts. But it is still not easy to catch fish in this lake. However, the fish caught are often a little larger. The best shore angling is during spring and fall.

➤ Since this lake is spring fed, Kinnickinick is not as susceptible to the summer doldrums. However, during the summer the fish can hold deeper. Try the typical trout baits here. For the larger trout, in-line spinners such as Mepps and Rooster Tails can work well, and flies often work the best.

➤ Wind can hamper fishing here when they sometimes roar across Anderson Mesa, where there are no tall stands of ponderosa pine to act as windbreaks. This is a good lake for night fishing during the summer, when Perseids meteor showers are underway. These high grasslands afford unrestricted views of the night sky with no competing light pollution. Keep your binoculars handy.

➤ This fishery has a very healthy population of crayfish, so crayfish-like lures work well. Conversely, when bottom fishing, it's best to have baits that float up off the bottom or they will be readily consumed by voracious crustaceans.

Special Notes: Boat-motor size is limited to single 10 hp. Access is usually not possible in winter due to snowdrifts across the gravel roads.

Its unobstructed sky views lure anglers to Kinnikinick Lake for night fishing in summer, especially during the Perseids meteor showers.

4 | FISHERY FACTS

LOCATION AND DIRECTIONS: GPS — 34°53′43.4034″N; 111°18′40.032″W
Kinnikinick Lake is located 38 miles south of Flagstaff on paved and graveled forest roads. Take Lake Mary Road to Forest Road 125 (near the turnoffs for Mormon Lake), turn north to FR 82, and follow the signs.

AMENITIES: There is a gravel launch ramp, restroom, and a parking area with eight trailer spaces. There are 18 single campsites with tables, fire rings, and cooking grills. Drinking water is available for campground guests only when the campground is open, from May to October.

5 Long Lake

The difficulties of getting to this remote lake, plus its lack of amenities, are often enough to keep away all but the most dedicated anglers and those looking for an adventure away from the crowds. However, those looking for big trout and monster pike are often willing to overlook these inconveniences. For others, the more austere and primitive nature of Long Lake is itself an attraction. Think self-reliance — you are on your own here.

When full, Long Lake has 268 acres and is almost 2 miles long, making it a superb place to exercise your canoe or kayak, at least when water levels are up. Water levels can vary significantly from year to year, or even from season to season. At 6,800 feet in elevation, the lake is formed in a slight depression in the high grasslands and wind-blown piñon-juniper woodlands on the eastern edge of rocky Anderson Mesa. A productive lake, Long Lake has held the state record for northern pike, and may very well do so again in the future. It is

HISTORICAL NOTE

Long Lake was named after the legend of a long serpent-like creature reportedly seen by ranchers as they herded cattle near the lake.

Remote, austere, and lacking amenities, Long Lake still draws dedicated anglers hoping to land its large trout and pike.

also renowned for its larger trout — growth rates here are phenomenal. But while it has big fish, this lake can be a gamble, and lots of anglers get skunked. The old saying for Long Lake is that it can be the best-producing lake in the state on one day, and have anglers thinking of new swear words on the next, especially when the winds come roaring off the mesa.

On the other side of Forest Road 82 from Long Lake is Soldier Lake, with just 30 surface acres. This fishery at 6,700 feet in elevation has good populations of largemouth bass, bluegill, walleye, and big catfish.

Launching from the shoreline at Long Lake.

Fishing Tips: Long Lake is a good place to use trout-like swim baits for the huge northern pike. Spinners are another good bet for pike and trout. The lake is also full of crayfish, so crayfish-like lures are a consideration. Since the lake doesn't usually attract casual anglers, you won't see many using Power Bait here. Trolling can be effective when the lake is fairly full. When the lake is low, it can be best fished from shore or by wading. Sometimes in summer, it can be a little challenged with aquatic weeds.

Special Notes: There are no boat-motor restrictions on Long Lake, but the long, bumpy roads leading to the lake can create a practical restriction worth considering.

5 | FISHERY FACTS

LOCATION AND DIRECTIONS: GPS — 34°47'18.1674"N; 111°12'59.796"W
Drive 48 miles south of Flagstaff on Forest Highway 3 (Lake Mary Road). Turn east (left) on Forest Road 211. Follow FR 211 about 8 miles to FR 82, then turn left (north) and drive 12 (bumpy) miles to Long Lake. The graded forest roads can be suitable for passenger vehicles in dry weather. However, high-clearance vehicles are recommended due to rutted and rocky roads. When the road is wet, the clay becomes slick and slimy, making four-wheel-drive necessary.

AMENITIES: There are two launch ramps and vault-style toilets, but not much else. There are no campgrounds, but dispersed camping is allowed. The Forest Service collects trash during the summer season, but the rest of the time it is a pack-it-in, pack-it-out area. Bring your own water and a sense of self-reliance.

WILLIAMS-AREA LAKES

6 Cataract Lake

If you enjoy the mystique of nearby freight trains rumbling down the tracks and fishing for largemouth bass and some rainbows in pine country, Cataract might be the lake for you. Don't expect an overly pretty lake, because this isn't it. Nor is it a superb fishery. Yet this 35-acre lake on the outskirts of Williams has lots of character — it's situated near the singing steel rails running east and west, and the local traces of Historic Route 66.

Cataract Lake does have the best largemouth bass population in the region, and is also home to channel catfish and crappie. The lake averages

Bulrushes add to the colorful character of Cataract Lake.

about 12 feet deep and sits at an elevation of 6,825 feet in the Kaibab National Forest.

The Arizona Game and Fish Department stocks rainbow trout from late spring through the end of summer. Stockings can be suspended when summer temperatures get too high.

If the fish aren't biting, you might want to take a ride on the Bill Williams Scenic Loop Drive. Also nearby are the Bill Williams Mountain hiking trail and the Devil Dog Loop mountain-biking trail, which in part follows the unpaved 1922 and 1932 alignments of Historic Route 66. The Grand Canyon Railway depot in Williams is not far away and is a place where you can often see vintage locomotives, especially in the summer.

Cataract might be small, but it is certainly a fishing hole surrounded by nostalgic mementos of bygone eras that will pique your imagination and wanderlust.

Fishing Tips: This is the spot to fish for largemouth bass. Try flipping and pitching weedless jigs in the abundant tule grass along the shoreline or work a Texas-rigged plastic worm along the bottom. This small, shallow lake has decent shoreline access and is a bait-fishing special for the whole family. Power Bait, night crawlers, corn, and salmon eggs are all good options. During summer when the trout bite slows, many anglers fish for crappie and sunfish. Try using mealworms or night crawlers.

➤ Cataract is fun to fish from a canoe, kayak, or float tube, but it is a bit small to fish from a powered boat, although some do. There are other area lakes better suited to motorized boats.

Special Notes: Power boats can have only single electric motors or single gasoline engines of 10 hp or less.

6 | FISHERY FACTS

LOCATION AND DIRECTIONS: GPS — 35°15′4″N; 112°12′16″W
Cataract Lake is about 1 mile west of Williams. From Interstate 40, take Exit 161; turn right onto Golf Course Drive if coming from the east, or left if coming from the west. After passing under the railroad tracks, turn right immediately and go about 1 mile to the campground entrance on your left. The road is paved and is open year-round. A short walk to the lake is required in the winter, when the campground is closed. The boat ramp area is also closed in winter.

From Railroad Avenue in Williams, turn north (right) on Seventh Street to Cataract Road. Turn left and follow Cataract Road west about 1 mile, then go under the I-40 underpass to the campground entrance on your right. This area is not accessible for large RVs.

AMENITIES: There is a cement boat-launch ramp and 18 campsites with picnic tables and fire rings. Camping fees apply. Pit toilets are provided, and drinking water is available but limited.

(7) Dogtown Reservoir

This 50-acre lake near the Town of Williams fishes a lot larger than its recorded size would indicate. This is often the top trout producer of all the small mountain lakes scattered about the Kaibab National Forest. Dogtown averages about 15 feet deep, and, at 7,070 feet in elevation, typically has larger holdover trout lurking in its depths, including some bruiser browns. Dogtown is stocked with rainbow trout from spring through the end of summer. This lake also has channel catfish, largemouth bass, and crappie. There is abundant shoreline access for anglers looking for plenty of elbow room.

Dogtown is also one of the most scenic of the Williams-area lakes. From its eastern shore, the imposing heights of Bill Williams Mountain dominate the near horizon. From its western shore, anglers can view the San Francisco Peaks looming on the horizon. Anglers fishing here can often hear the plaintive sound of faraway steam whistles as the vintage passenger trains leave the railway station in Williams bound for the Grand Canyon each day, or faintly hear freight trains rumbling down the Santa Fe Railway. Near the lake, visitors can enjoy a self-guided nature trail and a hiking trail that leads to a scenic overlook of the area from the top of nearby Davenport Hill.

HISTORICAL NOTE

Dogtown Reservoir got its name from the extensive prairie-dog towns that once covered open areas near the lake. In spite of the name, the lake is actually surrounded by tall ponderosa pines frequented by tassel-eared squirrels and camp robber jays.

Fishing Tips: The best fishing is in the spring and fall, but this picturesque mountain lake draws summer anglers like black bears to late-season manzanita berries. Bait fishing is very popular; try Power Bait, night crawlers, corn, or salmon eggs. During summer afternoons, many anglers switch from trout to fishing for largemouth bass, crappie, and even catfish — this lake has them all. Veteran spin anglers also like fishing the lake for larger fish while using spinners, small spoons, and crankbaits such as Rapalas.

➤ Don't plan on using your gasoline engine here — only electric trolling motors are allowed. In fact, trolling is a very popular fishing method. Try spinners, Rapalas, Cowbells, or Ford Fenders. This is also a good lake to fish using canoes, kayaks, and float tubes. During autumn, the large brown trout will exhibit spawning-like behavior, making them more susceptible to angler wiles. This is also a good time to use salmon eggs to catch larger holdover rainbow trout. Even anglers using lures may want to tip the hooks with single salmon eggs as a further inducement.

Special Notes: The roads are paved and graveled for passenger-vehicle use; however, they are usually closed by snow during winter months. Forest Road 140 is a high-use road and can become rough during peak season.

Veteran anglers like Dogtown Reservoir's shoreline, which offers plenty of elbow room.

7 | FISHERY FACTS

LOCATION AND DIRECTIONS: GPS — 35°12′15″N; 112°7′31″W
Dogtown Reservoir is about 6.5 miles southeast of Williams. From Williams, turn south on Fourth Street (County Road 73) for 4 miles to Forest Road 140. Turn left onto FR 140 and continue for 3 miles to FR 132. Turn left onto FR 132 and follow to the lake.

AMENITIES: There are 51 campsites with picnic tables and fire rings, and one group site. Camping fees apply. There is a concrete boat launch ramp. Vault toilets and water faucets are scattered throughout the campground.

8 JD Dam Lake

9 Elk Tank

10 Middle Tank

11 Perkins Tank

These small trout fisheries are located relatively close to one another southeast of Williams in the Kaibab National Forest.

JD Dam Lake is the most downstream of the three managed small waters on the JD Dam Wash drainage, but is by far the most popular. This is a small, marshy 6-acre pond at 6,458 feet in elevation that is located close to the rugged and remote Sycamore Canyon. While JD does have fish, it is also a really great place for wildlife-watching. Waterfowl often abound here, and elk, deer, and wild turkey routinely come to water. JD is periodically stocked with rainbow trout, but receives little fishing pres-

JD Dam Lake draws a variety of wildlife to its marshy waters.

sure and is catch-and-release only. This water is very marshy, and during summer you'll want to bring plenty of insect repellent. Some fly anglers like using float tubes here, but pontoons are a better bet due to aquatic vegetation.

Elk Tank is the most upstream impoundment on JD Wash. It is located 18 miles southeast of Williams and 4 miles southwest of Whitehorse Lake. The tank is less than 1 surface acre when full and has a depth of 30 feet. Elk Tank is a walk-in-only fishery with a small parking pullout and kiosk located off Forest Road 11.

Middle Tank is located 18 miles southeast of Williams and approximately 4 miles southwest of Whitehorse Lake. It is 2.19 surface acres when full. Middle Tank is the second and smallest of the three impoundments and is located 1.48 miles downstream from Elk Tank. Middle Tank is a walk-in-only fishery with a small parking pullout and kiosk located off FR 11.

Perkins Tank is located approximately 15 miles southeast of Williams off FR 110. It is a popular catch-and-release trout fishery for the local fly-fishing anglers of Williams, Flagstaff, and the surrounding area. Perkins Tank, with a lake elevation of 6,800 feet, on average is about 10 feet deep, with a maximum depth of 16 feet. This 3.5-surface-acre pond is part of an ongoing effort by the Game and Fish Department and the Northern Arizona Flycasters (NAF) to provide trophy catch-and-release fisheries close to the cities of Flagstaff and Williams. The members of the NAF have spent a significant amount of time, money, and effort to renovate and maintain this tank as a fishery.

Fishing Tips: All of these ponds or tanks are best fished with fly-fishing gear, but spin-angling is possible if you use weedless rigs or worms under a bobber. Fishing pressure is light, stocking levels are low, and catch rates are typically low as well.

Special Notes: JD Dam is a catch-and-release only lake with single barbless hooks. The graveled roads can be challenging in rain or snow.

8 | 9 | 10 | 11 | FISHERY FACTS

LOCATION AND DIRECTIONS: JD Dam Lake GPS — 35°4′5″N; 112°1′44″W
JD Dam Lake is 19.5 miles southeast of Williams. From Williams, turn south on Fourth Street (County Road 73) and drive about 9 miles to Forest Road 110. Turn left onto FR 110 and continue 7.5 miles to FR 109. Turn right onto FR 109 and go 2.5 miles to FR 12. Take FR 12 south (right) 4 miles to FR 110. Turn right and proceed approximately 0.1 miles to FR 105 and go 0.5 miles to the lake.

AMENITIES: Facilities are limited to parking, an outhouse, and trash receptacles. Camping is not allowed within a quarter-mile of the lake, as it is a popular wildlife watering hole.

(12) Kaibab Lake

This is a family friendly fishing and camping lake that is often the jump-off point for the Grand Canyon, which is about an hour's drive north. Whether you want to day fish or camp out, this 45-surface acre lake

Easily accessible Kaibab Lake offers a combination of family friendly fishing and camping.

located just a few miles from Williams in the pines is a convenient choice. Kaibab is easy to reach from Interstate 40 at the easternmost off-ramp for Williams.

Kaibab Lake averages 37 feet, making it the deepest of the Williams-area lakes in the Kaibab National Forest. The Arizona Game and Fish Department stocks Kaibab with rainbow trout from spring through summer, so catch rates are often pretty good here during this time. Because it is a deeper lake, Kaibab is known for harboring larger holdover trout. It seldom suffers from winterkill, but it can be subject to summer doldrums — at least for trout. Kaibab also has largemouth bass, channel catfish, and sunfish.

Kaibab Lake is also a favorite with campers. During the summer, the Kaibab National Forest will often put on evening campfire talks at the amphitheater overlooking the lake, especially on weekends. Many of these talks have interactive components for youth where they can learn and have fun at the same time. In the summer, you can sometimes hear train whistles as vintage steam locomotives commence their daily journey to the Grand Canyon. Because this lake is so close to Williams, when the morning bite is over you might jingle your spurs over to the Grand Canyon Railway depot (built in 1908) for the morning shootout at the adjacent Old West movie set.

Fishing Tips: The best fishing is in the spring, early summer, and fall, although this lake can be fishable at times in winter when snowdrifts don't block the entry road. During summer, the best trout fishing is at first and last light. But during the day, try switching tactics for largemouth bass, channel catfish, or sunfish. This lake is very amenable to shore fish-ing. During summer the trout will often hold deeper, making them more accessible to boat anglers. Trolling small spinners, spoons, and crankbaits is a popular technique here. Cowbells and Ford Fenders can be effective.

12 | FISHERY FACTS

LOCATION AND DIRECTIONS: GPS — 35°17'0"N; 112°9'31"W
Kaibab Lake is 2 miles east of Williams on Interstate 40; take Exit 165. Go north 1 mile on State Route 64 to the campground entrance on the west side of the highway. These are paved roads, but they are sometimes closed by snow in winter.

AMENITIES: There is a paved two-lane boat-launch ramp, handicapped-acces-sible fishing pier, restrooms, and RV dump. There are 70 campsites with fire rings and picnic tables. Camping fees apply. Vault toilets and water faucets are scattered throughout the campground. Water is not available during winter months. Tents, trailers, and RVs up to 35 feet can be accommodated, but no utility hookups are available. There are composting toilets and pit toilets, gar-bage bins, and recycle collection bins.

(13) Whitehorse Lake

This is a popular trout lake in the high pines where families enjoy camping not far from the edge of scenic Sycamore Canyon, which is renowned for its imposing bluffs and time-sculpted red sandstone formations. Although Whitehorse is a pleasing trout lake southeast of Williams, the area also offers families ready opportunities for hiking, mountain-biking, and wildlife-watching. The vast miles of dusty backcountry roads also make this region popular for those with all-terrain vehicles.

In drier years, this 35-acre lake can be challenged with low water levels. At about 15 feet deep and 6,650 feet in elevation, Whitehorse Lake can experience warm-water temperatures and lower oxygen levels during the height of summer, which can slow down the bite for cold-water fish. However, it also has channel catfish.

Whitehorse is a very scenic lake lined with tall ponderosa pines. The

At Whitehorse Lake, thunderstorms often cool the air on hot summer afternoons.

area is renowned for its elk, deer, and wild turkey. You can typically see tassel-eared squirrels and plentiful chipmunks in the area, making this lake popular with children who like to explore the forest. Osprey routinely fish the mountain lake, and an occasional bald eagle will glide by hoping for an easy fish meal.

Fishing Tips: Whitehorse has plenty of easy shoreline access, making it immensely popular for families. Rainbow Power Bait is often the most popular bait here. Salmon

A young angler at Whitehorse Lake concentrates on catching dinner.

eggs can be very effective in the spring and fall, but there are times when in-line spinners such as Mepps and Rooster Tails will put lots of feisty fish on the stringer. This is a classic put-and-take lake; most of the fish stocked are caught within a week to 10 days. However, you can also expect to catch some larger holdover trout here as well, especially in early spring and late fall. Anglers in the fall are often treated to the thrilling sound of bull elk bugling in the forest.

Special Notes: Power boats are limited to single electric motors of 10 hp or less. Drinking water is not available during winter months. This lake is often not accessible during winter.

13 | FISHERY FACTS

LOCATION AND DIRECTIONS: GPS — 35°7'9"N; 112°0'54"W
Whitehorse Lake is about 19 miles southeast of Williams. From Williams, turn south on Fourth Street (County Road 73) and drive about 9 miles to Forest Road 110. Turn left on FR 110 for 7.5 miles and turn left again onto FR 109. Go 3 miles to the campground entrance. The roads are paved and graveled but may be closed during winter.

AMENITIES: There are 94 campsites with fire rings and picnic tables. Two pit toilets are open only during the off-season. Composting toilets and water faucets are scattered throughout the campground and are open May to October. A concrete boat-launch ramp is available.

VERDE VALLEY-AREA FISHERIES

(14) Beaver Creek

This delightful small creek just a few miles east of Interstate 17 has two distinct characters. Near the old ranger station, you'll discover the small Wet Beaver Creek Campground and picnic area. This family friendly stretch of creek meanders through an imposing gallery of huge cottonwoods and giant Arizona sycamores. It is stocked with trout during late fall and early spring by the Arizona Game and Fish Department, but has smallmouth bass, largemouth bass, catfish, and even sunfish available all year long.

This section of the creek is lent additional character by a picturesque old bridge just below a deep pool bordered by flat rock shelves of dark pink-colored sandstone. Bring your camera. The riparian vegetation along this segment of the stream is rich and luxurious, attracting lots of wildlife, especially birds. Ringtail cats can sometimes be seen prowling the creek, especially in the evenings. Some anglers are treated to the sight of fox

Sandstone shelves along Beaver Creek are perfect spots for dropping a line.

and bobcat prowling the bottoms, but skunks and raccoons enjoy the dense riparian habitat, too.

The cool, clear waters of the creek provide an excellent place to fish, hike, swim, wade, and bird-watch, all within a few steps of the campsites or the picnic area. At 3,800 feet in elevation, it is a year-round camping, fishing, and hiking area the family will love to explore.

The area beyond this remarkable oasis nurtured by the stream is upper Sonoran Desert, with its characteristic rock gardens of prickly pear cactus and banana yucca providing a sharp contrast to the lush riparian zone along the creek.

Upstream, the creek takes on a different character when it is surrounded by the Beaver Creek Wilderness Area, which is dominated by a rugged high-desert canyon harboring deep secluded pools that can be an adventuresome challenge to reach. This is a superb area for those in good shape to hike, explore, and fish. The deep pools can harbor rainbow and brown trout, along with smallmouth bass, largemouth bass, and green sunfish.

A trailhead within easy driving distance from the campground (you'll see the parking area when driving in) provides access to hiking trails into the Beaver Creek Wilderness. This wilderness canyon is not the place to be when thunderstorms are visiting the watershed. Many a hiker in this imposing canyon has noted the high-water marks on the steep walls, testifying to the occasional flash floods roaring down the treacherous narrow waterway.

Fishing Tips: During the winter, fish for trout near the campground or head upstream to fish for smallmouth bass and trout in the more secluded areas. The area of stream below the campgrounds also has some largemouth bass lurking in the deeper pools. This is a great area to employ kid-friendly cane poles. Be sure to use light line — the usually clear water of this creek means fish can be very line-shy.

Special Notes: For more information, contact the Red Rock Ranger District at 928-282-4119.

14 | FISHERY FACTS

LOCATION AND DIRECTIONS: GPS — 34°40'6.77"N; 111°42'48.08"W
Leave Interstate 17 at Exit 298 (State Route 179) and drive 3 miles south on Forest Road 618 to the campground and picnic area along the creek. If you continue on this road, it will take you to West Clear Creek (follow the signs), which offers fishing adventures in the West Clear Creek Wilderness. FR 618 goes all the way to the General Crook Highway. It's a scenic but bumpy and dusty drive.

AMENITIES: The campground is sheltered by a stand of cottonwoods and Arizona sycamores clustered on the banks of Wet Beaver Creek. There are 13 single-unit sites, tables, fire rings and cooking grills, drinking water, and pit toilets. The road that leads to the campground is one of the Coconino National Forest's scenic drives. There is a free picnic area across FR 618 from the campground.

15 Dead Horse Ranch State Park

This state park offers readily accessible, family friendly fishing holes that are also very amenable to those with mobility issues. It's an excellent place for grandparents to take the kids fishing, whether for a day trip or campout.

There are two fishing lagoons nudged among an imposing gallery of giant cottonwood trees and tall willow trees in this beautiful state park bordering the banks of the Verde River. These lagoons are ready-made for those with physical limitations. There are even handicapped-accessible individual fishing piers immediately adjacent to the access road.

Dead Horse is just minutes away from the small community of Cottonwood and is a popular destination for winter visitors and those living in the Phoenix area. The developed portion of the Dead Horse Ranch State Park covers 423 acres. The 3,300-foot elevation accounts for the mild temperatures that are ideal for camping, mountain-biking in the Coconino National Forest, hiking along the Verde River, canoeing, picnicking, fishing, or just wading in the cool water. Keep an eye skyward in late spring and summer — hang gliders launching off a special launching facility on the top of nearby Mingus Mountain often provide an aerial treat to watch.

Fishing Tips: The Game and Fish Department stocks this stretch of river with trout in winter. It is also renowned for its flathead-catfish angling opportunities.

➤ All the trout baits work well here. Power Bait is by far the most popular. Night crawlers are a must-have. It's also a good place for beginner or novice anglers to use spinners — you might even catch a bass. In fact, some trout anglers have been surprised by catching 2- to 6-pound largemouth bass here. The bridge over the Verde River leading to Dead Horse is one of the areas stocked with trout in winter by the Game and Fish Department, so you might want to fish there as well.

➤ There are no flathead catfish in the Dead Horse Lagoons. It's all stocked with channel catfish, with some larger ones in the lower lagoon. There are not many flatheads in the Verde either until you get below Camp Verde.

Special Notes: To contact the park, call 928-634-5283.

HISTORICAL NOTE

The story of the park's name begins with the Ireys family, who came to Arizona from Minnesota looking for a ranch to buy in the late 1940s. At one of the ranches, they discovered a large dead horse lying by the road. After two days of viewing ranches, Mr. Ireys asked the kids which ranch they liked the best. The kids said, "The one with the dead horse, Dad!" The Ireys family chose the name Dead Horse Ranch. In 1973, when the State Parks Department acquired the ranch, the Ireys made retaining the name a condition of sale. The park borders a 6-mile reach of the Verde River known as the Verde River Greenway State Natural Area. Its unique ecosystem — the cottonwood and willow riparian gallery forest — is one of fewer than 20 such riparian zones in the world. It's a great area for birding.

LOCATION AND DIRECTIONS: GPS — 34°45'13.16"N; 112°0'32.17"W
From Interstate 17, go west at Exit 287 (State Route 260 toward Cottonwood). Continue approximately 11 miles to Main Street in Cottonwood (SR 89A) and turn left. Continue through Cottonwood on Main Street (the street will gradually curve to the left). Turn right (north) on North 10th Street. You'll see a brown information sign for the park before the 10th Street turn.

AMENITIES: A 23-site group campground is available by reservation. The loop contains modern restroom facilities providing hot water and showers, a large ramada, and a group fire ring. Most sites can accommodate two camping units.

(16) Fossil Creek

Fossil Creek is a relatively new and one-of-a-kind seasonal blue-ribbon and catch-and-release fishery with single barbless hooks for native roundtail chub, which were historically referred to as Verde trout by settlers in this area. Knowledgeable local anglers still use the term reverently. This is also one of the state's two travertine streams, with Havasupai Creek in the Grand Canyon being the other. It is one of only two designated Wild and Scenic rivers in Arizona. You can expect to encounter an ever-changing and growing series of rambunctious waterfalls, swift runs, cataracts, and deep aqua-tinted pools all tucked into a remote and rugged deep canyon.

The lush riparian vegetation, including willows, poison oak, wild grape, Gambel's oak, huge cottonwoods, and ancient Arizona sycamores, is so thick and luxuriant in places that it can inhibit creek access and make casting and travel difficult. Yet there are also long, turquoise-colored, deep pools that are so clear they seem to beckon one to cast an offering to the fishing deities, or possibly to jump into the water and become immersed in this Garden of Eden setting.

The Upper Falls, which is the upstream limit of the restricted 4.5-mile fishery, is one of the most picturesque waterfalls in the state. But you'll have to hike to it. Be sure to wear sturdy footwear — the cement-like travertine formations can be unforgiving and slippery in places.

This unique fishery borders the Fossil Creek Wilderness, adding to its allure. But getting there can be an adventure in itself. You have a choice of taking an hour-long drive down an often washboard-like dusty road or traveling 30 minutes down an often steep and narrow dirt road traversing a treacherous cliff overlooking Fossil Creek.

Fishing Tips: Spin anglers should use 1/32-ounce to 1/8-ounce crappie jigs (smaller is often better) in various colors, except red. The small crayfish-imitation lures can also work. Very small spinners worked via ultralight or microlight fishing poles are best, using the lightest line you can comfortably fish. The exceptionally clear water here is very line-revealing. For fly anglers, it is best to use flies that can be worked a little deeper, at least for the larger roundtails, which often hold in the shallows or the shadows. Anglers will often be able to see groups of smaller round-tails inhabiting the deep pools. These smaller fish can be readily attracted to flies hitting the water.

Special Notes: Fishing is allowed here from the first Saturday of October through April 30 each year. Fishing is allowed between the waterfall, approximately 1 mile above the Flume Trailhead parking along Forest Road 708, and the downstream powerline crossing immediately below Sally May Wash. This 4.5-mile area is catch-and-release only for roundtail chub. Roundtail must be immediately released unharmed; no chub may be kept. Use artificial lure and fly only, with single barbless hooks.

LOCATION AND DIRECTIONS: GPS — 34°23'39.41"N; 111°37'48.22"W (the bridge over Fossil Creek)

From Camp Verde, take State Route 260 east (General Crook Trail) approximately 7 miles to Fossil Creek Road (unpaved), turn right and travel approximately 21 miles to Fossil Creek — about an hour's drive on the bumpy dirt road. Or, from the town of Strawberry on the Mogollon Rim, take Fossil Creek Road (unpaved most of the way) and travel approximately 13.5 miles to Fossil Creek. This narrow dirt road with no guardrails traverses a steep cliff.

AMENITIES: The Forest Service has installed some portable restrooms, but there are no campgrounds or other such facilities. It is primitive dispersed camping and picnicking here. Most people visit for day trips.

A designated Wild and Scenic River, Fossil Creek is a rare travertine stream with gurgling cascades, rambunctious waterfalls, and enticing turquoise-colored pools.

(17) Oak Creek

Oak Creek is one of the most scenic fishing streams in the world. You'll find lots of interesting fishing opportunities along the 13 miles of Oak Creek Canyon, where you can experience millions of years of the Earth's geologic history dramatically exposed to both the eye and the elements. Some refer to Oak Creek Canyon as a dramatically sculpted cousin to the Grand Canyon. It's a visual treat. This famous stream has many characters, and even offers some quieter and more demure stretches of nutrient-rich water where river otters love to play in the shade of huge cottonwood and sycamore galleries.

The Arizona Game and Fish Department stocks rainbow trout at more than a dozen spots along this creek. In fact, Oak Creek has the distinction of being the only creek in the state that Game and Fish routinely stocks 10 out of 12 months (excluding January and February). Most of those trout-stocking sites are within Oak Creek Canyon, but not all of them.

There is also a lesser-known stretch of Oak Creek flowing to where it connects with the Verde River, almost 30 winding miles downstream from Sedona. Along its journey, Oak Creek flows past the Game and Fish Department's Page Springs Hatchery near Cornville. There are interesting wineries in the area, some of which have creek access where you can fish.

You can pick your spot and degree of fishing difficulty along Oak Creek. There are plenty of opportunities for classic put-and-take trout fishing made just for youngsters, such as the famous Slide Rock. Yet there is also a blue-ribbon stretch that is popular with experienced fly anglers where they can match wits with wily browns and larger rainbows. Below the popular canyon, you will also find stretches full of bass, catfish, and sunfish. Oak Creek is a convergence of fishing opportunities.

Geological Note: Oak Creek flows through a narrow gorge it has cut along a fault line in the same rock strata that form the Grand Canyon. This smaller cousin of the world's most prestigious chasm is much more accessible than its more famous relative — a road leads right down the middle of Oak Creek Canyon. If you'd like to get acquainted with these crimson cliffs and crystal pools, there are plenty of overlooks, picnic areas, hiking trails, and creekside paths to explore.

Fishing Tips: The various reaches of the creek in the canyon can vary, but many offer fast runs down slick sandstone stretches that energize deep hiding pools. These areas are best for fishing with bait such as night crawlers, grasshoppers, or cicadas in season. Small spinners, such as Mepps and Rooster Tails, can also be effective.

➤ In the upper end of Oak Creek Canyon, you'll find the catch-and-release blue-ribbon fishing area and the West Fork. Both are best fished with fly rod in hand and are usually fishable all year long, even when the occasional winter storm dumps snow in the picturesque canyon.

➤ Farther below the canyon, the creek takes on the nature of a small, slow-flowing river ambling past homes, pastures, orchards, and vineyards toward its meeting with the Verde River. The area is best fished with spin-

Oak Creek just might offer more miles of accessible fishing along a scenic byway than any other Arizona stream.

ners, crankbaits, and artificial plastics for the largemouth and smallmouth bass, or stink baits for the abundant catfish. Kids can use mealworms for the plentiful sunfish.

➤ In this more languid river-like stretch of Oak Creek, keep a watch for playful river otters, as they might try to steal your bait or possibly the fish on your stringer.

Special Notes: Between Junipine Crossing spanning the confluence of Oak Creek and along the West Fork of Oak Creek itself, it is catch-and-release only for trout. Trout must be immediately released unharmed; no trout may be kept. Only artificial flies and lures with single barbless hooks are permitted. There is no-limit fishing for smallmouth bass, largemouth bass, channel catfish, and flathead catfish.

17 | FISHERY FACTS

LOCATION AND DIRECTIONS: GPS — 34°56′45.33″N; 111°45′10.96″W (Slide Rock State Park in the heart of Oak Creek Canyon)
From Interstate 17, take Exit 298 to Sedona and travel on State Route 179 north for approximately 15 miles (just follow the signs). Sedona is the southern gateway to Oak Creek Canyon. Or drive south from Flagstaff on SR 89A; at 14 miles, the road drops nearly a thousand feet down a series of switchbacks to the canyon floor and continues for 13 more miles along the lush riparian zone beside cool, clear Oak Creek.

AMENITIES: There is a wide range of facilities, from campgrounds to high-end resorts and renowned restaurants. There are five developed campgrounds in Oak Creek Canyon proper, five picnic areas, hiking trails, developed services, and interpretation at Slide Rock and Red Rock state parks. Some campgrounds are seasonal. Manzanita Campground is open year-round. There are also RV parks nearby.

(18) Verde River (Verde Valley)

The Verde River holds the distinction as Arizona's first designated Wild and Scenic River. This classic Arizona river stretches approximately 180 winding miles from its origins in the high grasslands and chaparral north of Prescott until it merges with the Salt River in the upper Sonoran Desert habitat near Phoenix. The Verde watershed itself is larger than some states.

The Verde is one of the state's major life-sustaining arteries. The upper end of this river starts its life near the Game and Fish Department's Upper Verde wildlife area, which supports a restored riparian habitat that helps nourish this interesting river fishery near its headwaters.

In these uppermost areas, the Verde offers some limited fishing opportunities at a few remote access points for smallmouth bass, flathead catfish, green sunfish, and native roundtail chub. This rugged and remote area can best be accessed using high-ground-clearance vehicles via long and dusty dirt roads from Chino Valley, Williams, or Jerome. There are few if any flathead catfish above Camp Verde, and those few caught are typically less than 2 pounds. Yellow bullhead fishing would be better along the Upper Verde than would flathead fishing.

Portaging is required for canoes and kayaks on wilder reaches of the Verde River.

Once the river reaches the Perkinsville-Drake area, it makes a 38-mile jaunt mostly through the imposing Verde Canyon, where there is even more limited angling access, although this picturesque riverine chasm is traversed by the historic Verde Canyon Railroad. Access for this stretch is mostly by rail or shoe leather, yet experienced and hardy kayakers and canoeists skilled at portaging do navigate this uppermost and very wild stretch of river. There are also a couple of nearby access points via long, dusty, unpaved Forest Service roads that also serve as a jumpoff point for the Sycamore Canyon Wilderness.

Once the Verde River flows into the town of Cottonwood, it offers yet another fishing dimension — rainbow trout are stocked in winter. Trout are stocked biweekly from November through March at various road bridges of the Verde from Cottonwood to Camp Verde (see the list below). During the winter months, the Verde is at its lowest flows. It takes on more of a docile stream-like character in a cottonwood-lined riverbed that sometimes supports massive torrents of wild, frothing water, occasionally scouring out the riverbed.

Fishing Tips: Look for the fishing to pick up immediately following the winter trout stockings. Prepared trout baits can work for these stockers. Also try night crawlers, corn, small spinners such as Mepps and Rooster Tails, or small spoons such as Kastmasters. Some anglers target the abundant largemouth bass that prowl this river, or its channel catfish. Smallmouth bass can also be found in many stretches of river. An occasional native roundtail chub is caught as well. Bigger flathead catfish start showing up in the Childs area and downstream to Horseshoe Lake.
➤ In the upper reaches, you can use fly-fishing techniques to catch smallmouth bass, roundtail chub, and sunfish. Spin anglers should use ultralight equipment and try small crayfish-imitating lures, spinners, spoons, or crappie jigs. When seasonally available, try fishing with local terrestrials, such as grasshoppers and cicadas. Night crawlers and mealworms can be very effective at times and use little or no weight.

18 | FISHERY FACTS

LOCATION AND DIRECTIONS: GPS — 34°32'57.84"N; 111°51'3.34"W (bridge crossing in Camp Verde)
Take Interstate 17 to Camp Verde, which is 92 miles from Phoenix. From there you can access all the trout-stocking sites mentioned below.

TROUT-STOCKING SITES: Stocking sites are at Tuzigoot Bridge outside of Clarkdale, at the Dead Horse Ranch State Park access point called the Jacks, at the State Route 260 bridge (old White Bridge) in Camp Verde, and at Bignotti Beach (access off SR 260 and Thousand Trails Road).

AMENITIES: None are available at the trout-stocking sites, but the nearby towns of Cottonwood and Camp Verde offer all the amenities. A popular camping spot is Dead Horse Ranch State Park, which is also stocked with trout in winter.

(19) West Clear Creek

West Clear Creek on the east side of the Verde Valley suffers from a split personality when it comes to fishing, hiking, and adventure. At the Bull Pen area (3,200 feet in elevation), it is a fairly fast-flowing, family friendly creek with easy access and limited facilities. The Arizona Game and Fish Department stocks trout in the autumn and early spring.

However, upstream, past the Bull Pen parking area, awaits one of the most unique and sometimes challenging wilderness fishing experiences in the Southwest. It's almost a Jekyll-and-Hyde transformation, but not necessarily in a nightmarish way (unless you are caught by a flash flood). This energetic creek tumbles down through the West Clear Creek Wilderness, which slices through the rocky edge of the Mogollon Rim. This wilderness is really a connected series of steep, rugged canyons where Rocky Mountain bighorn sheep, mule deer, and javelinas are known to roam while dodging the attention of cougars and black bears. It is wild country.

There are sections of this deep gorge where the stream fills it from wall to wall, requiring you to wade or swim. There are also slick, treacherous waterfalls to negotiate. The landscape is both spectacular and, at times, dangerous. It's not the place to be when thunderstorms rattle the Rim Country and send walls of water and debris thundering down the narrow declines. These canyons can even test the mettle of those experienced at canyoneering. Be sure to tell people where you are going and when you will return.

Fishing Tips: The lower end of the creek near Bull Pen is best fished with ultralight fishing gear. Try night crawlers, corn, salmon eggs, or Power Bait for the trout. You might find some smallmouth bass, or maybe even a largemouth bass in a larger pool. There are some pools with catfish and sunfish as well. Try small spinners. Trout are also stocked near the Bull Pen parking area. This is a fast-running segment of creek best fished with a fly rod, or by wading out and tossing a night crawler into the riffles.

➤ A short hike upstream will introduce you to the lower reaches of the canyon and the wilderness area. The lower end of the canyon presents moderate difficulties, but you don't have to go far to reach areas best explored by experienced hikers. In these lower pools you'll find some trout, maybe even a smallmouth bass or two, and possibly some sunfish as well. It's rugged, challenging, and visually spectacular. But don't expect high catch rates — these are often wild fish hiding in small pools.

Special Notes: There is no-limit fishing for smallmouth bass, largemouth bass, channel catfish, and flathead catfish.

Portions of West Clear Creek flow through a rocky gorge on the edge of the Mogollon Rim. | DEREK VON BRIESEN

19 | FISHERY FACTS

LOCATION AND DIRECTIONS: From Interstate 17, take the exit for General Crook Highway, pass through the edge of Camp Verde and drive 6 miles to the West Clear Creek Campground. You can also access this area by taking Forest Road 618 north to FR 215 (follow the signs to the Bull Pen area) or by taking FR 618 from Wet Beaver Creek.

AMENITIES: There is an all-season campground with drinking water, cooking grills, and vault toilets adjacent to General Crook Highway. In the upper section, there is a primitive year-round campground at Bull Pen with vault toilets.

PRESCOTT-AREA LAKES

⑳ Fain Lake

This 3-acre lake in Prescott Valley is just 5 miles downstream from Lynx Lake, and although it may be small in size, it looms large when it comes to fun — especially for youngsters (and those who like to feel young). Fain Lake sits at 5,075 feet in elevation and is owned by the town of Prescott Valley and managed as a town park.

The Arizona Game and Fish Department stocks this lake annually with about 16,000 rainbow trout. The lake is typically stocked monthly except in July and August, when water temperatures and dissolved oxygen levels make stocking impractical. Fain is managed as a intensive-use, put-and-take trout fishery. Most of the fish stocked are caught within seven to 10 days, or sooner. Fain has also been stocked with channel catfish, brook trout, and bluegill. The lower elevation of this lake makes it fishable most of the year, although summer temperatures can soar into the triple digits.

Fishing Tips: This small lake is kid-friendly, with plenty of easy shoreline access. It is just made for bait fishing, especially worms and Power Bait. It is also a good place for beginning anglers to learn how to work in-line spinners, crankbaits, and plastic worms. Anglers often catch multiple species, adding to the enjoyment of fishing this small-town lake.

20 | FISHERY FACTS

LOCATION AND DIRECTIONS: Fain Lake is located near Prescott Valley. From Interstate 17, travel west on State Route 69 toward Prescott Valley and turn left on Glassford Hills road. Turn right on Second Street and go past the Arizona Department of Transportation yard. Follow Fain Park signs to the lake. This is a day-use-only facility.

AMENITIES: There is no established boat ramp. There is access to restrooms and a paved fishing area for physically challenged anglers.

(21) Goldwater Lake

This small lake near Prescott is a classic — you almost expect to see Andy and Opie sauntering down the lane carrying their fishing poles and jauntily whistling *The Fishing Hole*.

Grandparents looking for a location to take the grandchildren should put this lake high on the list. It's also a pretty nifty place to take grandparents, too, so they can once again experience the ageless thrill of catching fish.

Goldwater Lake is perched on the side of the Bradshaw Mountains just above Prescott. In fact, this lake is operated by the City of Prescott as a park and is therefore furnished with swings, picnic ramadas, and other such amenities. You can even play a round or two of horseshoes or have a family game of sand volleyball. Visitors to this picturesque fishing lake are treated to a drive up Senator Highway past historic Victorian homes before climbing the pine-clad, steep mountain with terrific views of Thumb Butte. The evocative drive sets a compelling stage for this family friendly fishing hole.

The 25-acre lake holds the state record for hybrid sunfish and is stocked in the fall and early spring with trout by the Arizona Game and Fish Department. At 5,990 feet in elevation, Goldwater also offers year-round fishing for largemouth bass, sunfish, and catfish. There are times

Goldwater Lake offers year-round fishing for trout, bass, sunfish, and catfish.

Operated as a park by the City of Prescott, Goldwater Lake is ideal for fishing and picnicking.

in winter when it can have ice forming along its edges; however, the ice typically melts by late morning. This lake is very popular with kayakers, but leave your gasoline engine at home — only electric boat motors are allowed. During the winter especially, Goldwater is routinely visited by bald eagles and osprey looking for fish meals.

Fishing Tips: Mealworms and night crawlers under bobbers are the Tom Sawyer specials here — they can hook you hybrid sunfish, catfish, bass, and even trout. In fact, you just might catch the next state-record hybrid sunfish here. Bring camp chairs for shore angling; there are also fishing piers. Even though this lake is only stocked in fall and early spring, trout fishing is viable from fall through late spring, with some trout being caught in summer as well. Just don't expect high catch rates all the time.
➤ This lake is perfect for fishing from kayaks, float tubes, and canoes.

Special Notes: Gasoline engines are not allowed on this lake. The park hours vary by season. Visit www.cityofprescott.net or call 928-771-1121 for more information.

21 | FISHERY FACTS

LOCATION AND DIRECTIONS: GPS — 34°29′55.03″N; 112°26′56.00″W
In Prescott, go south on Mount Vernon Street, which becomes Senator Highway, about 4 miles to the entrance to the lake. There is a small parking fee.

AMENITIES: Goldwater Lake's many amenities include a gravel boat-launch ramp, parking area, handicapped-accessible fishing piers, barbecue pits, a playground with swings, picnic tables, a sand volleyball court, horseshoe pits, hiking trails, restrooms, drinking water, and some vending machines.

(22) Lynx Lake

Lynx Lake's 55 acres are a family camping and fishing destination in the Bradshaw Mountains in the Prescott National Forest, just minutes away from the famous Prescott Courthouse Square and the infamous Whiskey Row. This pine-tree-lined lake sits at 5,530 feet in elevation and is renowned for its year-round mild weather. Fishing facilities are open all year long. Catch rates are seldom very high here, but Lynx Lake has a very relaxed atmosphere and most people don't seem to mind — anglers typically rate the fishing as "good."

The forested area also boasts other outdoor activities, such as hiking, mountain-biking, horseback-riding, and bird-watching. There are also ancient Indian ruins to explore.

Fishing Tips: Angling access is good because of a trail that contours the entire lakeshore. However, this trail is closed on the east side of the lake from December to June each year to accommodate nesting bald eagles. Lynx Lake has been managed as an intensive-use put-and-take trout-fishing location for more than three decades. Rainbow trout and bluegill are routinely stocked, but the Game and Fish Department also stocks brown trout, brook trout, and cutthroat trout. Lynx also has largemouth bass, black crappie, channel catfish, common carp, and goldfish.

HISTORICAL NOTE

Lynx Lake was built along Lynx Creek in 1963 by the Arizona Game and Fish Department to meet a growing demand for fishing. The Prescott National Forest completed renovations in 2002 in response to the ever-increasing popularity of the lake. The camping facilities especially were improved and expanded.

Special Notes: Lynx Lake is a Forest Service fee area. For more information, contact the Bradshaw Ranger District at 928-443-8000. Boat motors are restricted to electric only.

22 | FISHERY FACTS

LOCATION AND DIRECTIONS: GPS — 34°30'55"N; 112°23'2"W
From Interstate 17, travel west on State Route 69 toward Prescott. After passing Prescott Valley, turn left on Walker Road and follow the signs to Lynx Lake.

AMENITIES: There is a store with nonmotorized boat rentals; call 928-778-0720 for more information. There is a day-use area with picnic tables, toilets, and drinking water. The Hilltop Campground has 38 sites, with drinking water and toilets available. Lynx Lake Campground has 39 sites, with drinking water and toilets available. The campgrounds are seasonal. Accessible fishing is available for physically challenged anglers at a dock on the south-shore day-use site.

MOGOLLON RIM

Bear Canyon Lake requires a bit of hiking to reach its shore, but anglers are rewarded with terrific fishing for rainbow trout. | GEORGE ANDREJKO

Winslow

To Flagstaff

Ashurst Lake

Kinnikinick Lake

Clear C
Reser

40

Long Lake

99

East Clear Creek

Chevelon Creek

COCONINO
NATIONAL FOREST

87

FH 3

East Clear Creek

APACHE-SITGREAVES
NATIONAL FORESTS

FR 751

Clints Well

3

C.C. Cragin
Reservoir

FR 169

FR 169B

FR 504

87

FR 95

Leonard Canyon

Willow Creek

FR 34

4

Chevelon Canyon
Lake

COCONINO
NATIONAL FOREST

FR 300

FR 295

Bear Canyon
Lake

Chevelon Creek

APACHE-SITGREAVES
NATIONAL FORESTS

Heb

5

Knoll Lake

FR 89

260

FR 64

East Verde River

MOGOLLON

12

1

FR 300

Woods Canyon
Lake

7

Willow Springs
Lake

2

FR 86

FR 199

FR 289 →

11

FR 284

9

FR 149

6

FR 300

Black Ca
Lake

87

FR 622 →

13

Kohls Ranch

260

Christopher
Creek

FR 291

RIM

FR 512

8

Canyon Creek
← FR 188

East Verde
Estates

Payson

Star Valley

FR 200

Haigler Creek

Haigler Canyon
Campground

WHITE MOUNTA
APACHE INDIA
RESERVATION

87

10

FR 512

HELLSGATE
WILDERNESS

FR 129

Tonto Creek

FR 133

Rye

TONTO
NATIONAL FOREST

Young

288

Canyon Creek

To Phoenix

188

The sparkling mountain lakes and trout streams along the Mogollon Rim can provide you a lifetime of fishing adventures while exploring the largest contiguous ponderosa pine forest in the world. The Mogollon Rim Country is home to a series of clear mountain reservoirs that old-timers affectionately call the "Game and Fish Lakes." They were built in the 1950s and '60s by the Arizona Game and Fish Department to provide Arizonans increased water recreation, especially trout fishing. These mountain treasures have become more popular and successful than anyone's wildest imagination. Legions of Arizona youngsters and newcomers to the state routinely catch their first trout in Arizona while enjoying a Mogollon Rim trout-fishing expedition. For angling families across the state each year, fishing these waters for trout is a cherished outdoor tradition in the cool pines.

The Mogollon Rim Country, where the Western author Zane Grey and noted outdoors writer Jack O'Connor used to wander and write, also offers anglers ample stream-fishing opportunities. There are spritely creeks just off the beaten path where you will want to exercise some shoe leather on your trout quest. Some streams sport popular campgrounds where you can go to sleep at night with the rhythmic sound of a trout stream rushing by. Many creeks have quick runs and inspiring waterfalls. Others offer quality blue-ribbon fishing, where you can test your angling skills against wily brown trout hiding in shady, deep pools. The Mogollon Rim Country is also prime elk and turkey habitat, where omnivorous black bears prowl the forests and bald eagles soar the skies overhead.

This imposing 200-mile-long ridge along the southern edge of the Colorado Plateau also causes an uplift that affects weather patterns, resulting in significant annual precipitation in the form of winter snow and summer rain. This is one of the wettest areas of arid Arizona, with much of the moisture coming during summer afternoons. The Rim is renowned for tall, billowing clouds filling the summer sky and thunderous downpours that prompt people and wildlife to scurry for cover. You will return home with lingering memories of rising trout and sweet pine-scented mountain air that will refresh your spirit.

This remarkable mountainous area is also home to the Tonto Creek Hatchery and the Canyon Creek Hatchery, which combine to provide Arizonans thousands of quality hours of trout-fishing opportunities each year. Each is open to the public, so be sure to stop by and get acquainted with the trout you may catch in the future, or even the next day.

(1) Bear Canyon Lake

A beautiful, narrow, and canyon-bound mountain reservoir, Bear Canyon Lake is one of a series of mountain lakes built by the Arizona Game and Fish Department for angler recreation in the 1950s and '60s. This is a hike-in lake with no launching facilities and few amenities. Despite being several miles down a dirt road, it draws many anglers, especially fly anglers. The drive along the famous Rim Road is quite scenic, with several lookout points offering spectacular vistas from the edge of the steep Mogollon Rim ridge. Keep your camera handy.

Bear Canyon Lake consists of 60 surface acres with a maximum depth of 50 feet. It lies at 7,560 feet in elevation. Because of its depth and elevation, this lake does not suffer any water-quality problems, even during the

Despite its steep banks, there is a bit of shore angling at Bear Canyon Lake. | GEORGE ANDREJKO

heat of summer. The Game and Fish Department stocks it with catchable rainbow trout about six times each year, starting in late spring. Since it is deep, Bear Canyon also has larger holdover trout lurking in its depths. In fact, at one time it was managed as a blue-ribbon fishery. This lake is in prime elk, wild turkey, and bear country. There is only dispersed camping in the nearby forest, but you don't have to pay any fees to camp.

Fishing Tips: This lake is popular with float tubers, canoeists, and kayakers. Although there is plenty of shoreline access, this steep-sided, deep lake is not good for bottom fishing. There isn't much shallow water, except at the upper end of the lake.

➤ Spin anglers will want to use small spinners and lures. If fishing off the bottom, avoid casting out too far or you'll find the bottom very deep. Bait anglers should try fishing with a worm and bobber. Prepared trout baits don't always work well here. Fly anglers using a float tube can find solitude at Bear Canyon Lake, especially on weekdays. However, fly-fishing from shore or wading is not recommended because the tree line comes right to the water's edge, and the water gets deep close to shore. Most shoreline areas do not offer sufficient room for long back casts.

➤ During the summer, this deep canyon lake suffers less from increased water temperatures and decreased fish activity levels. Although stockings cease in late summer, the autumn action can be very good at times, especially for larger holdover trout.

Special Notes: Boat motors are restricted to electric only. Access is restricted in the winter when roads are closed due to snow, generally November to late April.

1 | FISHERY FACTS

LOCATION AND DIRECTIONS: GPS — 34°24'4.16"N; 111°0'18.95"W
Bear Canyon Lake is located nearly an hour's drive northeast of Payson. Travel west on Forest Road 300 (the Rim Road) from State Route 260 for about 12 miles. The road is paved to the Woods Canyon Lake turnoff, about 3 miles from SR 260; thereafter, the road is improved gravel. Turn north on FR 89 and drive 2 miles, then turn right onto FR 89A and drive to one of two access points. The left or northern spur leads to a parking area with a restroom. From this spot, hike 0.2 miles down a steep switchback trail to the lake. The shoreline is steep and narrow at this point. The right or southern spur leads to another parking lot with a restroom. A gentler hike, about a quarter-mile long, leads to the lakeshore. Here, the shoreline is wider and flatter.

AMENITIES: There is free, dispersed camping at the junction of FR 89 and 89A. There are also several barrier-free toilets along FR 89A and at the two trailhead access points. There is no boat ramp, and all boats must be carried in. You need to bring your own water. It is pack-it-in, pack-it-out at this beautiful lake.

② Black Canyon Lake

Black Canyon Lake is a survivor. Following the Rodeo-Chediski Fire in 2002, most biologists and foresters expected this lake to silt up and become unusable. Fortunately for trout anglers, they were wrong. It lost some capacity due to all the debris and ash flowing in, along with sediment from upstream drainages being scoured, but not to the extent predicted by some. The increased nutrient loading following the fire actually helped its productivity for several years.

Surprising biologists, Black Canyon Lake survived one of the worst recorded wildfires in Arizona's history.

The lake is currently managed primarily as a put-and-take trout fishery, with some put-to-grow still occurring. The Game and Fish Department stocks sub-catchable and catchable rainbow trout in the spring and early summer, with additional catchables stocked in the fall.

Black Canyon Lake has 78 surface acres, with a maximum depth of 60 feet and an average depth of 35 feet. The lake also currently contains illegally introduced green sunfish and largemouth bass. Although some trees around the lake are charred, the perimeter of the lake is forested and scenic.

Fishing Tips: There is plenty of shore access here. However, those fishing from boats often do better. Fly-fishing from a boat or float tube is a good way to catch large numbers of fish. Use prince nymphs, peacock ladies, hare's ear nymphs, or black, brown, or green wooly buggers. You'll get good surface bites in the evenings using dry flies. Trolling spinners, Super Dupers, or Rapalas early or late in the day would be a good way to go after some of the larger trout. Bait fishing is best with night crawlers off the bottom. Kids can do well catching green sunfish using night crawlers under a bobber. Try this technique from the shoreline wherever there are rocks or other cover. Catch and keep all you can of these illegally introduced fish.

HISTORICAL NOTE

Black Canyon Lake is another in a series of lakes the Arizona Game and Fish Department built in the 1960s along the Mogollon Rim.

Special Notes: Boat motors are restricted to electric only. Because of the Rodeo-Chedeski Fire, the entire area around Black Canyon Lake is open for day use only due to the danger of falling trees. Access is restricted in the winter when roads are closed due to snow, generally November to late April.

2 | FISHERY FACTS

LOCATION AND DIRECTIONS: GPS — 34°19'35.63"N; 110°42'7.22"W
This lake is located 15 miles southwest of Heber on the Apache-Sitgreaves National Forests. To access, turn south on Forest Road 300 from State Route 260, then drive 2.4 miles and turn east (left) on FR 86. Drive 3 miles farther to the lake turnoff.

AMENITIES: There is one boat ramp, usable at high water levels, and two barrier-free toilets. Camping is allowed only in two nearby campgrounds. The one closest to the lake is Black Canyon Rim Campground near the junction of FR 300 and FR 86. It has 21 sites, chemical toilets, water, and gravel road access. Approximately 2 miles farther down FR 300 is Gentry Campground, with six sites, a vault toilet, water, and gravel road access. Both campgrounds are fee-use areas, and no reservations are taken.

③ C.C. Cragin Reservoir (formerly Blue Ridge Reservoir)

C.C. Cragin Reservoir is a long and narrow serpentine lake winding through a steep, imposing canyon. This 70-acre lake on the Coconino National Forest sits at 6,720 feet in elevation and is one of the water sources used for the town of Payson 50 miles away. It is renowned for its shimmering beauty and big rainbow trout.

The overflow at C.C. Cragin (Blue Ridge) Reservoir.

With an average depth of 40 feet and a maximum depth of 100 feet, this is one of the deepest of the high mountain lakes. It can be challenging to fish unless you have a boat or other floating device. There are stately ponderosa pines and fir trees seemingly defying gravity on the steep and almost wedding-cake-like Coconino sandstone formations edging along the canyon slopes. The precipitous sides of this lake make it mostly unsuitable for shore angling.

Fishing Tips: C.C. Cragin can be a superb place to catch larger holdover rainbows, especially in early spring or fall. The lake is best fished from a small boat, kayak, canoe, or float tube. Many anglers work the steep shoreline with flies, lures, spinners, and spoons to catch the abundant rainbow trout. In fact, this lake is just made for slowly trolling the day away in a small boat. Rapalas, cowbells, and Ford Fenders are all popular.
➤ The rocky walls of the lake are crayfish heaven. The larger trout will feed on these small crustaceans, so you might want to try crayfish-like or crayfish-colored lures. You also might want to just catch a bunch of crayfish as well. A string with a piece of meat will work. Get a bucket of crayfish to go with your rainbow dinner and you'll have a gourmet treat to eat around your crackling campfire.
➤ In summer, this lake can be challenged with an algae bloom, which in turn affects the water quality, especially dissolved oxygen. Sometimes summer rains can ease the situation and prompt a better bite, but other times cloudy days can accentuate the bloom.

Special Notes: Boat motors are restricted to 10 hp or less. Access is restricted in the winter when roads are closed due to snow, generally November to late April.

At some points, serpentine C.C. Cragin Reservoir curves like a river.

3 | FISHERY FACTS

LOCATION AND DIRECTIONS: GPS — 34°33'16.18"N; 111°11'51.65"W
To reach C.C. Cragin Reservoir, drive 55 miles south of Flagstaff to Clints Well on Forest Highway 3 (Lake Mary Road). Turn northeast (left) about 4 miles on State Route 87 to Forest Road 751, then travel southeast about 6 more miles to the reservoir. All roads are paved except FR 751, which is graveled and suitable for passenger cars in most weather. In winter, FR 751 is closed and the reservoir is not accessible.

AMENITIES: There is a boat-launch ramp. The parking and restrooms are located just uphill from the boat ramp, although some vehicles also park on the sloped road nearby. There is a rough trail starting just behind the restrooms that also leads to the water. The closest camping is located 4 miles away at Rock Crossing Campground, where there are 35 single-unit campsites with tables, fire rings, cooking grills, drinking water, self-composting toilets, and hiking trails nearby. The facilities are maintained by the Forest Service. There is a country store, gas station, and restaurant at Clints Well just 10 miles away. The Blue Ridge Ranger Station is close by as well.

(4) Chevelon Canyon Lake

Chevelon Canyon Lake is a blue-ribbon fishery in the ponderosa pines that can take your breath away, both with its striking beauty and the need to hike in and out along a steep, challenging trail at 6,376 feet in elevation. Because of its remote location, steep topography, difficult access, special regulations, and lack of amenities, it typically draws only the most determined and physically fit anglers. On the plus side, this dazzling mountain lake is where you can expect to have a more solitary fishing experience for trout.

Chevelon Canyon Lake consists of 208 surface acres with an average depth of 35 feet and a maximum depth of 80 feet. It's the most difficult lake in the region to access, if not the most remote. But most anglers also come away impressed with its beauty as well. Chevelon is managed to produce large trout. It's stocked once in spring and once in fall with fingerling rainbow trout. The lake also contains trophy brown trout.

HISTORICAL NOTE

This lake was constructed by the Game and Fish Department in 1965.

Fishing Tips: You can expect to catch larger rainbow and brown trout, but due to its extremely steep sides, Chevelon is not shore-angler friendly. This lake is best fished via float tubes, kayaks, or canoes, but you must pack them up and down a steep, rocky trail leading to the dam and spillway.

Float tubes are popular at Chevelon Canyon Lake.

➤ Spin anglers should try Kastmasters, Panther Martin spinners, and Rapalas. Crayfish-imitating lures can also work well at times. Fly anglers should try wooly buggers or wooly worms in black or brown colors, crayfish-colored patterns, and brown or black semi-seal leeches, peacock ladies, or other large streamers. Try fishing near the inlet in the fall, when brown trout are spawning.

➤ Chevelon does not suffer water-quality or temperature problems during the summer. However, those looking for larger trophy-sized trout will want to fish this lake in the early spring or late fall. The huge brown trout go into spawning mode in late fall.

Anglers at Chevelon Canyon Lake must pack their gear in and out along a rocky trail.

Special Notes: Special fishing regulations apply at Chevelon Canyon Lake. Only artificial lures and flies are permitted. Trout between 10 and 14 inches may not be possessed, and trout taken from the lake must be killed immediately or released. Boat motors are restricted to electric or 10-hp-and-under gas motors. Vehicle access to the Chevelon Canyon Campground is restricted during winter when roads are closed due to snow, generally November to late April.

4 | FISHERY FACTS

LOCATION AND DIRECTIONS: GPS — 34°30′41.16″N; 110°49′30.76″W

The lake is located about 15 miles due west of Heber. Reaching it can take some effort. Traveling from Heber, turn north on Forest Road 504 and drive 18 miles to FR 169. Turn south (left) onto FR 169 and travel 9 miles to FR 169B. Turn east (left) on FR 169B and drive 2 miles to Chevelon Canyon Lake Campground.

Coming from Payson, travel west on the Rim Road (FR 300) from State Route 260 for 8.5 miles to FR 169. The road is paved to the Woods Canyon Lake turnoff; thereafter, the road is improved gravel. Turn north (right) on FR 169 and drive 12 miles to FR 169B.

You must park your vehicle and hike approximately 0.75 miles down a steep, closed road to access the lake.

AMENITIES: The lake itself has no amenities; you need to pack everything in and out. The nearby Chevelon Canyon Campground offers primitive camping with six sites and a vault toilet. Each site has a picnic table and fire ring. Chevelon Crossing Campground, on FR 504 near its junction with FR 169, is another primitive campground with five sites and a toilet. Camping is free at both of these sites. The closest community with stores, lodging, and gas stations is Heber-Overgaard, which is almost 30 miles away via narrow dirt roads.

5 Knoll Lake

Knoll Lake is one of Arizona's most secluded mountain reservoirs, but it offers a fishing adventure that can be well worth the effort. In fact, reaching this remote lake can be an adventure in itself. You must travel more than 20 miles along winding dirt roads — mostly via the famous Rim Road (Forest Road 300), which offers spectacular vistas off the steep Mogollon Rim cliff. It is one of the most scenic backcountry drives in Arizona for those who are not afraid of heights.

Knoll is often the last lake in Arizona to become accessible following snowmelt in the spring, which often adds to its appeal for those anglers with a pioneering spirit. However, four-wheel-drive might be necessary for those desiring to be the first anglers into this remote lake.

HISTORICAL NOTE

The Arizona Game and Fish Department built Knoll Lake in the 1960s.

Surrounded by ponderosa pines, this picturesque 75-surface-acre lake in Leonard Canyon has an island in its middle. Knoll averages 50 feet deep and is situated at 7,340 feet in elevation.

Surrounded by ponderosa pines, Knoll Lake is one of Arizona's most secluded mountain reservoirs.

Nesting ospreys are often seen diving into the water to catch fish. Bald eagles are also frequent guests to these sparking waters. This is prime elk and bear country, where you can sometimes be treated to the sight of wild turkey coming down to water.

Fishing Tips: Knoll is a productive rainbow trout fishery with plenty of shoreline access for anglers. The single access point for vehicles is at the dam, and most shore anglers

A young fisherman at Knoll Lake celebrates his catch.

don't get more than 100 yards away from that point. This is a superb lake for fishing from a canoe, kayak, small boat, or float tube. Those who like to hike and fish will find Knoll Lake a pleasing angling adventure.

➤ In early spring just after snowmelt, the holdover fish can be a little lethargic. While the catch rates for pink-fleshed holdovers can be low during this time, the quality of fish is typically good to excellent. The Game and Fish Department often stocks this lake for the first time in early May, and the catch rates pick up significantly. During the heat of summer, Knoll often produces when fishing at other lakes is slowing down. When the summer storms hit, fishing can be very good, but you don't want to be near the water when thunder and lightning are visiting this mountainous area. This lake is renowned for treating anglers to dramatic thunderstorms with tumultuous lighting displays.

Special Notes: Boat motors are limited to a single electric motor. Forest Road 300 is closed and Knoll Lake is not accessible in the winter.

5 | FISHERY FACTS

LOCATION AND DIRECTIONS: GPS — 34°25'53.04"N; 111°5'9.72"W
Knoll Lake can be accessed three different ways. Start on either end of Forest Road 300 (Rim Road), and travel either east from State Route 87 or west from SR 260 to FR 295, then travel the final 4 miles to Knoll. Either route is more than 20 miles of dirt road. While the roads to this lake are often negotiable by passenger cars when it is not wet or snowy, they are best traversed by high-ground-clearance vehicles.

AMENITIES: There is a boat ramp and restroom at the lake. The Knoll Lake Campground, just up the hill from the lake, has 33 single-unit campsites with tables, fire rings, cooking grills, vault toilets, and drinking water. The campground usually opens in early May and closes in mid-September. There is dispersed camping available nearby, as well as hiking trails.

6 Willow Springs Lake

Willow Springs is one of the largest, most popular, and easily accessible lakes along the Mogollon Rim. This narrow 158-acre reservoir provides lots of shoreline access among the tall ponderosa pines and mixed conifers in prime elk country.

Willow Springs Lake is situated at 7,500 feet in elevation and has an average depth of 60 feet, so it maintains good water quality even in summer. For this reason, it is stocked weekly from May through September with catchable rainbow trout. This large reservoir also contains illegally introduced largemouth and smallmouth bass and green sunfish. These illegal stockings can impact trout management in the lake, and are a serious threat to native fish populations downstream. Many anglers (and bald eagles) will often fish Willow Springs and Woods Canyon lakes on the same day — these two lakes are relatively close neighbors, as lakes go.

Camp chairs and small boats are excellent for fishing at Willow Springs Lake.

Fishing Tips: The lake is shore-angler-friendly. The most popular and successful fishing methods typically entail using night crawlers or Power Bait. Corn or salmon eggs can also work.

➤ This lake is also very popular with boat anglers. Try trolling with Super Duper, Panther Martin, or small gold Kastmaster lures. If all else fails, troll with cowbells or Ford Fenders. Trolling flies like wooly buggers can also be very productive, even on spinning outfits. Fly anglers should try flies such as wooly worms, wooly buggers, semi-seal leeches (black or brown), and peacock ladies. During the summer, try cicada or grasshopper patterns. Crayfish are plentiful, so please catch and eat all you can.

➤ Because of the size, depth, and topography of Willow Springs, it is less susceptible to warmer summer weather. However, fish will move deeper in the warmer months, and you'll want to fish 10 to 20 feet deep. Due to its close proximity to State Route 260, Willow Springs is often the first Rim lake to become accessible in spring.

Special Notes: There is no limit on warm-water fish, such as bass and sunfish. Please catch and keep all you can of these illegally stocked species. Boat motors are restricted to electric or 10-hp-and-under gas motors.

HISTORICAL NOTE

The Arizona Game and Fish Department constructed Willow Springs Lake in 1967 to provide water-oriented recreation opportunities for the public. In this respect, the department succeeded beyond anyone's expectations. Willow Springs is one of the most-visited lakes in the region.

6 | FISHERY FACTS

LOCATION AND DIRECTIONS: GPS — 34°18'48.67"N; 110°52'43.13"W
Willow Springs Lake is located 23 miles east of Payson on the Apache-Sitgreaves National Forests, immediately adjacent to State Route 260. Access the lake by way of Forest Road 149, which is paved.

AMENITIES: The lake has a paved boat ramp, a boat dock, barrier-free toilets, two picnic ramadas, and two boat beaches. Close to the lake, Sinkhole Campground is operated by a concessionaire and open year-round. It contains 26 camping sites, barrier-free toilets, and drinking water supplied from a tank. The much larger Canyon Point Campground is located 3 miles east of FR 149, adjacent to SR 260. It boasts 100 single-family sites, plus two group sites that can accommodate up to 40 people and 70 people, respectively. The campground has potable water, a shower building, dump station, and barrier-free toilets. Some sites have electricity. Daytime and evening programs on nature-related topics are presented in the campground amphitheater from Memorial Day through Labor Day. The campground is open from May 1 to October 31. Reserve a site at Canyon Point Campground by visiting www.reserveusa.com or calling 877-444-6777.

⑦ Woods Canyon Lake

Many a child or newcomer to Arizona catches his or her first rainbow trout at Woods Canyon Lake. This popular trout lake is stocked weekly during the prime fishing season, from May through September. It's a great place for youngsters learning how to fish.

Woods Canyon is a picturesque and delightful canyon-bound, deep lake that consists of 55 surface acres, with an average depth of 25 feet and a maximum depth of 40 feet. It lies at 7,510 feet in elevation. This is great place for grandparents to take their grandchildren fishing — it's very family friendly, with lots of easy-to-access shoreline. Like nearby Willow Springs Lake, the Game and Fish Department built Woods Canyon Lake for aquatic recreation. It gets intense angler use, and is the only Rim lake with a country store and boat rentals.

Fishing Tips: This is the classic put-and-take trout fishery — 80 percent or more of the trout stocked here are caught in the first seven days, which is why the lake is stocked weekly during the prime fishing season. Due to the weekly stockings, catch rates are typically good, making it a wonderful place to take youngsters to catch their first fish. Yet despite its high catch rates of stocker trout, Woods Canyon Lake has also produced winners for the department's "Big Fish of the Year" program in the brown and rainbow trout categories, including a 10-pound brown in 1999.

➤ If fishing for rainbow trout from shore, try Power Bait or worms. Boaters can try trolling a Super Duper or tiny gold Kastmaster. When it's hot in the summer, fish a little deeper, between 10 and 20 feet. However, don't fish too deep, because the lake stratifies in the summer, meaning there's no oxygen at the bottom. When summer thunderstorms pile up along the Rim and the barometer drops, trout will typically feed actively at the surface.

Morning mist shrouds the surface of Woods Canyon Lake.

Woods Canyon Lake can produce large brown and rainbow trout.

Special Notes: Boat motors are restricted to electric only, and there are no special regulations here. There is typically a seasonal closure for nesting bald eagles along a small stretch of shoreline, although it does not impact fishing opportunities. Vehicle access is restricted in the winter when roads are closed at the highway due to snow, generally December to early April.

7 | FISHERY FACTS

LOCATION AND DIRECTIONS: GPS — 34°20'1.72"N; 110°56'37.65"W
Woods Canyon Lake is located close to the edge of the Mogollon Rim, about 30 miles east of Payson. Take State Route 260 to Forest Road 300 (Rim Road), drive west about 4 miles, then drive north on FR 105 for 1 mile to the lake.

AMENITIES: Visitors to Woods Canyon Lake can enjoy a picnic area with restrooms, and a boat ramp. There is also a popular country store that rents boats and sells fishing licenses, bait, and tackle.

Campers can stay at one of four fee-use campgrounds. Spillway Campground has 26 sites, each accommodating a trailer up to 16 feet long, as well as barrier-free restrooms, drinking water, picnic tables, fire rings, and a campground host. Aspen Campground, along FR 105, has 136 sites and can accommodate trailers up to 32 feet long. It has the same amenities as Spillway. The Crook Campground is mainly a group camping area, with two loops and a total of 26 sites. Finally, Mogollon Campground on FR 300 has 26 units accommodating trailers up to 32 feet. Amenities are the same as Spillway Campground.

The campgrounds are open from April 15 to October 15, weather permitting. Get more camping information and reserve a site by visiting www.reserveusa.com or by calling 877-444-6777.

MOGOLLON RIM STREAMS

(8) Canyon Creek

Canyon Creek is one of those seemingly secret fishing spots, but in reality this fishery is so far off the beaten path down dusty dirt roads that it mostly attracts dedicated anglers looking for a quality stream-fishing experience. Canyon Creek flows off the rugged Mogollon Rim near the Arizona Game and Fish Department's Canyon Creek Hatchery. There are 6 miles of interesting fishing opportunities. The area elevation is 6,585 feet.

This creek has two characters: a stretch near the hatchery where you can catch and keep stocker rainbows and an occasional brown trout, and a stretch of stream below the OW Bridge that is a blue-ribbon fishery, where you are required to practice catch and release. This is an area where anglers are routinely treated to herds of elk coming down off the Rim, and even flocks of turkey coming to water. You can see the majestic Mogollon Rim dominating the horizon. This area was hit hard by the Rodeo-Chediski Fire in 2002.

Fishing Tips: Although there are certainly rainbow trout to catch here, the allure for most anglers is pitting their skills against secretive brown trout hiding in the deep pools or along shaded runs. Brown trout spawn in the fall, making this the optimum time to fish the creek.

➤ Canyon Creek is made for fly-fishing. The upper end near the hatchery is more thickly vegetated, while the lower end below the OW Bridge provides wider open areas where back casts are easier to perform. There are also some brown trout in the upper reaches of the creek between the hatchery and the spring head.

➤ Spin anglers should try small lures such as Mepps, Rooster Tails, and Panther Martin spinners. Fly-fishers may want to try wooly worms, wooly buggers, Yeager buggers, peacock ladies, prince nymphs, Zug Bugs, midge patterns, and small bead-head nymphs.

➤ During the summer and sometimes into the fall, try terrestrial

Orvis professional fly angler Cinda Howard chases trout in Canyon Creek.

Canyon Creek yields a huge brown trout.

patterns such as ants, grasshoppers, and cicadas. Try the following dry flies: parachute Adams, humpies, and caddis fly patterns.

Special Notes: From the creek source to the OW Bridge, the limit is four trout. From the OW Bridge to the Fort Apache Indian Reservation, trout must be immediately released unharmed, no trout may be kept, and only artificial lures and flies are permitted.

8 | FISHERY FACTS

LOCATION AND DIRECTIONS: GPS — 34°17'27.14"N; 110°48'22.59"W (Canyon Creek Hatchery)
Creek Access Point No. 1 (Airplane Flat/Upper Canyon Creek campgrounds): From Payson, travel 33 miles east on State Route 260. Turn right on the Young Road, Forest Road 512 (unpaved), and continue for 3 miles to FR 33. Turn left on FR 33 (unpaved) and travel for 5 miles to the site.
Creek Access Point No. 2 (OW Ranch Area): This access point is 42 miles east of Payson. From Payson, travel east 33 miles on SR 260. Turn right on Young Road/Forest Road 512 (unpaved), and drive for 5.5 miles to FR 188 (unpaved). Turn left on FR 188 and follow it for approximately 3.5 miles to the stream.

AMENITIES: Both Airplane Flat and Upper Canyon Creek campgrounds have a vault toilet equipped with grab bars. The nearby Canyon Creek Hatchery offers self-guided tours. Youngsters delight in feeding the trout, so be sure to bring some change for the fish-food dispensers.

⑨ Christopher Creek

Awaken your sense of fun for this 7-mile stretch of stream near the quaint mountain hamlet of Christopher Creek just below the imposing Mogollon Rim. This is a Tom Sawyer and Huck Finn stretch of stream just made for family adventure. For all you grandparents, this is a great choice to take the grandkids fishing. You can camp out or find nearby accommodations.

Christopher Creek attracts fishing pros like Cinda Howard and novices as well.

At 5,800 feet in elevation, it's slightly lower than many other popular trout fisheries in the cool pines. There are also many mountain lakes just a short drive away atop the Mogollon Rim. This is a classic put-and-take stream fishery that is stocked weekly by the Arizona Game and Fish Department during the prime fishing season. Catch rates are typically good following a stocking. Most of the stockers are caught within a week.

Fishing Tips: The best time to fish Christopher Creek is late spring through fall. Catching can slow down during summer, but fishing activity increases. At times, this is probably the most popular trout-fishing creek in the state, with good reason.

➤ Power Bait and night crawlers are favored here. Fly anglers routinely ply these waters with wooly buggers and parachute Adams. Small spinners can provide lots of fun in the deeper pools. This stream is just made for using cane poles. Starting in late spring, increase your catch rates by capturing grasshoppers for bait. Simply cast the hoppers into the riffles above the pools and let the current carry the wiggling offering into prime trout hiding territory. Watching a trout rise on a floating hopper will delight the youngsters (and the young at heart).

➤ Unfortunately, this creek also has plentiful crayfish. Crayfish are not native to Arizona, so please catch and eat all you can. Crayfish make a tasty side dish for a rainbow trout feast around the crackling campfire.

➤ On milder winter days, it is possible to fish this creek, but don't expect high catch rates, as stockings cease in September. There are also some wild browns in the upper reaches of See Canyon. The adventuresome might even find some trout up the tributaries off the upper reaches of Christopher Creek.

Special Notes: Christopher Creek's water can be a little cloudy in early spring, and that is typically why it isn't stocked until the flows subside.

9 | FISHERY FACTS

LOCATION AND DIRECTIONS: GPS — 34°18'28.61"N; 111°2'10.94"W (campground)
Travel 22 miles east of Payson on State Route 260 to reach the Christopher Creek Campground, or slightly farther to Forest Road 284 and turn left. Follow FR 284 to its end; it is a short hike to the creek.

AMENITIES: The Christopher Creek Campground has drinking water, picnic tables, grills, 43 camping units, six picnic units, and a vault toilet. There are plenty of other campgrounds in the area, but they fill quickly during summer. For more information, call 928-474-7900. The hamlet of Christopher Creek has a small store, restaurant, and cabins for rent.

10 Haigler Creek

This is a remote and often rugged small creek located just below the Mogollon Rim not far from the somewhat isolated community of Young, 14 miles away, although it can also be accessed from the mountain hamlet of Christopher Creek along State Route 89. Haigler sits at about 5,200

Small and remote, Haigler Creek offers hike-in fishing opportunities.

feet in elevation and mostly flows through a transitional vegetative zone from the ponderosa pine forest to chaparral habitat. This small creek is stocked during the late spring and summer by the Arizona Game and Fish Department. Occasionally, stockings are suspended due to warm water temperatures and low oxygen levels during summer.

There are a few places along this creek with easy vehicular access, such as Fisherman Point, but there are also rugged hike-in fishing opportunities as well, where the adventuresome can employ their wading and boulder-hopping skills. These rugged areas are challenging and not user-friendly to casual hikers and anglers.

Fishing Tips: Live bait such as night crawlers and grasshoppers can work well here, but in some places you might catch as many crayfish as trout. Power Bait might not be as effective as it is in lake environments, but can produce at times. In some of the deeper pools, small spinners can be used. As a rule, the thick vegetation makes casting a challenge at times. Fly anglers should think lightweight and small, although using terrestrial patterns during summer can be a good strategy. The most effective flies can vary with the season, so, as the saying goes, "match the hatch."

10 | FISHERY FACTS

LOCATION AND DIRECTIONS: GPS — 34°14'27.19"N; 110°57'18.24"W (Fisherman Point)

Fisherman Point: This is the most popular and accessible fishing area. From Payson, travel east for 24 miles on State Route 260. Turn right on Forest Road 291 (unpaved) and travel 3 miles to FR 200; turn right on FR 200 (unpaved) and travel for 5 miles. Take the trail for 0.25 miles to the creek.

Haigler Canyon Campground: From Payson, travel east for 24 miles on SR 260. Turn right on FR 291 (unpaved) and travel 3 miles to FR 200; turn right on FR 200 (unpaved) and travel for 5 miles to the site.

Alderwood Campground: From Young, take SR 288 for 3 miles and turn left on FR 200. Follow FR 200 (unpaved) for 7 miles to FR 202A and turn left. Follow FR 202A for 0.5 miles to the site. This site is 0.5 miles south of Haigler Canyon Campground.

Hellsgate Wilderness: From Young, go west on FR 129 for 7.5 miles. Turn left onto FR 133 for approximately 8 miles to the Smokey Hollow Trailhead. Hike north on Hellsgate Trail 37 for approximately 2.5 miles to the confluence of Haigler and Tonto creeks.

AMENITIES: These are mostly primitive (even at the campgrounds listed for access), although the town of Young and the hamlet of Christopher Creek are relatively close by, depending on where you choose to access the creek. The town of Payson is relatively close by as well.

(11) Horton Creek

Horton Creek is a hike-in fishery below the Mogollon Rim, not far from where the famous Western writer Zane Grey had his cabin along nearby Tonto Creek. Plan to hike if you want to fish this small creek, but don't plan to catch a lot of fish, or big ones for that matter. Few people are willing to hike very far to fish, so Horton is seldom crowded. This fishing hole is popular with Boy Scouts and Cub Scouts.

This creek sits at about 5,600 feet in elevation, and although it is a year-round fishery, the temperatures can get hot in summer — this hike is best accomplished in spring, fall, and winter, which are also the best fishing times. Don't be fooled; Horton Creek is typically dry at its confluence with Tonto Creek, but just upstream it is free flowing and then goes underground.

Fishing Tips: The fish here are wild trout that spook easily, so adjust your fishing accordingly. You must think stealth to be successful. Be sneaky. Do not let your shadow fall across the water.

➤ Horton is a small stream best fished with light tackle or fly rods. Night crawlers with little or no weight can be productive. During summer, youngsters often delight in catching live grasshoppers or cicadas to use as bait. Prepared trout baits, such as Power Bait, can work at times, but often aren't as productive as they are in lake environments. Fly anglers should think lightweight and small, although using terrestrial patterns during summer can be a good strategy. The most effective flies can vary with the season, so "match the hatch."

Special Notes: Be sure to carry plenty of water while hiking to Horton Creek. The rule of thumb is 1 gallon per day per person.

11 | FISHERY FACTS

LOCATION AND DIRECTIONS: GPS — 34°19'54.8"N; 111°05'38.1"W (trailhead at Upper Tonto Creek Campground)
To reach the Horton Creek day-use site and Upper Tonto Creek Campground, travel 17 miles east of Payson on State Route 260. Just east of Mile Marker 269 at Kohls Ranch, turn left (north) on Forest Road 289. Travel 1 mile north to these sites. At the parking area, cross the road and walk up the road to the campground. At the top of the hill, you will find a sign showing the start of the Horton Creek Trail. Follow the trail down to Horton Creek.

AMENITIES: This is a pack-it-in, pack-it-out fishing opportunity. However, at the Upper Tonto Creek Campground, which is the jump-off point to hike into Horton, there are six picnic units and nine camping units with picnic tables, grills, and vault toilets. Drinking water is also available. The hamlet of Christopher Creek is close by and Payson is about a half-hour away.

(12) Tonto Creek

This fast-flowing creek tumbles down the precipitous edge of the Mogollon Rim and flows through often-rugged canyons along its 30-mile journey to Theodore Roosevelt Lake in the Tonto Basin below. Along its journey through time and space, this creek has become a centerpiece in Western lore and Arizona angling traditions for more than 100 years. The narrow creek winds its way through the Tonto National Forest, providing anglers fast runs and deep pools to fish along its

HISTORICAL NOTE

Zane Grey, the famous Western writer who was also an avid angler, once had his cabin along Tonto Creek. The cabin burned down in 1990 during the infamous Dude Fire. The fire also came close to burning the Arizona Game and Fish Department's Tonto Creek Hatchery, which was saved by a group of conscientious firefighters.

upper end. Nearby small but picturesque waterfalls have inspired well-known authors and writers, including Zane Grey and Jack O'Connor.

The upper stretch of the creek is routinely stocked with rainbow trout by the Arizona Game and Fish Department from May through September, when weather and water conditions allow.

Tonto Creek takes on a different nature when it enters a remote and rugged area known as the Hellsgate Wilderness, where it often cascades down a demanding canyon that can be 1,000 feet deep along some stretches.

Fishing Tips: This is a small stream best fished with light tackle or fly rods. The upper reaches have mostly rainbow trout, but you can find some brown trout below the confluence with Horton Creek. The stretch of creek south of State Route 260 all the way past Bear Flat also holds some decent brown trout, although access can be challenging.

Waterfalls and pools dot Tonto Creek, which is a delight to fish, especially for youngsters.

➤ Catch rates can be good right after stocking. Night crawlers with little or no weight can be productive. During summer, youngsters often delight in catching live grasshoppers or cicadas to use as bait. Prepared trout baits, such as Power Bait, can work at times, but often aren't as productive as they are in lake environments. Fly anglers should think lightweight and small, although using terrestrial patterns during summer can be a good strategy. The most effective flies can vary with the season, so "match the hatch."

Special Notes: While the upper end of Tonto Creek below the Mogollon Rim provides year-round fishing, snowstorms can make access challenging at times. This stream can be cloudy in early spring during snowmelt.

Sandstone terraces give Tonto Creek plenty of character.

12 | FISHERY FACTS

LOCATION AND DIRECTIONS: GPS — 34°19′54.8″N; 111°05′38.1″W
Tonto Creek Fish Hatchery: Travel 17 miles east of Payson on State Route 260. Just east of Mile Marker 269 at Kohls Ranch, turn left (north) onto Forest Road 289. Travel 4 miles to the parking area just outside the entrance to the fish hatchery. FR 289 parallels Tonto Creek most of the way to the hatchery. Park in the lot.
Horton and Upper Tonto Creek recreation sites: Travel 17 miles east of Payson on SR 260. East of Mile Marker 269, turn north onto FR 289.
Bear Flat: Travel 14 miles east of Payson on SR 260, just past Mile Marker 266. Turn right on FR 405 and follow it for 4.5 miles to the creek.

AMENITIES: At the Upper Tonto Creek Campground, there are six picnic units and nine camping units with picnic tables, grills, and vault toilets. Drinking water is available. The hamlet of Christopher Creek is close by and the town of Payson is about a half-hour away.

(13) East Verde River

The segment of the East Verde River flowing off the Mogollon Rim near Payson is a small stream at about 4,900 feet in elevation that is usually stocked with rainbow trout by the Arizona Game and Fish Department in spring, typically starting in April. Summer temperatures are often too high for trout stockings, and the creek is usually at its lowest flows in fall and winter, which also precludes stocking. However, it is typically a good place to picnic most months of the year, as snow seldom stays on the ground long at this elevation.

The East Verde is managed as an intensive-use, put-and-take trout fishing area. But the stocking sites can vary, depending on flows. When it is stocked, this creek gets lots of angler use, especially from those living in the adjacent communities of Payson, Strawberry, and Pine, or from those who have cabins in the area.

Fishing Tips: The only viable sport fish in this section of the creek is rainbow trout. The Game and Fish Department can stock as early as April. Trout fishing is best in May and June, prior to the dropping of the stream flows and the increasing air and water temperatures of summer. Stockings are possible in July and August in some years, but not in others. Night crawlers and grasshoppers are the preferred bait for spin anglers. Fly anglers should "match the hatch."

13 | FISHERY FACTS

LOCATION AND DIRECTIONS: GPS — 34°13'34.61"N; 111°30'52.79"W (East Verde River and State Route 87)
East Verde Picnic Site: At the junction of SR 87, turn west on East Verde Estates Road (Forest Road 622) and drive 0.25 miles to the picnic site. This stretch can be stocked in the spring if it has sufficient water.
Houston Mesa Road (FR 199) crossings: At the junction of SR 87 and Houston Mesa Road (FR 199), turn east and travel 6 miles to one possible fishing site, travel 1 mile more to another site (7 miles from the junction), or 2.5 miles more to another site (9.5 miles from SR 87).

AMENITIES: Vault toilets are available at some of the sites along this creek, but mostly the conditions are fairly primitive. It's pack-it-in, pack-it-out. However, there are campgrounds fairly close by, especially on Houston Mesa Road. Most segments of this small creek are a short drive away from the mountain communities of Payson, Strawberry, and Pine, where you'll find stores, lodging, and restaurants.

CENTRAL ARIZONA

Lake Pleasant is one of the most popular fishing lakes in the state. It is the only lake in Arizona with white bass, although striped bass have exceeded whites in popularity.

To Flagstaff
Camp Verde
169
Dewey
260
69
87
Mayer
17
Verde River

MOGOLLON
Leonard Canyon
Chevel

Childs
Pine
Kohls Ranch
260
RIM
59
Agua Fria River

TONTO
NATIONAL FOREST
Payson
Tonto Creek
Verde River

Young
288

Castle Hot
Springs Road
Black Canyon City
9
MAZATZAL
TONTO
NATIONAL FOREST

Lake
Pleasant
Horseshoe
Lake
Bartlett
Lake
8
MOUNTAINS
188
Theodore Roosevelt Lake
2

1
New River
FR 24
FR 19
Cave Creek
87
188

74
101
Canyon
Lake
Apache
Lake
4
3
Apache Trail
Salt R
88

Peoria
6
5
Saguaro
Lake
Bush Highway
Tortilla Flat
188

60
101
7
Phoenix
Mesa
Superstition Mountains
TONTO
NATIONAL FOREST
Glob
10
Salt River
Apache Junction
60
Tempe
Chandler
Superior
202
60
Gila River
GILA RIVER
INDIAN RESERVATION
79
Gila River
347
177
10
Florence
10
87
Hayd

Casa Grande
8
To Yuma
Santa Cruz River

TOHONO O'ODHAM
INDIAN RESERVATION
10
To Tucson

Central Arizona offers some of the best fishing in the state for bass, crappie, and catfish, but it also has plenty of seasonal trout-fishing opportunities as well.

In fact, knowledgeable anglers contend this section of Arizona offers some of the best year-round fishing found near any major metropolitan area in the nation.

Here's why:

There are nine major warm-water fishing lakes and two classic desert rivers within a two-hour drive from Phoenix, plus 16 Urban Fishing Program lakes and various canals to fish.

Central Arizona is home to the state's largest inland reservoir, Theodore Roosevelt Lake — anglers affectionately call it "Rosy" — which is renowned for its bass, crappie, and catfish angling opportunities. It's one of the best in the West.

Rosy is at the top of a chain of lakes along the Salt River, followed by Apache, Canyon, and Saguaro lakes. Each one of these popular fishing lakes has its own personality, but all are renowned for their rugged scenic beauty in a landscape where desert bighorn sheep, mule deer, javelinas, and mountain lions roam.

Below Saguaro Lake on the outskirts of Phoenix, there is even a unique desert river, the Lower Salt, where trout are stocked during the cooler months and a steady stream of tubers floats downstream during the summertime.

Another remarkable fishery, Tempe Town Lake, is an engineering marvel. In a normally dry desert riverbed — the water is usually diverted to municipal use — the lake is tucked between two inflatable dams.

That's not all: About 45 miles from Phoenix, along the Verde River, Bartlett and Horseshoe lakes provide a fun tandem fishery in a wilderness-like setting that will make you want to return time and again.

There's more: Lake Pleasant, just north of Phoenix, is a dynamic angler-pleasing fishery with striped bass, white bass, largemouth bass, and smallmouth bass.

Then there are the lakes on the nearby San Carlos Apache Indian Reservation, including San Carlos Lake, which is renowned for its big bass and pie plate–sized crappie. San Carlos, when full, is the second largest inland lake in the state (see Indian Lands, page 246).

① Lake Pleasant

Lake Pleasant, just north of Phoenix, is one of the most versatile fishing lakes in the state — which is quite a feat, since it is also one of the busiest water-recreation attractions in Arizona.

Pleasant's breezy nature makes it a popular lake for sailing and wind-surfing, as well as water-skiing and riding personal watercraft. In addition, this desert reservoir near the Bradshaw Mountains attracts oodles of camp-ers, picnickers, hikers, stargazers, and swimmers.

It almost seems a contradiction, but despite drawing swarms of out-door recreationists (especially in late spring and summer), Pleasant still maintains a well-deserved reputation as a superb fishing lake where you can fill a cooler with fish.

Pleasant is the only lake in the state with white bass. This fishery also abounds with line-stripping striped bass — it is the state's only inland fishery with stripers — and is renowned for its largemouth bass. In recent years, smallmouth bass have taken hold as well.

Pleasant also has channel catfish, bluegill, redear sunfish, white crappies, black crappies, and green sunfish, while also harboring plenty of large carp.

Lake Pleasant attracts many anglers from the nearby metro Phoenix area.

The key to Lake Pleasant's success is the canal built and maintained by the Central Arizona Project (CAP). In 1993, the New Waddell Dam was built, expanding the lake from 3,700 surface acres to about 10,000 surface acres to provide storage space for Colorado River water from the CAP canal, which stretches across the desert from Lake Havasu.

Author Rory Aikens shows off a bass caught from Lake Pleasant.

Every year, starting in October, CAP water from Lake Havasu is pumped into Lake Pleasant. Throughout the winter, the lake level steadily rises, and it is kept stable during the vital spring spawning period. Starting in about May, water is pumped out to meet municipal and agricultural needs in the metro Phoenix area, so the lake level declines until it reaches its low ebb in late October once again. It's a systematic up-and-down cycle ardent Pleasant anglers know well.

The CAP water has brought with it several species from Lake Havasu, including striped bass, flathead catfish, and smallmouth bass. The Colorado River has also transported a tiny, prolific invader: quagga mussels. These invasive filter-feeding mussels have rapidly colonized throughout the lake. As the water level falls each year at Lake Pleasant, you can readily see vast colonies, or carpets, of these invading mollusks exposed on most hard surfaces. These opportunistic mussels will even coat lost fishing rods or other items resting along the lake bottom (see Invasive Species Note, p. 129).

Lake Pleasant also periodically gets a water and nutrient influx from the seasonally dry Agua Fria River, which starts life near Prescott along the Bradshaw Mountains. When there are river flows in late winter and early spring, both white bass and striped bass will spawn in the current, creating some fun fishing opportunities.

Fishing Tips: On most mornings, especially in spring, summer, and fall, there is a breeze rushing down the slopes from the Bradshaw Mountains just north of the lake. These northerly breezes across the lake usually last until midmorning, and then the prevailing westerly breezes take over. Weather fronts can disrupt or change this pattern.

There are two biological zones to fish at Lake Pleasant.

➤ **Zone No. 1:** The more shallow northern coves with abundant sub-merged vegetation constitute one biological zone. These shallow coves, which often have submerged creek channels, are the first to warm up in spring and have active fish, especially spawning bass. The northern coves are the first to experience significant plankton and zooplankton produc-tion. They also receive the most nutrient loading from runoff, which adds to their ability to warm up sooner.

**Anglers at Lake Pleasant are wise to
avoid the heat of the day in summer**

As the lake fills each year from Colorado River water — and sometimes from runoff — water slowly creeps up the length of these coves, inundating vegetation that has grown up along the fertile exposed lakebed.

These sheltered northern coves include Cole's Bay, Goose Bay, Humbug, and Bass Bay. The Castle Creek and Agua Fria arms of the lake also offer both shallow and deeper submerged creek channels that act as major fish thoroughfares. If the Agua Fria River is running in January, February, and March, striped bass and white bass can be found spawning in the inflows.

➤ **Zone No. 2:** During late spring and into summer, the biotic activity will pick up significantly in the second zone, which includes the much deeper main lake and its associated larger coves, such as Honeymoon, Jackass, Two Cow, Cottonwood, and Pipeline, especially during the prime daylight hours.

The main lake is up to 100 feet deep, so it takes longer to warm up. The largemouth bass that spawn in the main-lake coves can be two to three weeks behind the northern coves in their prime activity levels. Each year is a little different. Spawning in these areas can start in early March but not hit full stride until April, with some bass still on beds in May.

➤ Near the dam, the water-intake towers — the large structures sitting on pillars — typically create a zone of highly oxygenated water. Both striped and white bass are attracted to this oxygen-rich water.

➤ A typical late-spring (post-spawn) fishing pattern is for the stripers to feed actively on shad in the coves at first light. This bite will slacken as the sun rises into the sky, but the bite will pick up for largemouth bass. By late morning, when the wind shifts, the bite for both largemouth bass and striped bass typically moves out onto the main lake points, islands, and reefs. This pattern can often hold through the summer and early fall as well.

➤ In summer, the water in the shallow northern coves is often very warm and sometimes lacks oxygen, especially if there is a pronounced thermocline, or thermal layering of the water. You'll typically find the most active biological zones in the main body of the lake or in its associated deeper coves. At these times, the deeper portions of the Castle Creek and Agua Fria arms of the lake can also be active if water quality and temperatures remain satisfactory, especially at night.

➤ In the fall, the greatest biological action can shift back and forth between the coves and the main lake, so anglers will have to be in a searching pattern to see which zone is harboring the most active sport fish. Sometimes both areas are active simultaneously. However, in the fall the size of the lake will have diminished significantly, concentrating the

HISTORICAL NOTE

Lake Pleasant was originally created in the mid-1920s when the Waddell Dam was built to impound water from the Agua Fria River. The lake was named after Carl Pleasant, the engineer who designed the dam. To expand the size of the lake to hold CAP water, the New Waddell Dam was completed in 1992, flooding almost 7,000 acres of Upper Sonoran Desert habitat. The new dam tripled the size of Lake Pleasant.

The Agua Fria Arm of Lake Pleasant is a prime spot for white and striped bass.

aquatic communities, often with dramatic results.

➤ During winter months, the main lake's biological zone will seem almost dormant — except near the oxygen-rich water intakes near the dam — and the shallow northern coves will become the most biologically active. The vast numbers of waterfowl and shorebirds attracted to many of the northern coves attest to the biotic activity in winter.

Striped Bass Fishing Strategies: Although Pleasant has been renowned as a largemouth and white bass fishery, striped bass have taken over as the premier species anglers are targeting. Keep in mind that stripers hunt in schools and are open-water cruisers. However, they like to ambush shad up against prominent geological features, such as major points, islands, and reefs.

During the spring, summer, and fall, striped bass will often chase shad into the coves at first light. During the day, they can usually be found patrolling the main lake in search of balls of threadfin shad.

Because they hunt in packs, stripers are forever on the move. Once you catch one, the secret to catching more is chumming, especially with anchovies. Chumming can hold the school in the area so you can catch more fish. Some anglers like to mix corn into their anchovy chum. This can draw other fish species and possibly create a multispecies feeding frenzy.

During summer, anglers often fish at night over the submerged creek channels in the northern coves — since those channels act as fish highways — using submerged lights and chumming with anchovies, or else they anchor off major lake points and the mouths of coves.

During winter, stripers and white bass almost disappear from the main lake, except near the water intakes at the dam, and can be found congregated in the northern coves, especially the Agua Fria and Castle Creek arms of the lake. Sometimes Cole's Bay, Castle Creek, or Humbug can erupt with schools of stripers chasing schools of shad, creating sporadic winter topwater opportunities.

If the Agua Fria River has late-winter or early spring flows, stripers will actively spawn upstream or in the current from the inflows. Stripers can spawn in colder water than white bass, so they are first to spawn, usually in February or early March.

Special Notes: Lake Pleasant has a bald eagle nesting closure from December to June each year along a segment of the Agua Fria Arm of the lake. There are well-marked buoy lines for anglers to avoid the area. Also, to help this fishery, please catch and keep all the striped bass you can.

Invasive Species Note: Because quagga mussels have really taken hold at Pleasant, *be sure to clean, drain, and dry your boat after each outing,* as required by law. Day-use boaters are also required to wait five days before launching at another lake; this dry-out period is intended to kill the microscopic quagga larvae.

1 | FISHERY FACTS

LOCATION AND DIRECTIONS: GPS —
Lake Pleasant Regional Park entrance: 33°51'52.67"N; 112°19'2.20"W
Castle Creek launch ramp: 33°54'21.93"N; 112°18'29.69"W
Lake Pleasant Harbor entrance: 33°50'47.61"N; 112°14'50.38"W

For Lake Pleasant Regional Park, from Phoenix take Interstate 17 north to Carefree Highway (State Route 74). Exit Carefree Highway and travel west 15 miles to Castle Hot Springs Road, then turn in at the park entrance (follow the signs).

To reach Castle Creek's four-lane launch ramp entrance to the lake, travel past the main entrance along Castle Hot Springs Road and drive north 2.3 miles.

For Lake Pleasant Harbor and Marina, exit I-17 at Carefree Highway, head west 8 miles, turn right on West Harbor Boulevard (within sight of the dam), and travel less than a mile to the main entry gate (follow the signs).

AMENITIES: Lake Pleasant has two marinas: one public, at Scorpion Bay in Lake Pleasant Regional Park on the west side of the lake (operated by Maricopa County); and one private, at Lake Pleasant Harbor on the east side of the lake. Boat rentals and slips are available at both marinas.

There are four-lane and 10-lane launch ramps in the regional park and two launch ramps serving the private Lake Pleasant Harbor.

Lake Pleasant Regional Park offers 148 sites for RV and tent camping. All sites in the campground are available on a first-come, first-served basis.

Lake Pleasant is 20 minutes away from the northern edge of Phoenix, where there are ample shopping centers, gas stations, and restaurants.

SALT RIVER WATERSHED

(2) Theodore Roosevelt Lake

Roosevelt Lake is the granddaddy of the warm-water fishing lakes in Arizona, in more ways than one. This popular year-round fishery draws a steady stream of anglers in all four seasons and occupies a special place in the history and development of the Southwest (see Historical Note).

Roosevelt Lake has another distinction as well — with 21,493 surface acres spread across 22 miles and supporting 128 miles of shoreline in the Tonto Basin, it is by far Arizona's largest inland lake.

Roosevelt, also known as "Rosy," is just 80 miles from downtown Phoenix and is one of the most productive fisheries in the Southwest. Rosy is renowned far and wide for its largemouth bass, smallmouth bass, crappies, channel catfish, and flathead catfish. Carp, buffalo fish, bluegill, and green sunfish are also plentiful.

Rosy is shaped kind of like an elongated, overly plump barbell. Its two huge basins, the Tonto and Salt, are connected by a slightly narrower middle section where the dam and full-service marina are located, as well as a road south to Apache Lake. At times Rosy can fish like three different lakes all tied together.

Roosevelt Lake is one of the most productive fisheries in the West.

Roosevelt is liberally fed with water and nutrients from the Salt River, which has its origins in the White and Black rivers rushing down from the White Mountains. It is also fed by Tonto Creek, which flows down from the Mogollon Rim escarpment near Payson.

Theodore Roosevelt Dam was raised 77 feet in 1996, but then followed an almost decade-long drought. Not only did Rosy not fill during this period, the lake shrank dramatically.

During the spring runoff of 2005, the lake almost filled, covering all the vegetation that had grown up in the fertile lake bottom over the years, plus inundating about 6,000 surface acres of habitat that had never been covered with water.

At Roosevelt Lake, crappies are a mainstay for many anglers.

Most of the inundated landscape was prime Upper Sonoran Desert habitat, but the rising lake also covered a small forest of huge cottonwoods and mesquite trees, especially where Tonto Creek enters the lake.

The snowmelt and corresponding runoff in 2009 caused the lake to fill and spill for the first time since the dam was raised. In 2010, the lake filled in the late winter, which meant there had to be sustained water releases from Rosy throughout the spring for the first time ever.

All these events are important for anglers because Roosevelt is going through what biologists call "new lake syndrome." The fertility of the lake has been phenomenal, and the corresponding fish production and grow-outs have been exceptional.

Roosevelt may be a granddaddy, but it's behaving like an overactive teenager with a voracious appetite and raging hormones.

HISTORICAL NOTE

Roosevelt Lake played an integral role in the development of Phoenix and the entire western United States. Theodore Roosevelt Dam was originally constructed on the Salt River between 1905 and 1911, resulting in what was then the largest man-made lake in the world. President Theodore Roosevelt, who was instrumental in passage of the Reclamation Act of 1902, dedicated the dam in March 1911. In fact, Roosevelt Lake was the first impoundment ever built under the Reclamation Act, which created the U.S. Bureau of Reclamation. Dams have since been built by reclamation across the West. Roosevelt Dam is also unique in the way it was originally constructed. It was the world's largest "cyclopean-masonry" dam, a Greco-Roman style of building that uses huge, irregular blocks. This original dam is now covered by concrete. In 1996, the height of the dam was raised 77 feet, increasing the water-storage capacity of the lake by 20 percent (enough to serve 1 million more people).

Fishing Tips: Rosy is a popular four-season fishery offering anglers lots of fishing choices.

There are three major zones to fish: the two major basins, the Tonto and Salt arms, which can have significantly different fishing dynamics at times, plus a center section of the lake that can also have its own fishing character. If you can't find action in one zone, try another. But even exploring one arm can consume a whole day, making Rosy a destination fishery where people spend whole weekends, or whole vacations.

➤ **Zone No. 1:** The Salt River Arm on the eastern end of the lake is more alluvial in nature. The tremendous inflows each year from the Salt River keep this area charged with plentiful nutrients. Sandbars and mudflats (catfish heaven) abound. The irregular southern shoreline is where you'll often find salt cedars, willows, and mesquite trees either along the lake edges or submerged.

The northern shoreline, adjacent to a rising upland, is rockier in nature, and you'll find steeper banks, sometimes with nice fish-holding 45-degree angles or shelves with adjacent drop-offs.

During winter, flotillas of crappie anglers are often found in the deeper parts of this huge arm of the lake because that is where vast schools can congregate to feed on suspended plankton.

➤ **Zone No. 2:** On the western end, Roosevelt Lake's Tonto Arm starts with very rocky terrain supporting large coves near the middle of the lake, but as it progresses toward Tonto Creek inflows it gradually evolves into huge mudflats and sandbars, leading to areas with dense vegetation.

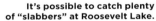

It's possible to catch plenty of "slabbers" at Roosevelt Lake.

Next you'll find a submerged mesquite bosque or forest that many anglers describe as "a submerged jungle" where Tonto Creek enters the lake. There is also a cottonwood gallery where 100-foot-tall trees are partially submerged when the lake is full. This area is ideal for flipping and pitching and for working spinner-baits. Be sure to use stout line.

Bald eagles typically nest in one of the cottonwoods, so watch for the warning buoys during winter and early spring; the young eagles normally fledge in June.

➤ **Zone No. 3:** The rockier, slightly narrower center section of Rosy, with its reefs, islands, coves, marina, and dam, can also have its own fishing dynamics. As you might guess, this section of the lake can harbor lots of smallmouth bass. The very sheltered and large elongated bowl of Salome Cove can also act like a

Open, grassy Bermuda Flat offers dispersed shoreline camping at Roosevelt Lake. The area is closed November to February for a large flock of wintering Canada geese.

lake within a lake. In some years, Salome Cove can be the first to have spawning bass.

During spring runoff, when both Tonto Creek and the Salt River dump tons of sediment into the lake, the center section can provide the clearest water, although it too can look like "chocolate soup" at times.

Seasonal Patterns: Roosevelt Lake contains lots of potential spawning habitat for all species, giving anglers plenty of territory to explore. A good strategy from spring through fall is working vegetation transition zones. Try those areas where you can see a transition of vegetation or habitat types, such as going from submerged cockleburs to brush, from brush to submerged trees, or rocks and boulders to submerged brush and cockleburs. Also be sure to work the edge of the vegetation adjacent to open, clear water.

➤ During the spring, anglers are treated to superb fishing opportunities for prespawn and spawning bass, crappies, and carp. Largemouth bass

Roosevelt Lake hosts a number of bass-fishing tournaments.

typically prefer shallows in the sheltered coves or large flats for spawning. Smallmouth bass prefer rocky ledges or shelves. Prespawn crappies can often be found in the mouths of coves or in the deeper water adjacent to the huge flats, such as in the Tonto Basin. For spawning crappies, look for submerged flats — especially those with submerged cockleburs — or in the shallow backs and sides of coves.

The spring runoff can create lots of turbidity, making this a superb place to use spinnerbaits along the vast acres of submerged vegetation for bass. In early spring, try slowing down the presentation by using trailers and rattling jigs flipped into the dense vegetation. Some anglers like to use slightly lighter tackle to flip and pitch smaller flutter-down lures, especially along the leading edges of the vegetation. Drop shots are also popular here.

Springtime bowfishing for carp is also popular, especially in the jungle-like submerged vegetation in the Tonto Arm. March is often the prime time for spawning carp.

Once bass have recovered from the spawn, the postspawn bite in late spring can also put smiles on anglers' faces. Bass can be in the coves at first and last light, but during the day, try working the major points, islands, and reefs.

➤ During the summer, most anglers switch to nighttime fishing under lights, especially off major points or along the secondary points just inside coves.

➤ Starting in late summer and continuing through the fall, bass can often be found chasing shad at the surface of the lake, creating what anglers call a "topwater bite," which can be some of the most exciting fishing of the year. These shad "boils" can also occur in open water. Keep a watch on the activity of fish-eating birds, such as great blue herons, to help determine where the action is located.

➤ During the winter, most anglers fish deeper for bass, catfish, and carp. However, starting in about January, the winter crappie fishing can really pick up in the Salt River Arm, the Tonto Creek Arm, or both.

Although the majority of anglers fish for bass and crappie, there are those who target the huge flathead catfish, especially in the Salt River Arm. Roosevelt holds the potential each year to produce a new state-record flathead. Try using live bluegill or small carp as bait. The upper Salt River where it flows into Roosevelt Lake is a prime location for flathead catfish.

Special Notes: This lake is located in the Tonto National Forest, so you will need a Tonto Pass (daily-use recreation pass).

2 | FISHERY FACTS

LOCATION AND DIRECTIONS: GPS — 33°40′18″N; 111°9′40″W
Roosevelt Lake is 80 miles from downtown Phoenix. Take Beeline Highway (State Route 87) north 45 miles to SR 188, then take SR 188 34 miles to Roosevelt Lake. Or from Globe, take SR 188 for 27 miles to Roosevelt Lake.

AMENITIES: Roosevelt Lake has the most developed campsites of any lake in the state — 764 sites spread across three major areas, plus there are other specific areas where dispersed camping is allowed (often at the water's edge), such as Bermuda Flat and Cholla Cove.

Rosy has 11 launch ramps spread across the lake. However, most people launch at one of the four most popular camping and recreational sites: Windy Hill (Salt River Arm), Cholla (Tonto Creek Arm), the marina (four-lane), or Schoolhouse Point (eastern end).

There is a full-service marina with boat fuel, a store, snack bar, boat slips, boat rentals, and houseboat rentals available. There are also fish-cleaning stations and group campsites.

Small grocery stores, gas stations, and restaurants are not far from the lake, with some local lodging available and nearby bait and tackle stores. The closest towns are Globe and Payson, and the small village of Pumpkin Center.

③ Apache Lake

Apache Lake offers a remote but scenic angling adventure the whole family will love.

Tucked between the Superstition Wilderness on one side and the Three-Bar Wildlife Area and Four Peaks Wilderness on the other, Apache Lake is a narrow band of water between wild and rugged wilderness areas in the Tonto National Forest full of steep terrain best suited for desert bighorn sheep, mule deer, javelinas, mountain lions, and Gambel's quail.

This narrow, winding lake seems much larger than its full 2,654 acres. It is 17 miles long and has 41 miles of shoreline with lots of rock shelves and other irregular features to fish. This is a fairly deep lake that can reach depths of 255 feet, especially near Horse Mesa Dam.

Apache is the second-largest lake in the Salt River chain, exceeded only by its wide-shouldered neighbor just upstream, Roosevelt Lake. It is located approximately 65 miles from Phoenix along the Apache Trail, but its relatively close proximity to a major urban area belies its remoteness. In fact, getting there along the unpaved portion of the Apache Trail can be an adventure in itself.

Apache Lake is renowned for its rugged scenic beauty and abundant wildlife, such as desert bighorn sheep.

Being the second lake in the chain with few significant inflows from other drainages, Apache is not the most productive of the Salt River lakes for anglers. However, it can be one of the most interesting to fish, providing a wilderness-like feel to any fishing escapade.

Fishing Tips: At 1,900 feet in elevation, this is a year-round fishery. The best fishing is during the spring and fall, but Apache is also popular during the winter. During the summer, triple-digit daytime temperatures often keep anglers away but draw water skiers and swimmers looking for a cool escape.

HISTORICAL NOTE

Apache Lake was formed by Horse Mesa Dam, which was completed in 1927. Nearby Horse Mesa was so named because thieves sometimes hid stolen herds there. The dam measures 660 feet long and 300 feet high and includes a 32,000-kilowatt hydroelectric generating unit.

Long and narrow, Apache Lake is the most remote of the four Salt River lakes.

➤ Apache offers anglers lots of irregular shoreline to work their lures. Expect to encounter many narrow, rocky shelves adjacent to steep drop-offs. There are also some inviting deep coves, extended points, and rocky cliffs to fish.

➤ This rocky-sided reservoir is full of crayfish; anglers will want to carry a decent arsenal of crayfish-like lures, especially in winter and early spring.

➤ Prior to golden algae blooms, Apache had been Arizona's premier smallmouth bass lake, and it might be again in the future. In more recent times, Apache has experienced a resurgence of largemouth bass. Feisty yellow bass are plentiful. Apache also supports a good population of walleye.

➤ Carp and black buffalo fish also abound in this lake. Those who fish for them often experience line-stripping fun. Apache also has a small population of crappies and plenty of catfish, both flatheads and channels.

➤ Because of its hydroelectric capacity, during nonpeak electricity-use hours, Salt River Project will often pump water back into Apache from Canyon Lake just below. This creates a slight flow away from the dam at those times. Predatory sport fish will often face into the current to feed.

Special Notes: Apache Lake is located in the Tonto National Forest, so you will need to obtain a Tonto Pass before arriving at the lake.

3 | FISHERY FACTS

LOCATION AND DIRECTIONS: GPS — 33°34′43″N; 111°15′48″W
From Phoenix, take the Superstition Freeway (U.S. Route 60) to Idaho Road, head north 2.3 miles to the Apache Trail (State Route 88), and follow the Apache Trail for 31.3 miles, past Canyon Lake, to the Apache Lake Marina (the downstream end of the lake).

You can also access Apache Lake from Roosevelt Lake. At the Roosevelt Lake Dam, take the Apache Trail south approximately 11 miles to the Burnt Corral campground and the launch ramp at the northern or upstream end of Apache Lake.

The unpaved portion of the Apache Trail is often narrow, and in some places, such as Fish Creek Hill, even treacherous. It's not a road for anyone afraid of heights or intimidated by narrow, winding dirt roads traversing steep cliff faces. If you pull a boat trailer or have an RV, it's advisable to make a scouting trip beforehand. This road is not suitable for larger RVs.

AMENITIES: The Apache Lake Marina and Resort offers paved launch ramps, bait and tackle, boat rentals, a restaurant, a store, lodging, RV camping with hookups, picnic tables, grills, toilets, and showers.

The Burnt Corral Recreation Site, which is operated by the Forest Service, offers a paved launch ramp, courtesy dock, fish-cleaning station, and camping units with fire rings, tables, toilets, drinking water, and a public pay phone.

The barrier-free fishing pier at Canyon Lake's Boulder
Recreation Area is open to anglers of all ages and abilities.

(4) Canyon Lake

Slang terms anglers use to describe big bass include "lunkers," "hawgs,"
and "toads." But no matter what you call them, Canyon Lake is where
behemoth bass reside.

But don't expect high catch rates. In fact, you might go the whole day
and not catch a single bass; it's not an easy fish, but a quality one.

Canyon Lake typically attracts veteran bass anglers, especially those
looking to get into the record books. At one point, it held the state-record
largemouth bass at 15 pounds. Many firmly believe it harbors a new state-
record bass, maybe even a world-record one.

At 950 surface acres and 1,700 feet in elevation, Canyon Lake is the
smallest of the chain of lakes along the Salt River and sits between its two
sister lakes, Saguaro and Apache. Canyon has largemouth bass, smallmouth bass, walleye, catfish, bluegill, green sunfish, and carp. Trout are
stocked from November through March.

This 10-mile-long lake can be difficult to fish for bass. However, novice
anglers often enjoy success in the family friendly Boulder Recreation

Area, where they can catch everything from bluegill and yellow bass to catfish and carp during the warmer months. This is almost like a lake within a lake — it's a moderately sized shallow basin connecting to the main lake by a narrow channel that passes through the marina.

Canyon has a large bowl-like section of lake with a very long and narrow portion that is almost river-like in nature. Despite its relatively small size, Canyon has 28 miles of shoreline to fish, attesting to its narrow nature, and a maximum depth of 131 feet.

The narrow portion is in a rugged canyon where desert bighorn sheep roam and peregrine falcons nest. In many stretches, the near-vertical canyon walls plunge well past the water level, making it challenging to fish.

When there are torrential rainstorms, the steep sides of Canyon Lake can turn into a wonderland of cascading waterfalls.

Fishing Tips: Canyon Lake is full of crayfish but also has a decent population of threadfin shad; you'll want to arm yourself with both crayfish- and shad-like lures for the big bass.

At Canyon Lake, you may catch a "hawg" bass like this one. | BILL LARSON

➤ Canyon is subject to pump-back water operations, especially from spring through the fall. Water is released downstream into Saguaro Lake during peak electricity-use times, but is typically pumped back into Canyon Lake during times of nonpeak use. This can create a tidal-like effect in the lake, with the current switching directions, especially close to the dam. Predatory sport fish will often face into the current to feed, so it behooves you to determine which way the current is going or you may be making your presentations to the tail of the fish, rather than its head. Some anglers contend that the bass will also feed more aggressively during peak flows.

➤ The steep, rocky sides along the narrow portion of the lake can make it challenging to fish, especially for novice anglers. However, large walleye and lunker bass can lurk in the dark depths along these submerged canyon walls, which provide excellent habitat for crayfish.

➤ During winter, Canyon takes on a different appeal: From November through March, it is stocked biweekly with rainbow trout. Trout anglers — especially winter visitors to the state — often catch some nice yellow bass as well. Anglers don't need a boat to fish for rainbows. Rainbows are stocked near the launch ramp and in the Boulder Recreation Area. But this stocking regime also sets up a different dynamic; anglers looking for huge bass will often use trout-imitating lures called swim baits.

➤ This lake has another shore-fishing appeal: channel catfish. Many shore anglers target these bottom feeders using stink baits. At Canyon, it is possible to catch catfish all year long, although the best fishing is from the spring through the fall.

Special Notes: This lake is located in the Tonto National Forest, so you will need to obtain a Tonto Pass before you arrive.

4 | FISHERY FACTS

LOCATION AND DIRECTIONS: GPS — 33°32'37"N; 111°26'12"W
Canyon Lake is 15 miles from Apache Junction. Take the Superstition Freeway (U.S. Route 60) to Idaho Road, head north 2.3 miles, turn right on the Apache Trail (State Route 88), and travel 13.8 miles to Canyon Lake. The scenic Apache Trail is narrow, winding, and steep along some segments.

AMENITIES: There is camping, picnic tables, paved launch ramps, and a barrier-free fishing pier. The full-service Canyon Lake Marina offers bait and tackle, ice, food, beverages, a restaurant, fuel dock, boating supplies, boat rentals, a store, and a paddlewheel excursion boat.

⑤ Saguaro Lake

Saguaro Lake might be at the bottom of the Salt River chain of lakes close to Phoenix, but, for a host of knowledgeable anglers, this sparkling jewel ranks at the top of their must-fish list, thanks to its plentiful angling opportunities and scenic beauty.

As its name implies, this lake is surrounded by picturesque Upper Sonoran Desert with lots of giant saguaro cactuses. Boaters and anglers are treated to terrific views of the rugged Four Peaks to the north, which may have a dusting of snow in winter.

At 1,529 feet in elevation and a maximum depth of 110 feet, Saguaro is a popular year-round fishing lake within a short drive from metro Phoenix. This 1,264-surface-acre reservoir has long been known as great place to catch large bass, but the 10-mile-long fishery was challenged with golden algae blooms and corresponding fish die-offs in 2005 and 2006. It's been on a comeback ever since.

Saguaro is also very family friendly — there are plenty of fishing piers where you can catch everything from sunfish and yellow bass to the trout stocked during the winter months.

The Keyhole area, also known as Saguaro del Norte, has multiple fishing piers where boats are excluded. The Butcher Jones Recreation Area is a popular location for shore anglers; there is also

HISTORICAL NOTE

The Stewart Mountain Dam was completed in 1930 and was named — along with nearby Stewart Mountain — after the old Stewart Ranch. The dam is 1,260 feet long and 208 feet high and includes a 13,000-kilowatt hydroelectric generating unit.

Saguaro Lake combines superb fishing with a striking Sonoran Desert landscape.

Flipping and pitching along the shoreline grass is a good strategy at Saguaro Lake.

a fishing pier here located in a large cove.

This lake also has something unique compared with others in the chain: 30 boat-only camping spots at Bagley Flat Campground, where there is also a boat dock with adjacent restrooms and picnic tables.

Saguaro is renowned as a water playground that attracts throngs during the late spring and summer; during these prime recreation times, most anglers switch to night fishing. In fact, sometimes you have to wait your turn just to get onto the lake (see Special Notes).

Fishing Tips: Although Saguaro has long been known as a big bass lake, it has gained prominence as a location to catch multiple fish, such as largemouth bass, yellow bass, channel catfish, smallmouth bass, walleye, carp, and bluegill.

➤ The lake has two basins. The larger basin, where the launch ramps are located, provides plenty of shoreline-fishing opportunities, but the second and smaller basin just upstream past the narrows gets the most fishing pressure from boat anglers. This smaller but more elongated basin is mostly fringed with cattails, which provide good hiding cover for forage fish and excellent ambush cover for predatory sport fish. There are plenty of small coves to work. Flipping and pitching the abundant tule grass is a popular technique.

➤ Saguaro has a healthy population of crayfish, but the primary food source for sport fish is threadfin shad; select your lures accordingly. Drop shots, jigs, crankbaits, spinners, and spinnerbaits can all work well here.

➤ Trout are stocked from November through March in the Butcher Jones Recreation Area and the Keyhole area, where the launch ramps are located. Trout are accessible to both shore and boat anglers.

➤ Bass anglers in winter and early spring will use trout-like swim baits to catch lunker-size largemouth bass.

➤ Saguaro is also known as an early spring producer for channel catfish; even bass anglers will often catch channels on shad-like lures.

➤ In late spring and summer, there are outflows into the Salt River to provide water for municipal and agricultural uses. There are also inflows from Canyon Lake, especially during prime electricity-use times in the late afternoon and evening. But at nonpeak times, water is pumped from Saguaro back into Canyon Lake. This can create a cyclic two-way current in the lake, depending on the time of day. Knowledgeable anglers at Saguaro know that as the current goes, often so goes the bass bite.

Saguaro Lake can yield lunker bass.

Special Notes: There is limited vehicle and boat-trailer parking available, which can fill up rapidly during the spring and summer, especially on weekends. It's first-come, first-served. Entry to the lake is closed by the Forest Service when capacity is reached. Boaters may wait at the Pobrecito boat waiting area to access the lake when allowed by the rangers. Plan accordingly by arriving early or late in the day to avoid waiting.

Saguaro is located in the Tonto National Forest, so you will need to obtain a Tonto Pass prior to arrival.

5 | FISHERY FACTS

LOCATION AND DIRECTIONS: GPS — 33°33′56.16″N; 111°32′9.96″W
From Mesa, travel east on U.S. Route 60 to Bush Highway. Turn left and follow the signs to the lake. From Phoenix, take Shea Boulevard to State Route 87 (Beeline Highway). Travel 8 miles north to the Saguaro Lake turnoff.

AMENITIES: Services include two boat-launch ramps, a full-service marina, picnic areas, a restaurant, sheriff's aid station, fishing piers, vault toilets, boat storage, boat rental, boat repairs, slips, a fuel dock, and bait and tackle. There is also an excursion boat. There is no drive-up camping available, but there are some boat-only camping sites 4 miles up-lake at the Bagley Flat Campground.

⑥ Lower Salt River

The Lower Salt River below Saguaro Lake is a unique fishery in that it is the only desert river adjacent to a major metropolitan area that provides seasonal trout-fishing opportunities. Just a short drive from the Phoenix area, the Lower Salt is stocked with rainbow trout from November through March by the Arizona Game and Fish Department.

Because water is released from the bottom of Saguaro Lake, it is often a chilly 52 to 54 degrees in the river, even in late spring when the air temperatures can soar into the triple digits. Fly anglers sometimes experience having their legs almost numb with cold in the water while their upper torso is sweating in the hot desert air.

This river is popular with both fly and spin anglers. You'll often see anglers fishing for trout before and after work, sometimes shoulder-to-shoulder with amazed winter visitors. Anglers new to this fishery often

A unique desert fishery, the Lower Salt River offers seasonal trout fishing adjacent to a major metropolitan area.

marvel at catching rainbow trout in a desert river lined with giant saguaros.

The Lower Salt is a great place for both novice and veteran anglers, especially fly anglers who will find lots of room for back casts without catching on brush or trees. But on some days, spin anglers have been known to out-fish the fly anglers.

Even though it is close to Phoenix, the Lower Salt River Recreation Area is within the Tonto National Forest. Anglers are routinely treated to sightings of mule deer, desert bighorn sheep, and javelinas. Bald eagles nest in the area and can often be seen foraging for fish along the river. Peregrine falcons nest along the nearby cliff faces.

The back-casting technique on the Lower Salt River.

Flow regimes and trout-stocking locations in winter and spring can vary. During early winter, Salt River Project (SRP) will typically release water from Bartlett Lake down the Verde River, but not down the Salt. During such times, trout are stocked at the Phon D. Sutton and Granite Reef recreation areas, located at and below the confluence of the Salt and Verde rivers, respectively.

During late winter or early spring, SRP will often switch and release water from Stewart Mountain Dam at Saguaro Lake, and trout will be stocked at the Water Users and Blue Point Bridge areas, making the entire 11.5 miles of the Lower Salt River fishable.

However, in wet years things can change. For instance, in 2005 and again in 2010, the entire stretch had flows and was stocked with rainbows throughout the winter. Due to the productive nature of the river, trout grow-outs at such times are superb, providing anglers some larger hold-over trout in spring.

During late spring and summer, the Lower Salt attracts droves of water recreationists, primarily to "tube the river." These tubers will typically put in at the Water Users area just below Stewart Mountain Dam and float the 10 miles to the Phon D. Sutton Recreation Area. The prime tubing season often starts in May. You'll see tubers fishing along the way, and catching trout!

Fishing Tips: Spin anglers should try small spinners, small casting spoons (such as Kastmasters), and live bait such as night crawlers or mealworms. Live grasshoppers or even cicadas can work wonderfully when available in late spring. Small crankbaits (such as Rapalas) can work at times. Prepared trout baits such as Power Bait are often less effective in the faster runs, but can work where there is less current, such as in the

Granite Reef area.

➤ Bait anglers should cast slightly upstream and let the current carry their bait down the riffles. Be sure to mend your line to keep contact with the bait. With spinners, try casting slightly downstream and let the current engage the spinner while slowly reeling it in.

➤ Spin anglers should also experiment using flies. Get a casting float or a bubble float and tie on a tapered fly leader with something like a wooly bugger on the end. It's a way to fly-fish without needing a fly rod.

➤ For fly anglers, bring a little bit of everything. Bead heads are often necessary to get the nymphs down in the fast flows. Popular flies include wooly worms (green and brown), semi-seal leeches, hare's ear nymphs, prince nymphs, San Juan worms, caddis flies, minnow imitations, grasshopper patterns, ants, and mayflies.

➤ Bring waders if you have them; if not, most anglers can easily wade and fish the river without them.

➤ Besides trout, anglers along the Lower Salt can catch largemouth bass, catfish, sunfish, smallmouth bass, carp, and native suckers. If a fish species is found in the Salt River lakes, it will show up in this river.

Special Notes: The Lower Salt River Recreation Area is located in the Tonto National Forest, so you will need to obtain a Tonto Pass prior to arrival. There are no passes available on site.

6 | FISHERY FACTS

LOCATION AND DIRECTIONS: GPS —
Water Users parking lot: 33°33'19.88"N; 111°32'37.30"W
Blue Point Bridge: 33°33'14.74"N; 111°34'32.40"W
Phon D. Sutton Recreation Area: 33°32'49.57"N; 111°39'36.72"W
Granite Reef Picnic Area: 33°30'55.63"N; 111°41'28.79"W

From Mesa, exit U.S. Route 60 at Bush Highway. Travel north 7 miles to Granite Reef Dam (lower end of the river).

From north Scottsdale or Fountain Hills, take Shea Boulevard east to State Route 87 (Beeline Highway); turn north (toward Payson) and travel 10.3 miles to Bush Highway (Saguaro Lake turnoff or Forest Road 204). Head east 5.4 miles past Saguaro Lake to the Water Users parking lot just below Stewart Mountain Dam (upper end of the river).

AMENITIES: There are vault toilets at the four recreation sites, but there is no drinking water available. Some of the areas have picnic tables, but there are no campsites. The nearest commercial facility for food, water, ice, and phones is likely the Saguaro Lake Marina. However, Mesa is just 20 minutes away. There is also lodging, food, and horse stables at the Saguaro Lake Ranch Resort just below the dam. Tube rentals and snacks are available at Salt River Tubing; watch for the signs.

The inflatable dams on Tempe Town Lake quickly release and recapture water to control Salt River flooding and also keep the lake filled.

⑦ Tempe Town Lake

This marvelously unique 220-acre lake is tucked between inflatable dams along the normally dry Salt River bed adjacent to Tempe.

Besides being an engineering marvel, the 2-mile-long lake, which averages 12.3 feet deep, has become a respectable year-round warm-water fishery and a popular seasonal trout fishery. Trout stocking begins each year the week before Thanksgiving, usually with lots of fanfare and celebration, and continues through March. This fishery also has plentiful largemouth bass, yellow bass, sunfish, carp, and catfish.

Besides gaining popularity as a quality fishery, the lake is truly a community recreational hub for greater Phoenix, attracting millions each year. It has an enjoyable cosmopolitan outdoor ambience all its own. Anglers and other recreationists witness large commercial jet planes routinely flying overhead to land at Phoenix Sky Harbor International Airport. The relatively quiet METRO Light Rail train routinely zips across a bridge spanning the lake. Built in 1931, the historically picturesque Mill Avenue Bridge lends character from a bygone era. There are even modern skyscrapers sprouting up near the Tempe Town Lake shoreline, and Arizona State University's Sun Devil Stadium is located nearby.

The linear-oriented lake combines attributes of popular city-based waters, such as the Charles River in Boston and the River Walk in San Antonio, with the warm Arizona sunshine and our fondness for healthy

In addition to anglers, Tempe Beach Park and Tempe Town Lake attract festival-goers, joggers, rowers, and triathlon participants.

The concept for this lake was created by Arizona State University in 1966. It was ultimately opened in 1999. Tempe Beach Park, a centerpiece of the lake with many connected parks and trails, was originally built in 1931 and completely renovated in 1999 when the lake was constructed.

outdoor activities.

You'll often see rowing sculls racing across the tranquil waters, especially in the early morning desert light. The U.S. Olympic rowing team sometimes uses the lake for training. Joggers and bicyclists routinely ply the many paths.

Visitors are often intrigued by the lake's inflatable dams. Each dam is 240 feet long. The dams hold back about 977 million gallons of water in the lake. Each of those dam bladders weighs 40 tons. The dams are lowered during major runoff events, such as during the tumultuous spring flows of 2010.

Fishing Tips: Tempe Town Lake is great for shore fishing. No matter what time of year you are fishing, one strategy is to try the shade lines beneath the bridges, where fish can sometimes congregate.

➤ Those anglers fishing from boats (see Special Notes) will often focus on working the Mill Avenue Bridge supports. This lake is very flat and fairly shallow, without a lot of submerged structure, so the bridge pillars can act like fish magnets.

➤ Predatory sport fish will sometimes wait to ambush schools of forage fish swimming along the cement-lined shoreline, especially where there are pockets of shade.

➤ During winter, anglers primarily fish for trout using all the popular methods, from Power Bait, corn, and night crawlers to in-line spinners such as Mepps and Rooster Tails.

➤ The lake's flat, fairly smooth bottom allows beginning or novice anglers to experiment with different fishing techniques, such as drop shots, Carolina rigging, or Texas rigging, without experiencing a lot of snagging. Plus there can be some nice payoffs: decent-sized largemouth bass.

➤ Trout anglers using small spinners often find some striped surprises on the ends of their lines — yellow bass abound in this fishery. Yellow bass, which are related to striped bass and often misidentified as stripers, seldom grow big. A 2-pounder is considered huge. But what they lack in size they make up for in ferocity, especially on the end of a line. A good lure to use specifically for yellows is a gold Kastmaster, which is a casting spoon. Try slowly retrieving the Kastmaster with a stop-and-go action, letting the lure bounce periodically off the bottom.

Special Notes: All public water-craft require a Tempe Town Lake boat permit prior to use on the lake. Gas motors are not allowed, only electric. Permits are available at 132 E. Sixth Street, Tempe. For more information, call 480-350-8625 or visit www.tempe.gov/lake.

In winter, Tempe Town Lake is liberally stocked with trout.

7 | FISHERY FACTS

LOCATION AND DIRECTIONS: GPS — 33°25'52.92"N; 111°56'32.72"W
Tempe Town Lake is located at 620 N. Mill Ave., along the Salt River adjacent to Arizona State University, just off Loop 202 between Priest Drive and Scottsdale Road.

AMENITIES: This lake is served by the Phoenix METRO Light Rail system and sits adjacent to the 2,000-acre Papago Park, the Mill Avenue District with its popular shops and restaurants, and Arizona State University Sun Devil Stadium. The Tempe Center for the Arts is located along its rambling shoreline. There are plenty of picnic sites available, as well as bike paths, restrooms, jogging paths, and a series of parks stretching into Scottsdale along or near the riverbed.

Fun events are staged throughout the year, from fishing clinics and bathtub races to triathlons and open-air concerts. The Fourth of July fireworks display has become a major annual event for the whole region.

VERDE RIVER WATERSHED

8 Bartlett Lake

9 Horseshoe Lake

Since its inception in 1939, Bartlett Lake near the Town of Cave Creek has been renowned as a great fishin' hole; it's just fun to fish. This lake along the Verde River is less than 50 miles from the heart of Phoenix, yet it's surrounded by rugged wilderness in the Tonto National Forest.

Its fans are quick to point out that at 2,815 surface acres, Bartlett is larger than both Saguaro and Canyon lakes combined. The lake's maximum depth is 174 feet at the dam.

Situated at an elevation of 1,798 feet, Bartlett is a popular year-round

warm-water fishery with largemouth bass, smallmouth bass, crappie, bluegill, flathead catfish, channel catfish, green sunfish, and carp. The productive lake has a robust population of threadfin shad, a forage fish, but its rocky terrain provides superb habitat for abundant crayfish, which is a very nutrient-rich food source for bass and other sport fish.

Twelve miles long, Bartlett Lake is fairly narrow and winding, providing anglers with 33 miles of shoreline to fish. The meandering lake is dotted with reefs, rock piles, rock stringers, and lots of irregular shore features that can sometimes make boating challenging while providing anglers superb submerged habitats to fish.

As you will see when coming down the fairly steep and sometimes winding paved road into Bartlett Lake, the reservoir is bordered on its eastern flank by the Mazatzal Mountains and along its western flank by gradually rising highlands of prime Upper Sonoran Desert habitat, creating kind of a long desert trough.

The lake is popular for those who favor dispersed camping along the

Less than 50 miles from Phoenix on the Verde River, Bartlett Lake is surrounded by the rugged landscape of the high Sonoran Desert.

shoreline, but when the lake is full of spring runoff water, most of the prime camping beaches are submerged.

Anglers, campers, picnickers, and hikers will routinely see mule deer, javelinas, coyotes, quail, and bald eagles. During the warmer seasons, keep an eye out for rattlesnakes. Mountain lions are occasionally seen. Keep pets on a leash and children within sight.

Although Bartlett is not technically the reservoir at the top of the line along the Verde River, it is on a seasonal basis. Here's why:

Horseshoe Lake, just upstream, is used as a flood-retention basin during times of heavy runoff. But it typically holds water just temporarily or seasonally, even when it fills to capacity. The water in Horseshoe is gradually released to replenish Bartlett. When Horseshoe empties each year, the Verde River water flows through it directly to Bartlett. This can also mean that the much-shallower Horseshoe Lake can act as a seasonal nursery for both shad and sport fish that will eventually end up in Bartlett.

Named after Bill Bartlett, a government surveyor, Bartlett Dam was completed in 1939. It was the first dam on the Verde River. This multiple-arch dam is 308 feet high and 800 feet long.

HISTORICAL NOTE

Horseshoe Dam just upstream was built in 1946 and was named for the horseshoe-shaped bend in the Verde River at the dam site. This earthen dam is 144 feet tall.

Although Bartlett has a greater water-storage capacity than Horseshoe, when full, Horseshoe can have a larger surface size. Horseshoe can be a popular waterfowl area in winter, but the dirt road leading to it is subject to washouts from storms.

This lake can also get visits from one of the state's more playful mammals, river otters. River otters are normally found higher up along the Verde River watershed, but sometimes they work their way into this reservoir, much to the astonishment of anglers fishing here.

Fishing Tips: Bartlett is one of Arizona's premier bass and crappie fisheries. You can expect to catch lots of small bass about 1 pound in size and occasional medium-sized bass ranging from 2 to 3 pounds or more, but this fishery is not known for producing big "hawg" bass over 5 pounds or so. No one is really sure why. However, Bartlett is known for producing plate-sized black crappie. It is also a renowned fishery for huge flathead catfish; use live bluegill as bait.

➤ Due to the abundant crayfish, crayfish-like lures work well here, especially in spring. Staging bass and typically postspawn bass will feed heavily on crayfish, but will eat shad as well; go armed with both.

➤ When the water is turbid from spring runoff, try for staging bass using spinnerbaits, crankbaits, and rattling jigs worked along the major points and irregular terrain features, such as rock stringers and reefs. Those adept with drop shots will also love fishing this lake.

➤ For postspawn bass, you'll find lots of reefs, major lake points, and plenty of irregular shore to fish — this lake is ideal for bass-boat anglers who like to work shoreline.

Water releases can be dramatic at Horseshoe Lake, which provides flood control on the Verde River.

➤ During summer, the river valley seems to radiate the heat, so most anglers switch to nighttime fishing. But be careful: This winding lake has a lot of boating hazards.

➤ In the fall, Bartlett can provide some of the best topwater fishing action around. Look for bass chasing shad at the surface.

➤ In winter, Bartlett is favored by both bass and crappie anglers. Many anglers will fish small jigs suitable to catch either of those sport fish. Live minnows are also favored by many. Bass and crappie anglers often find surprises on the end of the line: huge flathead catfish.

Special Notes: You will need to obtain a Tonto Pass prior to arrival at Bartlett Lake.

8 | 9 | FISHERY FACTS

LOCATION AND DIRECTIONS: GPS — 33°49'7"N; 111°37'55"W

Bartlett is about an hour's drive from the heart of Phoenix. From Carefree or Cave Creek, take Cave Creek Road (which turns into Forest Road 24) to Bartlett Road (FR 19) and turn right, then travel 13 miles to the reservoir.

AMENITIES: There is a full-service marina with a store and boat fuel (on the water), slips, boat storage, and boat rentals. There is also a sheriff's aid station, two launch ramps, a barrier-free fishing pier, campsites, picnic areas, vault and portable toilets, and an angler trail from Rattlesnake to S.B. Cove. There are also full services, including lodging, shopping, and restaurants, available in either Carefree or Cave Creek about 30 minutes away.

COLORADO RIVER NORTHWEST

The Colorado River runs cool and smooth at Willow Beach, just downstream from Hoover Dam.

COLORADO RIVER NORTHWEST

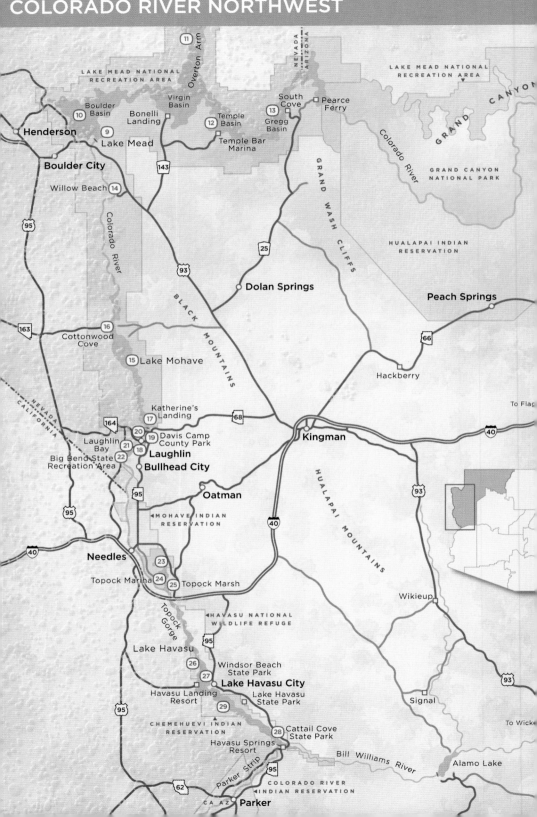

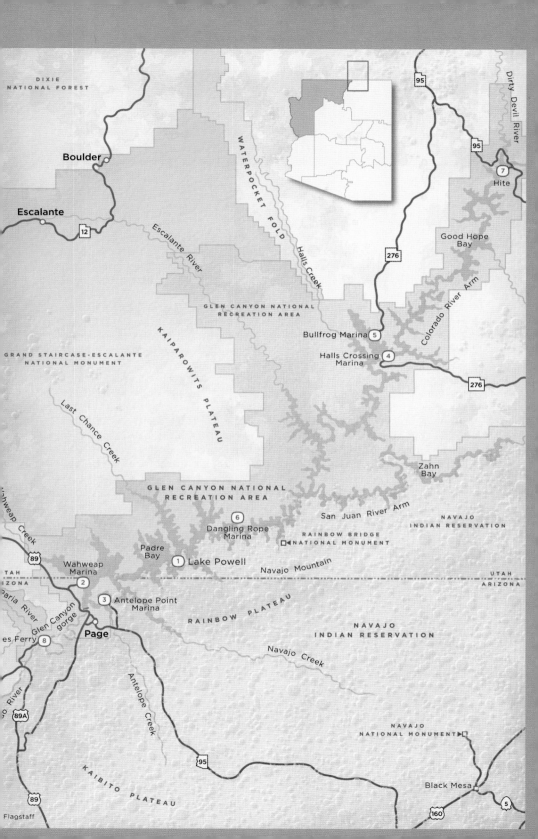

The taming of the mighty Colorado River this past century created a series of immense impoundments and renowned stretches of river amid timeless desert landscapes and geologic wonders that beckon and astonish millions of visitors each year.

This section of the Colorado River is home to four major reservoirs, including North America's largest man-made lakes, Powell and Mead. Lake Powell alone has more shoreline than the entire West Coast of North America. The Lake Mead National Recreation Area, which includes both Mead and Lake Mohave, is twice the size of Rhode Island. You'll also find widely renowned tail-water fisheries, such as Lees Ferry, which could be considered North America's cathedral of fly-fishing. You can discover lesser-known stretches of river, such as Willow Beach, where monster stripers search the current for rainbow meals. You might even want to explore fishing opportunities along the mighty Colorado River as it makes its often tumultuous journey through the majestic Grand Canyon.

The Río Colorado is a study in recreational contrasts — there's even a stretch of river where you can gamble on catching trout and stripers amid the glitter of huge gambling houses hugging the Colorado River shoreline along Casino Row in Laughlin. But you'll also discover a more relaxed, meandering stretch along Arizona's border with both Nevada and California where Huck Finn and Tom Sawyer would feel right at home, especially in scenic places like Topock Gorge. This section of river is also home to an extremely popular water-recreation reservoir that provides superb fishing opportunities for both recreational and tournament anglers: Lake Havasu. You might even catch a tiger-striped smallmouth bass in the shadow of the famous London Bridge.

① Lake Powell

Besides being one of the West's scenic natural wonders, Lake Powell is also one of the foremost fishing lakes in the western United States.

Yet despite its popularity, Powell is a desired destination for those seeking angling solitude in the remarkably clear desert air.

While visiting the Glen Canyon Recreation Area encompassing Lake Powell, you can experience 1.2 million acres of time-etched sandstone cliffs, colorful limestone bluffs, majestic buttes, imposing mesas, towering pinnacles, delicate sandstone arches, lush hanging gardens, immense rock grottos, mushroom-shaped hoodoos, daunting sandstone monoliths, and incredibly narrow slot canyons. All these remarkable terrain features are situated in a high-desert landscape, where ribbons of rock strata stained with subtle sandstone hues are starkly contrasted by the brilliant blue paradox of Lake Powell's 8.5 trillion gallons of water. You might even discover intriguing Moqui Marbles to play with. There is no landscape quite like it on Earth.

The Powell fishing experience is unlike any other. Powell is the second largest man-made lake in North America — Lake Mead is the largest. These two sister lakes along the Colorado River, which are separated by the Grand Canyon, also share another distinction. Mead and Powell provide what many consider to be the best freshwater fishing in the nation for voracious striped bass. It is a close contest on which lake is No. 1.

There is no bag limit on striped bass at Lake Powell. You are encouraged by Utah and Arizona fishery managers to catch and keep all the stripers you can to help this dynamic fishery in the high desert of the Colorado Plateau. Powell also provides some of the best smallmouth bass fishing in the West (the limit is 20 smallies), along with good angling action for delectable walleye and decent opportunities for crappie. Catfish, carp, and sunfish abound and can easily be caught at night off the back of houseboats or from shoreline camps.

It seems an enticing irony that despite receiving about 3 million visitors a year, Powell offers us anglers vast opportunities to escape the crowds and experience a sense of exploration and discovery in remote hidden canyons, secret coves, mysterious slot canyons, and amazing sandstone grottos deep enough to swallow a houseboat or two.

With 1,960 miles of shoreline (when full) encompassing 96 side canyons spread across this remote and meandering 186-mile-long lake, you can fish for days and not see many, or even any, other anglers if you so desire. It is also not difficult to find vast stretches or even whole canyons that have not received recent fishing pressure. You might even encounter the angler's Holy Grail — aggressive sport fish that have never seen a lure before. The slang term for this piscatorial phenomenon is "dumb

HISTORICAL NOTE

Glen Canyon Dam was begun in 1956 and completed in 1966. Lake Powell began backing up when the diversion tunnels were sealed on March 13, 1963. It took 17 years for this huge reservoir to finally fill, in 1980. Glen Canyon Bridge was constructed between 1957 and 1959.

fish," where it is possible to catch a gullible country fish on every cast. Anglers at Powell have been known to grow arm and shoulder weary from catching so many fish, especially hard-fighting stripers, whirling-dervish smallies, or mouth-watering walleyes. You can routinely fill your live well with excitement, memories, and dinner.

One of the reasons you can easily escape the visiting hordes of tourists is that Powell only has three primary land access points: Wahweap and Antelope Point near Glen Canyon Dam; Halls Crossing/Bullfrog, about two-thirds of the way up-lake; and Hite, where the Colorado River enters the lake.

While this immense impoundment has evolved over the decades, it seems a poetic contradiction that the drought-related fluctuating water levels this century have tremendously improved Powell's fishing persona.

Here's why. When the water level is low, vegetation, especially prolific, fast-growing salt cedar, develops in the fertile lake bed. When the water level comes back up, it floods this vegetation, providing added nutrients along with habitat for a host of other food items to grow, while also providing hiding cover for fry (newly hatched fish) and shad. The vegetation also provides ambush cover for aquatic predators, such as largemouth bass and walleye. The gradually rising and falling of the water actually acts like an immense desert irrigation system, ultimately growing huge crops of fat and feisty fish. In fact, Powell has evolved into a very good largemouth bass fishery, even though the vast majority of anglers target the plentiful striped bass. Therein resides an angling opportunity.

Geological Note: The distinctive brick-red rock dominating much of Lake Powell's landscape comes from iron oxide in the Navajo sandstone dating back to either the late or early Triassic period. Glen Canyon itself was carved from the slowly uplifting Colorado Plateau by the mighty Colorado River over an estimated 5 million years. The Colorado Plateau arose some 11 million years ago — these same tectonic and erosive forces also combined to create the Grand Canyon.

Fishing Tips: While Powell might be considered a year-round fishery, in reality few anglers fish it during winter, when most fish are lethargic and tend to hold deep in the cold water. Keep in mind that Lake Powell is an extremely clear water reservoir. You will want lighter fishing line that is smaller in diameter and less visible. The most successful anglers will use the most invisible fishing line — fluorocarbon. Try 8- to 10-pound test, unless you are working areas with brush or in stained areas, such as the San Juan Arm of the lake or the upper end where the Colorado River enters the lake near Hite. But if you are encountering fish in the 10-plus-pound range, it makes sense to go with stronger test line. Powell can go through cycles, so check the weekly fishing reports at www.azgfd.gov.

➤ **Striped Bass:** Most anglers at Lake Powell fish for striped bass, and with good reason. Stripers are abundant and can be readily caught, even by novice anglers, while also providing line-stripping fun and excitement. Expect to catch lots of stripers in the 1- to 2-pound range, with occasional larger fish ranging from 3 to 10 pounds, and sometimes even larger ones.

Stripers are schooling predators. They are continuously on the move.

Boat and houseboat campers receive their morning wake-up call on Lake Powell.

Devise your fishing strategies accordingly. Stripers prefer oxygen-rich water and don't function as well in warmer water. Their primary food base is threadfin shad, which are typically found in huge schools called balls. Shad feed on plankton; it's a food-chain effect. There is also a relatively new forage fish at Powell called the gizzard shad, which grows rapidly to immense sizes. Stripers prefer to spawn in moving water, but at Powell, moving water is not essential for spawning success.

Although most anglers fish for stripers using anchovies as bait, this pizza delicacy actually works best either when shad (the bait fish) are not abundant, or when stripers are not actively feeding on shad. Winter and spring are when shad abundance is typically lowest; they are most abundant in late summer and fall. When fishing with anchovies, use a No. 4 circle hook instead of anchovy hooks and possibly a small weight 18 inches up from the hook, or 6 inches in winter. There are times when it is also best to use no weight. Because stripers feed in schools that can move rapidly, once you catch a striper try chumming with precut pieces of anchovies to hold the school and hopefully create a feeding frenzy. For chumming, cut the anchovy either into thirds or quarters. You should also try chumming when locating a school of stripers with your fishfinder. Adding corn to the chum can help attract other fish as well and possibly create a feeding frenzy.

When stripers are feeding on shad, shad-imitating lures can work the best. Silver, white, and chartreuse can be the three best colors, or in some combination. A new color pattern to consider for the arsenal is gizzard shad. When stripers are close to the surface, try reaction crankbaits like Rat-L-Traps, Shad Raps, and Cordell Spots. When stripers are boiling and schools of stripers are actively chasing balls of shad to the surface, try topwater lures such as Zara Spooks, Zara Puppies, Sammys, and Jumpin' Minnows. Shad-like swim baits can be devastating at times.

There can be small striper boils in spring. Boils will continue to increase in number, duration, and size as you move through summer. During late summer and into autumn, striper-shad boils reach a crescendo, sometimes creating surface feeding frenzies that are spectacular in size and duration. For an in-depth discussion of striper boils, timing, duration, and fishing techniques, visit www.wayneswords.com. Wayne Gustaveson is a fisheries biologist with the Utah Division of Wildlife and has spent his lengthy career on Powell. He has compiled an outstanding website on fishing Lake Powell and produces a weekly fishing report, which can also be found at www.azgfd.gov in the Arizona weekly fishing report.

When stripers are holding deeper, try using jigs and spoons. In fact, a curly-tailed jig can be used both as a reaction lure worked at near surface, at moderate depths worked in a flutter-down fashion, or even worked across the bottom in a jigging fashion. You can even put an anchovy on a swim jig head, or tip your jig with a small piece of bait. Marabou jigs and spoons can also be effective at times, either worked on the fall to elicit a bite from striper schools passing by, or jigged off the bottom for those holding deep.

Trolling is another very popular technique for catching stripers at Powell and also allows one to explore and sightsee at the same time. Try any shad-colored crankbait. Trolling spoons can also be effective for deeper schools of stripers. Use your pliers and crimp the barbs of the treble hooks — stripers will flop around even when landed, sometimes impaling anglers with fish hooks.

➤ **Smallmouth Bass:** The same arsenal you have for stripers, except anchovies, can also be used for smallmouth bass, but where and how you fish will be different. Smallmouth will typically be found in more rocky areas, such as rockfalls, where you will see lots of piled-up rock along the shoreline in canyons and along the main lake. Half-submerged hoodoos make a beautiful bronzeback habitat. Rocky islands and reefs provide superb holding structure.

Although smallies will gobble up shad, they favor forage with much higher calorie content: crayfish. Texas-rigged craws can be devastating. The limit on smallmouth bass in Lake Powell (for both Utah and Arizona) is 20. Please catch and keep smallies in the 8- to 12-inch range and practice catch-and-release on the larger ones to help sustain this marvelous fishery. Filleted and fried, they make marvelous eating.

Probably the most versatile lure for smallmouth bass is the curly-tailed jig. Use a single-tail jig to work the top of the water column and get a reaction bite (work in like a crankbait or flutter-down lure). But for working the bottom, go to a twin-tailed grub or even use something like a shaky-head jig with a minnow-like soft-plastic lure, such as a Senko. If you don't know about shaky heads, do an Internet search and you'll find lots

At Lake Powell, striped bass are by far the most popular sport fish.

of good information. This method of fishing can be devastating for small-mouth, stripers, and even largemouth. Drop shots also work well here for smallmouth, and morning dawn Robo Worms are a good bet.

➤ **Largemouth Bass:** Largemouth are mostly ignored by anglers at Powell, which means they provide superb fishing opportunities. The best time to target largemouth bass is during April, when they are spawning and you can actually see them on the beds in the shallow, sheltered

backs of canyons, especially if there is submerged vegetation. The key is using soft-plastic lures you can see when sight fishing, such as bright red, bright chartreuse, bright orange, or glowing white. Largemouth in spring will feed more heavily on crustaceans, so crayfish-like patterns work well. Once again, the versatile curly-tailed jig works as well for largemouth as for stripers and smallies. Crankbaits can work well, but in early spring try crayfish-colored ones, such as orange or red.

Despite Lake Powell's high traffic, anglers who like the quiet can discover undisturbed side canyons.

Due to fluctuating lake levels and abundant cover, larger bucket-mouths prevail. You might even find pockets of black bass that have never seen a lure before and quickly tally up numbers of fish. When you see areas of submerged brush, especially in small coves or along points, you are probably looking at prime largemouth bass habitat, which can also hold walleye at times as well.

In the fall, largemouth bass get in on the autumn feeding frenzy. When schools of stripers attack balls of shad, largemouth bass have been known to lurk below and pick up on the dead and dying floating down. At such times, spoons and flutter-down lures can be devastating. It is possible to find areas, sometimes whole canyons, where largemouth have not been fished recently, allowing anglers to rack up impressive totals of fish.

➤ **Walleye:** While most anglers fish for stripers and many fish for small-mouth bass, only a relatively modest number routinely target the walleye at Powell. Yet walleye proliferate and provide delicious eating. Two secrets for walleye: they are light sensitive and they love night crawlers.

At most walleye waters across the country, the best time to fish for walleye is at first and last light, seldom during the prime daylight hours. Not so at Powell. Because of its deep canyons, huge sandstone overhangs with hanging gardens, dark grottos, cave-like rocky spaces full of water, plus steep and narrow winding slot canyons where direct sunlight seldom penetrates, it is possible to catch these light-sensitive fish at Powell 24/7, at least from spring through fall.

Even those looking to catch smallmouth bass will often find walleye lurking around the darker shaded areas, such as in huge cracks and fractures along cliffs extending below water lines, or along half-submerged hoodoos. Walleye also like to feed in recently submerged brush, especially in spring. When the lake level is coming up in May and sometimes June, look for the areas where the rising lake level has

Lake Powell abounds with feisty smallmouth bass.

covered brush and you might find both walleye and largemouth bass.

Try using the thicker-bodied soft plastics, such as Senkos and Bass Assassins, and rig them weedless for working the submerged vegetation. But no matter what lure you use, keep in mind that walleye love night crawlers. Even when using jigs, soft plastics, or crankbaits while targeting other fish species, tip your hook with a small piece of night crawler when you get into areas without light. Walleye spawn in February or March, but then go back deep again until sometime in May. The best place to catch spawning walleye is the stain line where any of the rivers come into the lake, but especially the mighty Colorado. It is also possible to catch stripers along these early season stain lines.

Fishing Tip for Using a Houseboat: When you beach your houseboat at night, leave the rear deck lights on. If you have a submersible light, which is recommended, use it as well. This will attract plankton, which will attract shad, which in turn will attract predatory sport fish such as striped bass, largemouth bass, smallmouth bass, and even channel catfish.

Special Notes: There is no limit on striped bass at Lake Powell, so please catch and keep all you can. The limit on smallmouth bass is 20. Those with a resident Arizona fishing license may want to get the special Lake Powell stamp or fishing privilege to fish the Utah portion of this sprawling lake.

You don't need a houseboat to explore Lake Powell, but if you plan to shore camp using your personal boat or even a rental, be sure to bring along a portable chemical toilet. In fact, one is required by the National Park Service. Also keep in mind that when the lake level is low, you'll probably find the most beaches available for camping.

Autumn, winter, and early spring are the best times to photograph Powell's spectacular landscapes. The more southerly azimuth of the sun bends the light rays and helps bring out the subtle hues of the multi-colored sandstone layers. The spectacular sunrises and sunsets at Powell can also add a colorful brilliance to the sandstone formations. Bring a tripod.

Invasive Species Note: Due to invasive quagga and zebra mussels, mandatory inspections by trained personnel are necessary for all watercraft launching at Bullfrog and Wahweap marinas. These requirements, and inspection hours, are subject to modification. Please visit www.nps.gov/glca for the latest information.

Wahweap Marina: GPS — 36°59'39.12"N; 111°29'4.99"W

This is the largest marina at Lake Powell and is located 8 miles from Page, Arizona. There are two launch ramps (Wahweap and State Line), two campgrounds (one with hook-ups), and picnic areas. The concessionaire, ARAMARK, provides a variety of services including lodging, food services (including elegant dining), gift shops, laundry, showers, and a service station. The full-service marina includes slips, buoys, boat rentals (including houseboats), tours (especially of Rainbow Bridge), repairs, dry storage, and fueling. There is a land-based gas station and marina-based boat fuel available.

For more information, please contact the following resources: National Park Service Information, 928-608-6200; National Park Service Emergency, 800-582-4351; ARAMARK Wahweap, 928-645-2433; ARAMARK, 800-528-6154.

The city of Page, 2 miles from the dam and visitors center, has stores, motels, restaurants, churches, a hospital, and a museum. Page can be reached by surfaced roads year-round, and by air from Phoenix.

 Antelope Point Marina: GPS — 36°57'57.38"N; 111°26'32.45"W

Antelope Point Marina is approximately 5 miles up-lake from Glen Canyon Dam on the main channel. Land access is from State Route 98. This marina features a public launch ramp, day-use area, and dump station. Antelope Point Holdings, one of the park's concessionaires, provides boat rentals (including houseboats), valet launching, slip rental, boat repair, boat pump-out, a floating restaurant, snack bar, dry storage (indoor and outdoor), and a small convenience store. There is also on-the-water boat fuel available. For more information, please call 928-645-5900.

 Halls Crossing Marina: GPS — 37°28'11.87"N; 110°43'7.74"W

This marina is 96 miles up-lake from Glen Canyon Dam and can be accessed off Utah Route 276. There is a full-service marina, launch ramp, a store with gas pumps, a campground on a bluff overlooking the lake, full RV hookups, and house-trailer rentals.

The State of Utah maintains a regularly scheduled ferry, capable of carrying cars, trucks, RVs, and boat trailers, which runs between Halls Crossing and Bullfrog. This is a fee service and it is available on a first-come, first-served basis.

The Halls Crossing/Bullfrog ferry is occasionally out of service for repairs. If ferry service is crucial to your trip, call ahead to National Park Service Halls Crossing, 435-684-7460; or ARAMARK Halls Crossing (ferry information), 435-684-7000.

 Bullfrog Marina: GPS — 37°30'44.99"N; 110°43'57.27"W

This is the second largest marina on the lake and is located 97 miles from Glen Canyon Dam. It can be accessed via Utah Route 276 and is connected with Halls Crossing via a large vehicle ferry. The National Park Service provides a launch ramp, portable toilet dump station, free boat pump-out station, a picnic area, fish-cleaning station, and a paved landing strip for aircraft.

ARAMARK, the park concessionaire, provides many visitor services, including housekeeping units, a grocery store, two campgrounds (one with hook-ups), laundry, showers, a service station, and boat repair. Cal Black Memorial Airport is located approximately 10 miles east of Halls Crossing.

 Dangling Rope Marina: GPS — 37°7'15.35"N; 111°4'54.95"W

This marina is only accessible by boat, or by a long hike overland. It is located 40 miles up-lake from Glen Canyon Dam. Even the gasoline and supplies are brought in via lake barges. There is boat fuel, limited boat repair (especially prop replacement), a store, restrooms, and a hot dog stand during the summer. There is also emergency communication available, but no public telephone. You can use credit cards here, if the data-link is functioning. Bring cash just in case. This marina is closed during the winter.

 Hite: GPS — 37°53'25.80"N; 110°22'16.46"W

Although subject to change in the future, there are no water-based facilities at Hite. The launch ramp became covered in mud and silt, making it unusable. While small boats can be launched at Hite, it is at your own risk. Four-wheel-drive is recommended, or car-toppers and inflatables. There is a land-based pay-at-the-pump gas station and a small convenience store that is open intermittently. There is a ranger station at Hite that is also staffed intermittently.

(8) Lees Ferry

Lees Ferry is the cathedral of fly-fishing in North America, where spin anglers also can experience a state of angling grace. This blue-ribbon rainbow-trout fishery below Glen Canyon Dam is situated in a spectacular 1,000- to 1,500-foot-deep gorge slashing 15.5 miles through the immense Colorado Plateau at the gateway to the Grand Canyon. The steep red walls of time-etched Navajo sandstone provide an epic backdrop to the swift waters of the Colorado River. There is no other wild trout fishery quite like it.

Since the completion of Glen Canyon Dam in 1963 and the resultant filling of Lake Powell, Lees Ferry has evolved and grown in importance as one of the nation's premier trout fisheries. The first rainbow trout were stocked in 1963. During its most productive years in the 1970s, while Lake Powell was filling with nutrient-rich water from the Colorado Rockies, huge rainbows ranging from 10 to 20 pounds were common. Biologists estimated that Lees Ferry provided anglers approximately 50,000 trout per linear mile, quickly gaining it an international reputation as a trout-fishing destination.

Biologists and other scientists have routinely kept this fishery under

Against a backdrop of red canyon and blue sky, anglers at Lees Ferry fish for trophy-sized wild rainbow trout.

close scrutiny. Lees Ferry is one of the most intensively managed and studied wild trout fisheries in the West, if not the world. Scientific studies show that its dynamics are intrinsically tied to the operations of Glen Canyon Dam and its resulting water releases, as well as the water levels of Lake Powell. Resource managers here utilize a tool called adaptive management, where a management experiment is instituted, and then what is learned from the experiment is implemented. Then scientists take the next step and also study the implementation to learn even more. It is a continuous process of learning and improving.

Once again since the turn of the 21st century, Lees Ferry has been gaining renewed prominence as one of the best places to catch trophy-sized wild rainbow trout, creating yet another set of "good ole days" that anglers will be reminiscing about for years.

A veteran guide, Terry Gunn, has described Lees Ferry as a series of parallel spring-creek-like waterways, all with different characteristics, flowing side by side at times. You might find a short, swift run sweeping past submerged boulders next to a rapid 500-yard stretch rippling down an older river channel, yet also discover a long, swift glide past a partially submerged gravel bar where rapacious rainbows lurk to gobble midges. There might even be seams in between the three where larger trout will wait in the shaded ambush cover of deep ledges and flow-scoured deep channels.

Unlike most other popular trout waters, Lees Ferry is not a seasonal rainbow fishery, nor is it stocked with trout. Lees Ferry is a year-round, naturally producing rainbow-trout fishery. During any season, you can expect to have high catch rates for quality wild trout in an unmatched setting stretching from Lake Powell to the Grand Canyon. The most popular fishing season is when the wild trout are actively spawning on their redds. Sight fishing a crimson-sided huge rainbow on a redd in this dramatic gorge will have you grasping for superlatives and seeking another day in angling paradise. In previous times, the prime spawning season commenced in late November or early December and ended in late March or early April. In more recent years, the spawning window has shifted, hitting a crescendo in late March or April. The spawning period could shift again as the fishery dynamics change, so be sure to check the weekly fishing reports at www.azgfd.gov.

This vibrant fishery is fed from the depths of Glen Canyon Dam, so the clear-flowing water ranges from 46 to 60 degrees while averaging between 52 to 56 degrees, even when air temperatures soar into the 100s at times during summer or plummet in winter. Lees Ferry sits at 3,120 feet in elevation, so it does not ice up and seldom gets snow.

Trout at the Ferry feed heavily upon midges and blackflies, along with the gammarus (freshwater shrimp) when available. The area has 50 or so species of midges, along with mayflies and caddis flies, plus other insects and aquatic organisms in season. The abundance of aquatic insects and the pink-colored shrimp called scuds results in mature trout having exaggerated crimson sides, especially those in late winter or early spring spawning regalia. Knowledgeable anglers from the "Continent" say these crimson-sided rainbows at "les Ferry de pêche" could hang in the Musée du Louvre in Paris and rival any artistic works of man.

In late spring and into summer, there is typically a terrestrial bite dominated by grasshoppers. There also can be a bodacious cicada hatch at times in summer. This ephemeral cicada bite at the Ferry can provide some of the most exciting rainbow-trout fishing in North America, but ironically it doesn't draw swarms of anglers. Watch summer fishing reports. Late autumn and early winter is the off-season, but it still offers great fishing. Look skyward while rhythmically casting a fly and you might observe a speeding flock of goldeneyes zipping downriver with the wind whistling off their wings. Desert bighorn sheep can also be found agilely traversing the precipitous slopes along Lees Ferry. Anglers any time of year might catch a glimpse of California condors soaring in the skies

In 1871, Mormon settler John D. Lee was directed by The Church of Jesus Christ of Latter-day Saints to establish a ferry on the Colorado River. The location had earlier been scouted by the Mormon explorer Jacob Hamblin on his numerous missionary expeditions to the Hopi and the Navajo east of the Colorado River. Previously, the river had been forded at the Ute Crossing or The Crossing of the Fathers, which is now under Lake Powell. With financing supplied by the church, Lee built the ferry from 1871 to 1872 near the confluence of the Paria River with the Colorado. Due to its proximity to the confluence, the site was originally named Paria Crossing. It features a natural slope from the cliffs to the riverbank, allowing safe crossing through the canyon and across the Colorado River in otherwise impassable terrain.

In the late 1800s and early 1900s, Lees Ferry was the only crossing of the Colorado River by ferry between Moab, Utah and Needles, California; it was heavily used by travelers between Utah and Arizona. Since Lee traveled frequently, the ferry was managed primarily by his wife, Emma Dean Lee. Lee was eventually forced to leave the ferry site to evade law enforcement officers for his part in the 1857 Mountain Meadows Massacre. He was executed by firing squad on March 23, 1877. In 1879 Emma Lee sold the ferry, for 100 milk cows, to the LDS church, which continued to operate it until about 1910. Coconino County, Arizona subsequently managed the ferry. The Lees' Lonely Dell Ranch and the ferry are now listed on the National Register of Historic Places, together with the wreckage of the riverboat *Charles H. Spencer*.

The ferry was closed in 1928 when Navajo Bridge was completed over Marble Canyon, which was built 4.5 miles to the south. While the "old bridge" was recently replaced with a more modern structure to carry the traffic of U.S. Route 89A, the original Navajo Bridge still stands as a pedestrian visitor viewing point spanning the canyon. Visitors can get a bird's-eye view of Marble Canyon, spy condors soaring above or even resting on the bridge, and watch with some envy the travelers embarking on extended trips through the Grand Canyon on inflatable boats and dories.

A steel wire cable basket for gauging the flows of the Colorado now crosses the river downstream of the old ferry site. The Lees Ferry gauge holds the distinction of being the point of compliance for complex rules governing delivery of water from the Upper Basin of the Colorado to the Lower Basin.

above the Marble Canyon or Glen Canyon gorges. Condors were reintroduced to Arizona on the nearby Vermillion Cliffs along House Rock Valley.

Fishing Tips: There are three ways to fish Lees Ferry, and two of them
require a boat, with shallow draft being best. Drift fishing from a boat,
either with fly gear or spinning gear, is not only popular, but at certain
times of year and during certain flow regimes almost a necessity. When
physically possible, fly and spin anglers both wade the riffles. Waders
really are required in the cold water. The third approach is via the area
called the "walk-in" area, not far from the launch ramp. Here, your only
choice is wading the riffles, but you get to fish an area the boaters cannot
reach, although white-water rafters pass through this stretch. Either way,
fly anglers at the Ferry need to deploy long, dead drifts. A drag-free drift
is a must for catching trout here. As a general rule, use long leaders, light
tippets (6x or 7x), and small flies. Always check the latest weekly fishing
report at www.azgfd.gov to ascertain what is working best.

➤ **Fly Anglers:** Scuds and midges are the two keys to fishing the Ferry.
You always want to be armed with scud patterns, just in case. Midges
will hatch year-round at the Ferry, but prolific midge hatches commence
in March. Nymphs, streamers, and buggers are used the most here, but
dry flies can be effective at times. San Juan Worms can work as well. Use
attractors as strike indicators, such as Irresistibles, Humpies, Royal Wulffs,
and Unbelievables.

➤ **Spin Anglers:** Try bouncing Glo-bugs on the bottom or using marabou
jigs. Pink is often best. Let the jig or Glo-bug get the bottom, keeping

**A diet of pink-colored shrimp and aquatic insects gives
Lees Ferry rainbows their heightened crimson coloring.**

contact with the lure. Once the lure hits bottom, pop the rod tip up once or twice to "jig" the offering, then let it sink back to the bottom. Repeat this process. Trout will often hit on the fall, so watch and/or be sure to feel the line. In-line spinners such as Panther Martins, Rooster Tails, and Vibrex can also work. Once again, think pink. A little pink dye can work to good effect on white-colored spinners. Also try narrow and smaller bass crankbaits in bright colors, such as orange, pink, and chartreuse, but not red.

For crankbaits, cast out at a 10- to 15-degree angle downstream. When the lure hits the water, begin a slow retrieve to keep tension on the line as the current carries it downstream. When the lure (especially a spinner) gets almost perpendicular to you, the fast-flowing water will enhance its action. This is often when trout will hit the lure, so be ready. Don't do a huge hook set, as trout have soft mouths. Simply do a quick flick of the wrist to pop the rod tip up and set the hook. Although the Ferry is known as one of the best fly-fishing tailwaters anywhere, on any given day spin anglers might have better luck and reel in more wild thrashing rainbows, and larger ones at that.

Special Notes: Lees Ferry has been governed by special regulations for decades. These regulations are subject to modification, so please check the Arizona Fishing Regulations for the latest updates.

8 | FISHERY FACTS

LOCATION AND DIRECTIONS: GPS — 36°51'57"N; 111°35'11"W
Lees Ferry is located approximately 126 miles north of Flagstaff, a two-hour drive along U.S. Route 89A. It's 42 miles from Page via U.S. 89 south and U.S. 89A west. It is 85 miles from the North Rim of the Grand Canyon via U.S. 89A and State Route 67. The Lees Ferry Junction and Recreation Area entrance is just west of the Navajo Bridge Interpretive Center. A paved road leads 5 miles to the Ferry area past huge balancing rocks.

Lees Ferry is the only place within Glen Canyon where visitors can drive all the way to the Colorado River in more than 700 miles of Canyon Country, and actually drive right up to the first "rapid" in the Grand Canyon.

AMENITIES: A National Park Service campground, ranger station, and public launch ramp are the only services available at Lees Ferry. There is a gas station, a store, a post office, a motel, a restaurant, and a fly shop at Marble Canyon, next to the recreation area entrance. More services, including another fly shop, are found just west of Marble Canyon on U.S. 89A at Vermillion Cliffs and Cliff Dwellers. The year-round launch ramp at Lees Ferry has a courtesy dock for temporary tie-up. Keep in mind that this is the launching point for all Grand Canyon white-water rafting trips, and the boat beach next to the launch ramp can be a busy place.

(9) Lake Mead

Houseboating is a great way to explore Lake Mead.

Lake Mead is the grand matriarch of the nation's impoundments and is still the largest man-made lake in North America. This immense lake sprawling across the Arizona-Nevada border can provide good year-round fishing opportunities for striped bass, largemouth bass, and smallmouth bass. Line-stripping stripers routinely constitute 80 percent of the fish caught from Mead.

Lake Mead and its behemoth sister lake upstream, Lake Powell, are typically the top two freshwater fisheries for striped bass in North America. However, Mead has the edge when it comes to monster stripers, tipping the scales at up to 50 pounds or more. Anglers at Mead can expect to have good catch rates for these hard-fighting stripers, especially from late spring through fall. Mead was once renowned for its largemouth bass fishing before striped bass took over as the paramount species to catch. In recent years, the crystal-clear waters of Mead have been providing decent action for smallmouth bass as well. Mead has channel catfish, carp, bluegill, walleye, green sunfish, black bullheads, and black crappie to help round out your fishing experience.

Despite its popularity, this immense impoundment provides ample opportunities for angling solitude in the clear and dry lower Mohave Desert air. With 550 miles of shoreline when full, it is not difficult to find whole coves you won't have to share with other anglers, especially on weekdays. In fact, much of this lake is remote and receives relatively light fishing pressure. The Lake Mead National Recreation Area totals 1.5

HISTORICAL NOTE

Boulder Dam, as it was originally called, or Hoover Dam, as it is now named, was completed in 1935. At that time, it created the largest man-made lake in the world. The lake was named after Elwood Mead, who was the commissioner of the U.S. Bureau of Reclamation from 1924 to 1936 during the planning and construction of the Boulder Canyon Project that created the dam and the lake. The Boulder Dam Recreation Area was created in 1936 and the Lake Mead National Recreation Area was created in 1964, but it includes Lake Mohave and the Shivwits Plateau as well. At the bottom of the lake is a B-29 Superfortress that crashed in 1948 while testing a prototype missile guidance system known as "suntracker." The wreckage of at least two smaller planes also lies within Lake Mead.

million acres, including Lake Mohave, and attracts 8 million visitors annually. Encompassing 247 square miles, it is almost twice the size of Rhode Island. However, most visitors are attracted to the Hoover Dam area.

While fishing on Mead, you'll encounter nearly 2 billion years of Earth's geologic history readily exposed in the often topsy-turvy rock formations bordering the lake's emerald-blue waters. Visitors can witness spectacular vistas of multi-colored rock formations nakedly exposed to the sculpting forces of windblown time in the arid Mohave Desert. This stark yet intriguing otherworldly landscape provided the backdrop for the movie *Planet of the Apes*. At night, the clear desert air results in a magnificent celestial display that will astound stargazers, especially during periodic meteor showers such as the summer Perseids.

Fishing Tips: With 150,000 surface acres spread across 100 miles, Lake Mead encompasses three major basins and two minor basins plus the huge Overton Arm. Anglers have lots of choices.

➤ Although Boulder Basin, the largest section of water on Lake Mead, is located within 30 miles of Las Vegas, Nevada, this sprawling lake spreads well into Arizona. Both the South Cove and Temple Bar areas are located approximately 80 driving miles from Kingman. By far, the most popular Arizona launching location for fishing Mead is South Cove, although there are those who prefer Temple Bar. This is the only basin to receive intense fishing pressure, especially in June, July, October, and November. It is stocked during winter with trout. This is also the area where huge stripers ranging from 20 to 50 pounds can put a strain on your angling equipment.

Solitude amid Lake Mead's stark landscape.

➤ The narrow channel, once known as Boulder Canyon, is now known as "The Narrows" and connects Boulder Basin to the Virgin Basin to the east. This basin may receive some of the lightest fishing and recreational boating pressure. The Virgin River and the Muddy River empty into the Overton Arm, which is connected to the northern part of the Virgin Basin. This arm can experience a little higher productivity due to nutrient loaded inflows. If there are sufficient spring inflows, stripers will spawn in this area, typically during February and March.

➤ The next basin to the east is Temple Basin, where Temple Bar is located, and following that is Gregg Basin, which is connected to Temple Basin via the Virgin

Temple Bar Marina is the launching point for many a Lake Mead adventure.

Canyon. Gregg Basin contains South Cove, where most Arizona anglers launch, although there is little in the way of amenities. In February and March, depending on flows, stripers congregate along the Colorado River inflows just up-lake, but lower lake levels can make access challenging.

➤ There is also a launch ramp at Pearce Ferry, where those rafting the Grand Canyon typically come out. Due to low lake levels through 2010, this ramp became challenged and may not be usable by the general public. Check before coming.

When the water level is high enough, a section of the lake farther upstream from Gregg Basin is flooded, which includes Grand Wash Bay and the Pearce Ferry Bay and launch ramp. In addition, there are two tiny basins, the Muddy River Inlet and the Virgin River Basin, that are flooded when the lake is high enough to inundate the areas where these two rivers flow into the lake.

Stocking History: Prior to the building of Boulder Dam in Black Canyon, the Colorado River contained carp, channel catfish, and four endemic native fish superbly adapted for the former wild and sometimes rampaging Colorado River. These native big-river fish such as the humpback chub, razorback sucker, and the Colorado pikeminnow, which grows up to 100 pounds in size, are now federally listed as endangered species. In 1954, threadfin shad were introduced to Lake Mead and the largemouth bass fishery flourished, drawing anglers from across North America and beyond. In 1969, the largemouth fishing was waning and management was changed to a two-stage reservoir, with warm-water fish stocked in the shallow shoreline zones and cold-water fish stocked into the deep cold-water zones, including seven species of trout and striped bass. By 1974, striped bass were reproducing and soon took over the reservoir. The trout fishery waned. Trout stocking ceased altogether from 1983 to 1990. In 1999, two new species, smallmouth bass and blue tilapia, were documented in the lake.

➤ **Striped Bass:** By 2010, biologists were also seeing a new trend — the 1- to 2-pound stripers were not as numerous as in other recent decades. Although the exact reasons had not been determined, the proliferation of invasive quagga mussels, which are filter feeders, could be one of the factors. Another trend was also being observed: Smallmouth bass were becoming more common.

If you plan to fish for stripers during the springtime, keep in mind that these fish don't spawn on beds; they prefer to spawn in current. Spawning stripers often congregate in the Overton Arm in either February or March, depending on flow regimes, which vary based on releases from the Glen Canyon Dam upstream. June, July, October, and November are often the premier months to fish for rampaging schools of striped bass, including huge fish up to 50 pounds at times. Stripers hunt in schools to attack huge schools of threadfin shad. Stripers will attack these balls of shad in open water but can also push them up against a shoreline, reef, island, or other structure. When shad are not abundant in spring and early summer, one of the most effective methods entails using bait. Try cutting anchovies into thirds or quarters and use a No. 4 circle hook, not an anchovy hook. Chumming is legal on Lake Mead. Try mixing anchovy pieces with corn. You can also use corn to catch bluegill and carp.

When stripers are actively chasing shad, live bait might not be as

Low water levels expose clean, sandy beaches at Lake Mead perfect for setting up camp.

effective and it's time to switch to your arsenal of lures. But even while using lures to catch one of these voracious marauders, remember to chum to keep the school of stripers from moving. Stripers are constantly on the move. If you can get a striper school into a feeding frenzy, it is possible to fill the live well with these aggressive foragers. Starting in late spring and continuing through summer, stripers can be spotted in "boils" chasing shad at the surface just about anywhere on the lake. At first, the boils are of short duration and are often dispersed. As summer progresses, the boils

A junior fisherman demonstrates his technique at Lake Mead.

increase in intensity and often in duration as well. By autumn, these boils typically hit a crescendo and there are times when acres of water erupt with stripers chasing shad at the surface.

Good topwater lures include Zara Spooks, Zara Puppies, Sammys, and Jumping Minnows. Spoons can work to good effect, especially when the stripers sound (go deep). Also try shad-like crankbaits, such as Cordell Spots, Shad Raps, and Rat-L-Traps, either in white or in shad colors. Never cast directly into a boil, as stripers can be spooky. Nor should you ever run your boat directly to a boil. Get the boat near a boil and cast past it, then work the lure back through the surface eruption. Also, watch the birds. If you see a flock of seagulls wheeling about the sky or great blue herons converging on an area of water, it most likely means the stripers and shad are actively working at the surface. Go join the melee.

During the summer, most striper anglers turn to night fishing under submersible lights. Keep in mind that this strategy works best on moonless nights.

➤ **Largemouth and Smallmouth Bass:** Also keep in mind that Mead can be a little windy in early spring, from March through May, but this is typically the prime time for largemouth bass and smallmouth bass to spawn. The clear waters of Lake Mead make it a superb place to sight-fish both largemouth bass and smallmouth bass on beds. Largemouth will typically spawn in the more sheltered coves, while smallmouth bass prefer rocky shelves. Drop-shot rigs can work well in this exceptionally clear reservoir. The most successful anglers will typically use fluorocarbon line in the 8- to 10-pound range fished on light- or medium-action spinner gear.

In spring and fall, Mead can also provide fly anglers some excellent opportunities to catch largemouth bass, smallmouth bass, and stripers.

In the fall, largemouth bass can also be caught actively chasing shad at the surface. You might even catch largemouth bass gobbling up pieces of shad beneath the striper boils at the surface. At these times, use flutter-down lures and spoons.

➤ **Bottom Feeders:** Catfish and carp abound in Lake Mead but are seldom fished for by most anglers. Channel catfish especially prefer fresh bait, although stink bait can work. Anchovies, shad, corn, or even hot dogs fished off the bottom rigged with slip sinkers are effective.

Special Notes: During the first decade of this century, drought and reduced snowpack in the Rocky Mountains have resulted in a reduced lake level at Mead, giving it a bathtub-ring appearance and making launching difficult at many locations. Whole marinas have had to be moved. In addition, diminished nutrient inflows and vast colonization by invasive quagga mussels are gradually altering the ecosystem at Lake Mead. Always check the latest fishing reports at www.azgfd.gov before going. While the lake level is low, vegetation often grows in the fertile lake bed, adding both submerged habitat and added nutrients when the lake level rises again.

LAKE MEAD ACCESS LOCATIONS/AMENITIES

10 Boulder Basin: GPS — 36°1'39.38"N; 114°46'26.65"W
(immediately behind Hoover Dam)

Lake Mead, Las Vegas Boat Harbor, and Callville Bay Resort marinas have boat rentals, fuel, general-store merchandise, restaurants or snack bars, dry storage, and slip rentals. Due to lowered lake levels, Lake Mead Marina moved to Hemenway Harbor and became part of Las Vegas Boat Harbor. Boat rentals range from personal watercraft to 16-foot fishing boats, 18-foot runabouts for water-skiing and exploring, 24-foot patio boats, and houseboats that sleep up to 12 people. Advance reservations are advised. Because of the growing popularity of houseboats, reservations for these should be made at least six months in advance.

Cruises are available on a paddlewheeler to and from Hoover Dam with Lake Mead Cruises. Daily boat tours, special cocktail/dinner cruises, sunset dinner/dance cruises, and breakfast cruises are available. For more information, please call 702-293-6180 or visit www.LakeMeadCruises.com.

11 Overton Arm: GPS — 36°26'58.13"N; 114°20'57.30"W

Echo Bay Resort marina has boat rentals, fuel, general-store merchandise, a restaurant, dry storage, and slip rentals. Boat rentals range from personal watercraft to 16-foot fishing boats, 18-foot runabouts for water-skiing and exploring, 24-foot patio boats, and houseboats

This has actually helped some with with fish productivity at this aging desert fishery.

Invasive Species Note: Because of large colonies of invasive quagga mussels at Lake Mead, boaters should *clean, dry, and drain* their boats as required by law and wait five days before launching in another lake.

9 | FISHERY FACTS

LAUNCH RAMPS: Launch ramps are at the following locations: Callville Bay, Boulder Basin; Las Vegas Bay, Boulder Basin (can be closed at low water levels); Hemenway Harbor, Boulder Basin; Boulder Harbor, Boulder Basin; Echo Bay, Overton Arm; Southcove, Gregg Basin (near where Colorado River enters the lake); Temple Bar (East Lake Mead); and Pearce Ferry (has been consistently closed due to lower water levels).

that sleep up to 12 people. Advance reservations are advised. Because of the growing popularity of houseboats, reservations for these should be made at least six months in advance.

12 Temple Basin: GPS — 36°2'15.78"N; 114°19'13.07"W (Temple Bar)

Take U.S. Route 93 from Kingman approximately 52 miles to Temple Bar Road, then travel 26 miles to the lake. Temple Bar Marina has boat rentals, fuel, general-store merchandise, a restaurant, dry storage, and slip rentals. This launch ramp is typically recommended for craft longer than 35 feet that are launching in this end of the lake. Boat rentals range from personal watercraft to 16-foot fishing boats, 18-foot runabouts for water-skiing and exploring, 24-foot patio boats, and houseboats that sleep up to 12 people.

13 Gregg Basin: GPS — 36°5'23.01"N; 114°6'5.36"W (South Cove)

The South Cove launch ramp has three paved parking lots, lights, and a few picnic tables. No marina or services are available. Come prepared to pack it in and pack it out. Meadview is 8 miles away if you need to buy any of those last-minute items. Just up-lake where the Colorado River comes into the lake is Pearce Ferry, which can be high and dry when the lake level is low, as it has been for the first decade of this century.

(14) Willow Beach

Willow Beach is home to stocked rainbow trout, monstrous striped bass, nimble desert bighorn sheep, and speedy peregrine falcons. But don't expect crowds of tourists, as they typically flock to the imposing mass of Hoover Dam or the enticing neon lights of Las Vegas. If it's possible to be a secret fishery that is also famous, at least in some circles, then Willow Beach might just be it. This extraordinary fishery is located just 11 miles downriver (17.5 driving miles) from historic Hoover Dam along the semi-tamed Colorado River, as the powerful waterway flows relentlessly down the precipitous Black Canyon to the vast, clear waters of Lake Mohave. With its 2,000-foot cliffs, often right up to the water's edge, Black Canyon is the desert haunt of bighorns, peregrine falcons, cliff swallows,

anglers, rafters, and kayakers. Between Hoover Dam and Cottonwood Cove on Lake Mohave, you have approximately 30 miles of flowing water to fish and explore.

Willow Beach is just 3.5 miles off U.S. Route 93 leading from Kingman to Las Vegas. Despite being such a popular highway, relatively few travelers are attracted to this side trip. Each Friday, the Willow Beach National Fish Hatchery stocks rainbow trout, attracting a small but dedicated core group of trout anglers from Boulder, Las Vegas, and Kingman. But these stocked trout also attract something else — huge striped bass, sometimes reaching 50 or 60 pounds. These larger stripers can be found year-round here, but are typically more abundant from spring through fall. In the winter, a good strategy is to fish from Willow Beach downstream to Cottonwood Cove. From spring through fall, try fishing from Willow Beach up toward Hoover Dam.

The Colorado is very calm below the dam, and the high canyon walls usually keep out winds. This makes Willow Beach a serene stretch of river for fishing, boating, rafting, and kayaking. Much of the time, the water is smooth and almost glassy. But don't be fooled, as the current can be deceptively strong, which most anglers or those who let their boat drift quickly discover.

No matter what time of year, bring plenty of water and sunscreen. The volcanic black walls of this desert canyon will reflect and magnify the desert sun like a giant solar cooker. Be prepared. Despite being in the lower Mohave Desert, also be prepared for cold water. This stretch of the Colorado River is fed from the depths of Hoover Dam and even in summer will be in the low to mid-50s. Those who jump into the water to cool off can find it a shocking experience. A 30- to 50-degree instant change in temperature can stun your body, causing you to expel your breath and

A well-kept secret among anglers, Willow Beach in Black Canyon is a haven for both sport fish and a variety of desert wildlife.

The imposing mass of Hoover Dam towers above Willow Beach.

possibly sink, to be swept away by the current. Always wear a life jacket here, especially if you decide to go into the water.

During summer, there is another treat for those willing to brave the heat — battling desert bighorn sheep in the rut. Although it is possible to see bighorns any time of year in Black Canyon, the rut in late June and July is typically the best time, before the monsoon rains. Anglers routinely see bighorns on the cliffs. They often hear them banging heads, which sounds like a rifle shot echoing off the canyon walls. On rare occasions, anglers get to see dominant bighorn rams butting horns in the classic desert clash. Try drift fishing or trolling while keeping the binoculars handy.

Anglers heading toward Hoover Dam will often stop at Weeping Springs Cove (Mile Marker 58), where they can nose their boat in and take a shower or take a detour at Mile Marker 59 to head up Petroglyph Wash and visit ancient rock art (difficult to get to). Just before Mile Marker 60 are the restrooms. There is a beach that you can nose your boat into and take a short hike to visit the soothing Ringbolt Hot Spring, also called Arizona Hot Springs.

Fishing Tips: Because of the regular pattern of trout stockings, the largest concentration of huge stripers will often be found each Friday when the Willow Beach National Fish Hatchery plants rainbows. Most anglers fish for the stripers using trout-like swim baits as lures. Some of these large baits are up to 10 or 12 inches in length. Others are much smaller. Some are made of plastic, wood, or even rubber. They can be jointed or solid. There is a wide choice of such lures on the market, but to work best here they need to have one thing in common: they should look like a stocked rainbow trout.

Rigging a swim bait is relatively easy for veteran anglers, but those who have not used them before may want to consider buying prerigged ones. They are called "swim" baits for a reason; you will want to swim them versus cranking them in. Try short hauls by swinging your rod tips steadily. Experiment with the speed and duration. Some anglers like to stop and shake the lure, like an injured stocked trout. Also, many anglers choose to troll these swim baits rather than the sometimes arduous practice of casting and retrieving them.

➤ Another tried-and-true striper fishing technique is using bait, such as anchovy, squid, or sardine. Remember that stripers swim in schools and are constantly on the move. You will want to chum to hold the stripers, and to possibly get them into a feeding frenzy. A good rule of thumb is if you catch one striper, chum to hold the others. If two or more anglers are fishing out of a boat, while one angler is battling a striper, another angler should be chumming, and possibly grabbing for a big net. For anchovies, use a No. 4 or No. 6 hook, cut the anchovy into thirds or quarters, and fish it with just enough weight to get it down. The actively feeding stripers will probably not be deep, but the current can be an issue. There are some anglers who will use a larger and heavier No. 2 or No. 1 hook and will slowly troll a whole anchovy or squid. Live shad can also work very well. Veteran anglers in this area will sometimes head to Cottonwood Cove in Lake Mohave to net shad.

➤ Keep in mind that the water is exceptionally clear, and stripers can be line sensitive. Yet because of the possible huge size to the stripers, it's necessary to use fishing line of 18 pounds test or more. It is best to use fluorocarbon line, as it is the most transparent.

Special Notes: Black Canyon, the canyon from Willow Beach to Hoover Dam, is managed as a primitive zone where people can experience a variety of motorless recreational opportunities in a natural setting. Personal watercraft (PWC) and vessels with motors are prohibited on Sunday and Monday year-round. Between Labor Day and the Friday of Memorial Day weekend (Tuesday through Saturday), Black Canyon is managed as a semi-primitive zone. PWCs remain prohibited, and boating is restricted to vessels with 65-hp engines or less.

Between the Saturday of Memorial Day weekend to Labor Day (Tuesday through Saturday), Black Canyon is managed as a rural-natural zone. During the busy boating season, there are no horsepower restrictions and PWC are allowed. House-boating, water-skiing, and wakeboarding are prohibited for safety reasons in this narrow canyon.

Accessing Arizona Hot Springs requires scaling a sheer rock wall with the ladder you will find there. The water harbors an amoeba that can be a health hazard; do not get any in your nostrils or ears, and do not use the spring if you have an open wound or are susceptible to infection.

14 | FISHERY FACTS

LOCATION AND DIRECTIONS: GPS — 35°52'9.98"N; 114°39'44.09"W
Willow Beach Harbor is located on the Arizona side of the Colorado River. The turnoff is just 14 miles south of Hoover Dam and another 3.5 miles off U.S. Route 93. It is approximately a 50-mile drive from Las Vegas.

AMENITIES: Willow Beach has a convenience store with fishing tackle, a launch ramp, boat rentals (including canoes and kayaks), and a marine fueling facility.

(15) Lake Mohave

Lake Mohave, part of the Lake Mead National Recreation area, is a crystal-clear boating and picnicking jewel in the Mohave Desert that also offers good shoreline-camping opportunities. At 67 miles long and typically about 4 miles wide, it averages about 120 feet deep, although many areas are fairly shallow. Its largest basin is Cottonwood Cove and its most popular area is around Katherine's Landing near Davis Dam. Unlike Mead upstream or Havasu downstream, Mohave does not have a ready source of nutrient inflows and relies instead on flash floods down washes for its occasional nutrient shots, thus making it a much less productive lake. However, it typically does have something Mead lacks: fairly stable water levels, although this too can change at times. The main access area for Lake Mohave at Katherine's Landing is also relatively close to one of the area's popular attractions: Laughlin, or more precisely, Casino Row.

This 26,000-acre impoundment on the Colorado River is a place you can sometimes catch larger fish. Fish species include striped bass, largemouth bass, smallmouth bass, redear sunfish, rainbow trout, bluegill sunfish, crappie, carp, and channel catfish. Forage fish include threadfin shad and red shiners. Mohave also has a remnant population of razorback suckers and some bonytail chub, which are both endangered big-river fish. Don't expect a stringer full of smaller 1- to 2-pound stripers, as they aren't as prevalent as they used to be, possibly due to the invasion of colonizing quagga mussels.

But there is also good news — hard-fighting smallmouth bass have

Gasoline Alley, on the Arizona side of Lake Mohave, can be somewhat chaotic with boaters, personal watercraft, and cliff-climbers.

become more common here. Plus, it's likely that redear sunfish, also called shell-crackers, will become more prevalent to feed on the invasive mussels. Two Nevada state records have come from Lake Mohave; a 63-pound striped bass was caught in 2001, and a 16-pound, 4-ounce rainbow trout was caught in 1971. Lake Mohave has also produced a 30-pound, 8-ounce carp; an 11-pound largemouth bass; a 26-pound, 4-ounce channel catfish; a 2-pound, 12-ounce black crappie; a 1-pound, 1-ounce bluegill sunfish; and an 11-pound, 6-ounce cutthroat trout.

It isn't the fishing that necessarily draws most anglers here. Mohave is a picturesque place to boat and fish where you can find secluded coves of emerald-colored water and sandy beaches tucked between rolling desert hills, timeless wind-buffeted bluffs and ragged mountains. In fact, there are hundreds of beaches that can only be accessed by boat. Boat camping is allowed, but don't expect any crowds, as Mohave doesn't usually attract them. What it lacks in popularity it makes up for with wide-open spaces to explore.

Fishing Tips: Striped bass are the most sought-after fish here. The best time of the year to fish for stripers is April through November, with the peak in September and October when stripers are actively chasing shad at the surface. First and last light are typically the most productive fishing times. For much of the year, try frozen anchovies or squid on No. 4 hooks and avoid anchovy hooks. Stripers are schooling fish and are constantly on the move. Chumming is legal on Lake Mohave and can help hold a school of stripers so you can catch multiple fish. Trolling is also a popular form of fishing on Mohave. Try shad-like crankbaits, such as Cordell Spots, Shad Raps, and Rat-L-Traps, either in white or in shad colors. When stripers are actively chasing shad at the surface, anchovies won't be as effective. Try topwater lures, such as Zara Spooks, Jumpin' Minnows, or Sammys. To spot feeding activity, watch the skies for fish-eating birds,

HISTORICAL NOTE

Spanish explorer Melchior Diaz traveled through this area in 1540, 80 years before the *Mayflower* landed on the East Coast. In 1776, Spanish missionary-explorer Francisco Garcés crossed the Colorado River here, nearly a month before the Declaration of Independence was signed.

From 1852 to 1909, steamboats made regular trips up the Colorado River from Port Isabel in the Gulf of California. These sternwheeler riverboats played an important part in the early development of the areas bordering the Colorado River.

In October 1857, a caravan of 28 camels crossed the Colorado River below the present Bullhead City. On his presidential-appointed survey to establish a 1,000-mile wagon road across the southern part of the country, Lt. Edward F. Beale was testing the camels, which had been imported from Tunisia, as pack animals for desert travel for the War Department. With him was Hi-Jolly (Hadji Ali), a trained camel handler from Asia Minor.

The site for Davis Dam was selected in 1902, but construction did not start until 1942. It was discontinued in December of that year due to World War II. Construction resumed in April 1946, and the dam was completed in 1953.

Sun, shade, sand, and water combine for a day of fun at Lake Mohave.

such as seagulls. When seagulls are actively wheeling in the sky and div-ing into the water, you'll want to join in on the action. It's always good to have binoculars on board.

➤ During the summer, the best fishing is on moonless nights, as daytime temperatures can reach well past the 110-degree mark. The two best areas to target stripers are near Davis Dam or at the other end of the lake at Cottonwood Cove. The Nevada Department of Wildlife stocks rainbow trout at Cottonwood Cove, Placer Cove, and the Aztec Wash area, typi-cally from November through March. The trout stockings at Cottonwood Cove draw more than anglers, as large stripers gravitate here to feed on the stockers. Those seeking to catch monster stripers should consider using swim baits resembling rainbow trout. There are many varieties on the market. For largemouth bass, March through June is generally best, but bucketmouths can often be found on beds all the way into June and July as well. During the spring spawn, the clear waters of Mohave make it a good place to sight fish for spawning bass in the coves.

➤ Smallmouth bass prefer rocky areas to feed on crayfish, which means they are providing a welcome angling dimension at this rock-bordered lake. Smallies especially like areas with cobble or boulders. They spawn on rocky shelves, typically in March and April. For lures, think crayfish, espe-cially for soft plastics or crankbaits. In-line spinners such as Mepps and Rooster Tails can be effective as well. Curly tailed jigs on swim heads are probably the most popular bait.

➤ Mohave also has a superb and often ignored population of bottom fish, such as catfish and carp. Dough bait and corn can get your family a lot of action, even fishing from shore, which is just perfect for those visiting a remote sandy cove for a picnic. A good rule of thumb is to always carry a couple of cans of corn to chum with. The corn will attract a variety of fish, from catfish and carp to bluegill. Increased fish activity can also attract predatory species, such as striped bass and largemouth bass.

Special Notes: In 1999, more than 4,000 square feet of fish habitat was placed in Box Cove, which is immediately north of Cottonwood Cove;

Carp Cove, located on the Arizona side about 2 miles southeast of Cottonwood Cove; and Princess Cove, on the south end of the lake, north of Katherine's Landing. All habitat structures were placed in less than 25 feet of water and are often visible on a calm day.

Desert winds can whip up the waves in this long, thin lake. When that happens, it is best to head your boat into shore and seek shelter until the choppy water calms down. Mohave is known for its closely spaced waves that make it treacherous to negotiate for small craft when the winds arise.

15 | FISHERY FACTS

AMENITIES: There are three marinas with launch ramps, two in Arizona (Willow Beach and Katherine's Landing) and one in Nevada (Cottonwood Cove). There is also a launch ramp at Princess Cove on the Arizona side near Katherine's Landing (just follow the signs). Shoreline camping is permitted. Campers should carry out their trash and provide for adequate sanitation. Summer temperatures can exceed 110°F.

LAKE MOHAVE ACCESS LOCATIONS/AMENITIES

16 Cottonwood Cove: GPS — 35°29'30.82"N; 114°41'12.22"W

This access point is about an hour's drive from Bullhead City, Arizona and Laughlin, Nevada. There is a full-service marina with boats for rent, including houseboats. There is also a restaurant. There are 145 campsites with a 30-day limit. Park concessionaires provide RV sites with full hookups, including electricity, water, and sewage. For marina services, contact Cottonwood Cove Marina at 702-297-1464. For RV park information, call 877-386-4383

17 Katherine's Landing: GPS — 35°13'9.83"N; 114°33'53.40"W

This is the most popular access point on Lake Mohave, and there is a year-round, 24/7 launch ramp. Located 9 miles north of Laughlin on the Arizona side of Lake Mohave, Katherine's Landing features RV facilities, boat rentals, boat slips, a picnic area, a marina, dry storage, a restaurant and snack bar, a general store, and other resort amenities. Boat rentals range from personal watercraft to 16-foot fishing boats, 18-foot runabouts for water-skiing and exploring, 24-foot patio boats, and houseboats that sleep up to 14 people. For more information, call 928-754-3245.

18 Below Davis Dam
(Casino Row and Beyond)

The stretch of Colorado River below Davis Dam between Arizona and Nevada, known as "Casino Row," can spoil you. In this tri-state area, the river starts in a world of glitter, neon, and slot machines along Casino Row and then enters a rural stretch, rambling 40 miles between states to the Interstate 40 Bridge at Needles. In fact, you can boat all the way from here to Lake Havasu if you so desire, and there are boats to rent and tours available to do just that.

Let's start with Casino Row and the Bullhead City area just across the river. The U.S. Fish and Wildlife Service stocks the river below Davis Dam with rainbow trout starting in October and continuing through March each year. There are two stocking sites: Davis Camp, which is just below Davis Dam on the Arizona side; and near the Riverside Casino along Casino Row. The trout come from the Willow Beach National Fish Hatchery upriver, past Lake Mohave. Anglers in this area also fish for striped bass. But in recent years, the striper fishing has not been as dependable, although stripers can be caught any time of year. The diminished striper population has resulted in another angling bonus though — some larger holdover trout. There are also largemouth bass, channel catfish, and panfish (bluegill and redear).

Fishing this area is an unusual treat for most anglers. You can fish at first light, maybe grab an all-you-can-eat breakfast or lunch buffet, take an air-conditioned nap in your well-appointed hotel room (where rates are cheaper during the week), have your choice of superb restaurants for dinner, see a stage show or two, amble down the relaxing Laughlin Riverwalk, and maybe grab another snooze. Then you do it all over again

Casinos on the Colorado River at the Arizona-Nevada border offer boat tours and rentals of personal watercraft.

the next day, or some variation of that recreational theme. For those who don't have a boat, some anglers rent the more affordable personal watercraft and drift fish effectively with the river current. It's a hoot. There are also fishing boats for rent at some casinos.

The best fishing times are from fall through the end of spring, and the river can be extremely busy with water recreationists in summer. But even then, you can travel a few miles downriver and find relaxing areas to fish for a variety of species. Expect to find largemouth bass ranging from 11 to 20 inches, with an occasional "hawg" in the backwaters or marsh areas. Stripers average around 14 inches, but fish weighing 28 to 30 pounds are sometimes caught. The areas with little or no current also harbor abundant channel catfish and bluegill. Some areas have been known to produce plate-sized bluegill weighing up to 2 pounds.

The time-ravaged jagged peaks and volcanic mountain ranges in this area of the Colorado River give it a rugged and desolate desert countenance that makes some want to stick close to civilization, yet captivates others and provokes a keen sense of appreciation and exploration.

Fishing Tips: In the Davis Camp through the Casino Row area, most anglers either drift fish or troll the stretch, and down to River Bend as well. Shore anglers don't usually do as well. Some anglers use prepared trout baits or night crawlers. Rapalas and small in-line spinners such as Mepps and Rooster Tails can be effective. Spoons, such as Kastmasters and Z-Rays, can work as well as Super Dupers.

➤ For the striped bass and catfish, frozen anchovies, squid, or sardines are the preferred baits. Some anglers like to use trout-like lures, such as swim baits, but trout-colored Rapalas can sometimes catch trout and striped bass.

➤ Farther down the river, look for largemouth bass along small pockets off the main channel, along inlets, or in backwaters. Flipping and pitching soft-plastic baits along the edges of the vegetation, especially bulrushes and cattails, is a popular fishing method. From late spring through the fall, topwater frogs can be effective, especially in areas with less current. The Topock Marsh is also a good area for bucketmouths. For smallmouth bass, try working crayfish-like lures and jigs along the more rocky areas along the shoreline, especially where there is current. Small rocky points before inlets, coves, or backwaters can be prime locations for smallmouth.

Fishing for catfish is also popular along this stretch, especially in backwaters and inlets. Try stink baits, such as chicken liver. Channel catfish also like live bait, so minnows and shiners can work at times. Frozen anchovies are by far the most popular bait. Catfishing is extremely popular in Topock Marsh.

18 | FISHERY FACTS

LOCATION AND DIRECTIONS: GPS — 35°10′22.12″N; 114°34′2.80″W (Laughlin Bridge)
This stretch of river is 223 miles from Phoenix and 33 miles from Kingman. From Kingman, take U.S. Route 93 and just outside town take State Route 68 to Bullhead and Laughlin.

AMENITIES: Along Casino Row there are nine hotel-casinos providing more than 10,000 rooms, 60 restaurants, two museums, and all the other attractions and amenities. Bullhead City also has restaurants, stores, parks, and motels. There are launch ramps at Davis Camp, Big Bend State Recreation Area, Fisherman's Access, Bullhead Community Park, and Rotary Park (Bullhead City).

RIVER ACCESS LOCATIONS/AMENITIES

 Davis Camp: GPS — 35°11'3.23"N; 114°34'3.97"W

This camp is located just below Davis Dam on the Arizona side of the river. There is a three-lane boat ramp, 157 full-service hookups, 30 hookups with water and electricity, five restrooms with shower facilities, laundry facilities, a dump station, a group picnic area with a ramada, a large open area for dry camping, two cottages, and a day-use area with four ramadas. Boat and RV storage is available.

 Fisherman's Access: GPS — 35°10'10.97"N; 114°34'12.22"W

Located on Casino Drive in Laughlin along the Colorado River and just south of the Laughlin Bridge, this area offers a green, grassy area perfect for picnicking. There's a boat launch ramp, ample parking and restrooms. Here you can also access the Laughlin Riverwalk along the Colorado River. This is the only launch ramp with no fees.

 Laughlin Bay: GPS — 35°7'25.20"N; 114°37'42.43"W

This large lagoon on the Colorado River just south of the casino area offers fishing and sandy beaches, with launch ramps provided at the Laughlin Bay Marina and Bayshore Inn. The marina features 110 boat slips, a fuel dock, a store, a restaurant and cocktail lounge, plus a climate-controlled dry-storage facility.

Fun on the Colorado River.

 Big Bend State Recreation Area:
GPS — 35°6'39.53"N; 114°38'34.99"W

This area is located on the shore of the Colorado River, 2 miles south of Laughlin's resort area. This Nevada state park offers camping and day-use facilities, plus a launch ramp, swimming area, and lots of sandy beaches with ramadas and barbecues. Hiking, fishing, and bird-watching are among the many activities offered in the park. For information, call 702-298-1859.

(23) Topock Marsh/Havasu National Wildlife Refuge

Just downriver from Casino Row, the Colorado River meanders 40 miles over sandbars and past various resorts, agricultural fields, and the Fort Mojave Indian Reservation, providing fishing opportunities along the way until reaching the shallow 4,500-surface-acre backwater Topock Marsh and the Havasu National Wildlife Refuge. This huge marsh just east of Needles, California is another world, located in an arid desert landscape that attracts great numbers of waterfowl and shorebirds, while providing lots of fishing opportunities for a variety of fish species. The Havasu National Wildlife Refuge encompasses the marsh and extends downriver through the picturesque Topock Gorge until it almost reaches Lake Havasu itself.

Fishing Tips: Topock Marsh has modest numbers of bass, crappie, bluegill, catfish, and carp. Levee Road follows the Colorado River to a turnaround just before Topock Marina and the Interstate 40 bridge. Fishing is popular near this turnaround. Along the way there are numerous rock jetties, sandy beaches, and pullouts to fish from after a short walk. These sites are also excellent for wildlife photography.

Topock Marsh offers anglers plenty of fishing opportunities.

Special Notes: Local boat launches that allow access to the Colorado River include the Topock Marina (Exit 1, Interstate 40), Park Moabi (located 11 miles south of Needles, California, on I-40), and Havasu State Park at Windsor Beach (on London Bridge Road in Lake Havasu City). There are many other private and public boat launches along the Colorado.

RIVER ACCESS LOCATIONS/AMENITIES

24 Topock Marina/Levee Road:
GPS — 34°43'9.38"N; 114°28'58.14"W

A lot of anglers desiring to access Topock Marsh and the Colorado River as it flows down to Topock Gorge will launch at the Topock Marina. Many use the Levee Road access off of Barrackman Road and State Route 95.

25 Topock Marsh: GPS — 34°44'26.53"N; 114°29'18.38"W

Three sites offer boat access to the marsh: North Dike, Fivemile Landing, and Catfish Paradise.

North Dike marks the northern boundary of the marsh, where water diverted from the Colorado River enters the marsh. North Dike offers a boat launch as well as fishing directly from the dike. Fivemile Landing has a boat launch with some fishing from its shorelines. South Dike is about a quarter-mile hike into a water-control structure that controls the return flow of Topock Marsh water to the Colorado River. Anglers can hike or bike into this area. A highway sign marks this area for parking. Catfish Paradise has a handicapped-accessible fishing pier and boat launch with a nonwater restroom facility. New South Dike is a quarter-mile hike to a bridge where water flow from the South Dike continues on to the Colorado River.

(26) Lake Havasu

The brilliant blue-green waters of Lake Havasu encompass one of the premier fisheries in the West, drawing recreational and tournament anglers from across the country. In fact, Lake Havasu is a veritable water-recreation playground, receiving about 3.5 million visitors a year. However, the fishing popularity and efficacy of this aging impoundment along the Colorado River was waning in the 1980s. An ambitious $14 million fisheries improvement project — the largest in the world — revitalized this recreational goldmine along the Arizona-California border. The 10-year improvement program in the 1990s resulted in 875 acres of fish-habitat improvements, including 67,482 bass shelters, 54,724 catfish houses, 3,484 bass ambushing cover structures, 1,050 tire towers, and 11,800 brush bundles placed around the lake. Brush bundles continue to be placed in the lake at the rate of about 1,000 per year. An important component of this project was improving shoreline access for anglers, including building fishing piers at strategic locations along with improving launch ramps, restrooms, and other facilities. Havasu is now shore-angler friendly — it certainly wasn't before.

Striped bass are probably the most sought-after fish by casual anglers. Striped bass are dependent on threadfin shad for forage. Schools of shad move around, and populations tend to fluctuate. Historically, the majority of striped bass in Lake Havasu tended to be smaller fish of 1 to 2 pounds, with an occasional 20- to 30-pound fish. That trend has changed. By 2010, smaller stripers weren't as prevalent, which also meant an increased size for the stripers being caught. This same trend was being seen in Lake Mohave and Lake Mead as well. The cause of these changes could be related in some degree to the vast proliferation of invasive, filter-feeding quagga mussels in these reservoirs.

Lake Havasu is also well known for large, 2- to 3-pound redear sunfish. With the proliferation of the quagga mussels in the lake, large redears became more common. Redear sunfish are also known as "shell-crackers" due to their preference and ability for eating clams and mussels. A record redear sunfish weighing 4.14 pounds was caught in Lake Havasu in 2010. You might even catch the next record redear here.

Smallmouth bass are becoming more and more common in Lake Havasu. Bass tournaments have been showing almost a 50/50 mix of largemouth and smallmouth bass. Smallmouth bass are very aggressive and scrappy. Perhaps because of the exceptionally clear water in Lake Havasu, both smallmouth and largemouth bass here are strikingly colored. Havasu can be an early-bird lake for spawning bass. There are years when it vies with Alamo Lake to the east (up the Bill Williams River) and Martinez Lake to the south (a Colorado River backwater) for the annual honor of being Arizona's first lake with spawning largemouth bass. However, it is also susceptible to windy winter storms. The more sheltered London Bridge Channel often provides a superb shallow and early spawning ground for both largemouth and smallmouth bass, sometimes within yards of one another.

Havasu is also a relatively shallow lake, averaging 35 feet deep with

At Lake Havasu, fishing the man-made channel created for London Bridge is a good strategy, especially during the spring spawn.

a maximum depth of 75 feet. The lake is surrounded by gradually rising uplands and adjacent mountains, creating a solar-cooker effect that can readily warm up Havasu even in winter, especially the main basin. There are also crappies in Havasu, but the population has fluctuated. Havasu is home to monster flathead catfish exceeding 40 pounds. This lake also abounds with channel catfish and carp. The predominant forage fish is the threadfin shad, but other important species include red shiners, mosquitofish, and fathead minnows. Crayfish, insect larvae, and young-of-the-year of various fish species are also important forage items. Havasu has 19,300 surface acres to fish. There is an almost bowl-like main basin in the upper end near Lake Havasu City and also a long, narrow segment of the lake leading to the Parker Dam downstream.

Parker Dam, a concrete arch gravity dam, was built by the U.S. Bureau of Reclamation between 1934 and 1938. The dam's primary purpose is to store water for pumping into two aqueducts. The Havasupai Indian word *havasu* means land of the blue-green water.

White sturgeon from San Pablo Bay, California were stocked in Lake Havasu in 1967 and 1968. While some dead sturgeon were found downstream from Havasu (probably killed during passage over dams), living fish have not been recorded. However, it is believed that some still exist along the southern end of Lake Havasu near Parker Dam. Sturgeon have been known to grow upwards of 20 feet long and can live in excess of 100 years.

Fishing Tips: Lake Havasu is mostly a clear-water reservoir, and it is important to use the most transparent fishing line possible. You should consider using fluorocarbon or the most transparent, smallest-diameter monofilament or braided line you are comfortable with. Fishing for striped bass is popular here year-round. Striper boils will begin sporadically in spring with dispersed "slurps" occurring, even in open water. During summer, the surface action will keep picking up. By fall you might see acres of surface action with stripers busting shad at the surface.

➤ Good topwater lures include Zara Spooks, Jumpin' Minnows, and Sammys, but there are lots of others to choose from as well. You might rig two or three poles with your favorite topwater lures. Also try shad-like crankbaits. It is always good to have a pole rigged up with a spoon as well to get deeper fish when a boil wanes. Watch the birds. Seagulls and other fish-eating birds circling in the sky can lead you to active surface feeding frenzies. Take along binoculars. Keep in mind that stripers are easily spooked. If you zoom straight to a boil, it might just sound (go deep). Try approaching a boil at a slight angle, then cast past the boil and bring your lure or other offering back through the schooled fish.

➤ If you are not sure where to fish, trolling can be a good method to

The fishing pier at Havasu Springs is one of a half-dozen around Lake Havasu.

locate active fish. Try trolling large lures, like Bomber Long A's, Rat-L-Traps, or Storm ThunderSticks. Keep in mind that stripers often prefer thin-sided lures where largemouth bass often prefer fat ones, but not exclusively so. During times when threadfin shad are not as abundant, such as early spring and summer, it is good to use frozen anchovies, squid, or sardines as bait. Try a No. 4 circle hook with little or no weight. Also, live shad is superb bait. But while stripers are aggressively chasing shad, anchovies and other such baits aren't typically as effective, except at night.

➤ Remember that stripers hunt in schools and are constantly on the move. A good fishing strategy to hold a school is chumming pieces of anchovies mixed with some corn, especially after you catch a fish. Adding corn also helps attract other fish, such as sunfish and catfish. You want to create the most dynamic feeding frenzy as possible, with as many species as possible.

➤ Keep in mind that redear sunfish are less likely to be caught on artificial lures, such as spinners or poppers. They prefer small live baits such as worms, grubs, insects, and sometimes shrimp.

➤ Many anglers in summer will fish at night using submersible lights, especially on moonless nights. The submerged light attracts plankton, the plankton attracts shad, and the shad attracts predatory fish such as stripers, largemouth bass, and sometimes smallmouth bass as well. You might even catch a huge flathead or channel catfish. Chumming is almost essential. Night fishing using these methods can be effective most months of the year. In winter, stripers occasionally can be found actively feeding on shad, but often hold in deeper patterns and are much less aggressive; instead of feeding multiple times a day like they do in summer and fall, they might only need to feed every few days to maintain body condition.

➤ Use the fishfinder to locate schools and chum. Some anglers have found that using drop-shot rigs with anchovies or other baits placed up the line 18 to 24 inches can work exceptionally well at times. Spoons and deep-diving crankbaits can be effective. Good spots to try for stripers include Site Six, Havasu Springs, Windsor Basin, and the main channel. You might even try upriver in the picturesque Topock Gorge. When stripers are actively spawning, typically in late February, March, or early April, try areas of inflow, such as where the Colorado River enters at "the sandbar," or the Bill Williams River, if it is running.

➤ Largemouth bass can be caught all over the lake, but they especially like to hold around artificial habitat or submerged weeds. In early spring, you can often find largemouth on spawning beds in the backs of the more shallow coves and along the London Bridge Channel. It's a common sight in spring to see anglers on bass boats actively working the shoreline and docks while people amble down the cobbled walkway a close cast away. For post-spawn largemouth bass, try the major lake points, islands, and reefs throughout the main lake. Sometimes largemouth bass will get in on the action when stripers are ambushing shad. But the bucketmouths will typically hang near the bottom below the melee and gorge themselves on falling dead shad or shad parts. Spoons, jigs (shad-like), and flutter-down baits like Senkos and curly tails can be deadly at times.

➤ In fall, largemouth can also be actively chasing shad at the surface off the points or in the coves, often at first or last light, sometimes in conjunction with stripers and other times on their own. In winter, largemouth bass will typically be deep, but can come up into the sheltered shallows on warm, sunny winter afternoons. These fish can be lethargic, but might respond to reaction baits, such as spinners or wide-wobble crankbaits. Slow down your presentation and lower your catch-rate expectations in winter. With their lowered metabolism, the bass might miss when they

26 | FISHERY FACTS

LOCATION AND DIRECTIONS: GPS — 34°28'11.98"N; 114°21'9.74"W (London Bridge, Lake Havasu City)

Lake Havasu is a 200-plus-mile drive from Phoenix, either to Parker and then going north on State Route 95 along the Colorado River, or to Kingman and heading west toward Needles on Interstate 40 until reaching the Lake Havasu turnoff (almost to Needles) and then heading south along SR 95.

Havasu Springs is located northeast of Parker Dam on SR 95. Mesquite Bay on the Havasu National Wildlife Refuge is located on London Bridge Road north of Windsor Beach State Park.

BOAT LAUNCHING: Take-Off Point and Havasu Springs Resort near Parker Dam off SR 95, on the south end of the lake; Cattail Cove State Park, 9 miles south of Lake Havasu City; Havasu Marina at 1100 McCulloch Blvd. (across London Bridge); Site Six, in Lake Havasu City, off McCulloch Boulevard west over London Bridge to the end of the island; Windsor Beach State Park; Sandpoint Marina (10 miles south of the city on SR 95); and Lake Havasu Landing Resort and Marina (across the lake on the California side).

FISHING PIERS: Site Six, Havasu Springs, Take-Off Point, Bill Williams River National Wildlife Refuge Headquarters, and Mesquite Cove (two).

RESORTS: There are two private resorts, Havasu Springs and Black Meadow Landing, which are located on leased public lands along the lakeshore. These provide many recreational opportunities and facilities, including camping, boat ramps and marina, a swim beach, stores, restaurants, laundry, and long-term mobile-home spaces.

Havasu Springs is located northeast of Parker Dam on SR 95. While Havasu Springs is a privately run resort, the fishing pier located there is open to the public free of charge. Black Meadow Landing is west of the dam. Turn west on the first public road south of Parker Dam and follow the signs to the resort.

SHORELINE CAMPS: There are 105 shoreline camps available along the Arizona side of Lake Havasu, from Lake Havasu City south to Parker Dam. Most sites have a picnic table, shade ramada, barbecue grill, pit toilet, and a trash can. The camps are available on a first-come, first-served basis.

AMENITIES: Lake Havasu City has a year-round population of about 56,000 people. This popular resort city has all the amenities, from top-notch dining to fast food, along with motels, hotels, and a plethora of stores.

strike at the reaction bait. Keep a second pole rigged with a flutter-down bait, such as a Senko, curly-tailed, or small swim bait that you can cast when a bass tried but failed to attack your lure.

➤ Smallmouth bass have been adding yet another fishing dimension in recent years. Two- to 5-pound bronzebacks have become fairly common. Smallmouth prefer rocky areas full of crayfish, although they will also feed on shad. Rocky areas abound at Havasu, providing miles of viable habitat to fish. For smallies, think crayfish. Soft-plastic baits can be terrific, whether Texas-rigged or on jig heads. Shaky heads can be devastating at times. Drop shots have proven very effective, but typically in more crayfish colors. Crayfish-colored crankbaits are also worth a try, but the old standby for smallies is a curly-tailed jig.

Special Notes: The Havasu National Wildlife Refuge protects 30 river miles (300 miles of shoreline) of the Colorado River from Needles, California to Lake Havasu City, Arizona.

LAKE HAVASU ACCESS LOCATIONS/AMENITIES

27 **Windsor Beach State Park:**
GPS — 34°28′34.23″N; 114°21′18.17″W

This park offers three boat ramps, 47 campsites (all are nonelectric and on a first-come, first-served basis), a fish-cleaning station, picnic area, and beach area. There are restrooms, showers, hiking trails, a dump station, and a gift shop. To contact the state park, call 928-855-2784.

28 **Cattail Cove State Park:** GPS — 34°21′4.45″N; 114°10′9.92″W

There is a beach, boat ramp, fish-cleaning station, gift shop, 61 campsites, restrooms, showers, a dump station, picnic tables, and hiking trails. There are also 28 primitive boat-in camping sites with a picnic table and access to pit toilets, but no firepits or campfires. Propane stoves are acceptable. All boat-in camping sites are first come, first served.

29 **Chemehuevi Indian Tribe:** GPS — 34°17′48.75″N; 114°7′17.37″W
(Lake Havasu Springs Resort)

Boating, fishing, camping, and other facilities are available on the Chemehuevi Indian Reservation. Permits are required. For more information, call the tribal office at 760-858-4301.

COLORADO RIVER SOUTHWEST

Hidden backwaters like this one along the Imperial Division of the Colorado River are often home to big fish, as well as scenic beauty.

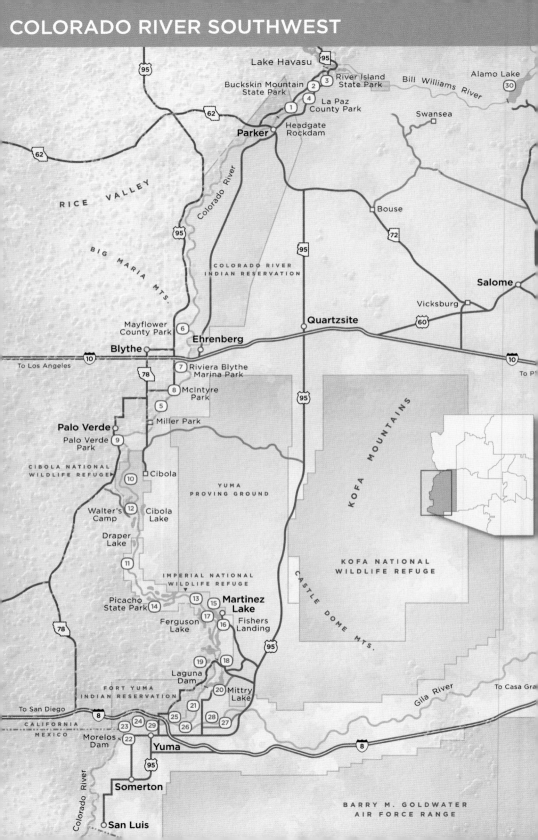

COLORADO RIVER SOUTHWEST

The Colorado River from Parker Dam above Parker to Morelos
Dam near Yuma along the border with Mexico could serve as an
impromptu time machine traveling back from modern-day use to
presettlement days.

The bustling Parker Strip downstream from Lake Havasu epitomizes
the modern-day river where intensive recreational use is coupled with
sprawling development on both sides of the river, all hemmed in by rugged mountains where desert bighorn sheep roam.

Yet you'll also encounter remote stretches of river, such as beyond
Walter's Camp below Blythe, where you won't see much evidence of
human occupation. These more tranquil stretches of river provide an
inkling of what the Colorado River was like back when paddlewheelers
navigated upstream from the Gulf of California to the goldfields of Picacho and beyond.

Along the way, you'll encounter marshy backwaters lush with bulrushes and cattails that can offer you a lingering taste of an era even
before the Colorado Basin was visited by Spanish soldiers under the
command of Francisco Vásquez de Coronado in 1540. These picturesque
backwaters and side channels are often referred to as "Arizona's Everglades," and some harbor largemouth bass exceeding 12 pounds. There are
also enormous flathead catfish here tipping the scales at 90 pounds or more.

You'll also encounter a stretch of river near the Imperial Dam offering
a watery world with more intensive recreational options and amenities,
but in this same river segment you can also discover nearly hidden waters
with a wilderness feel, such as Ferguson Lake and the Arizona Channel.

It's a land of extremes, including extreme temperatures; summer days
can reach 120 degrees. Yet winter days hover in the pleasant 60s and 70s.

The Colorado River flows are typically higher in the warmer months,
and lower in the milder months of year. January flows can be very low.
That's often when they do annual work on the diversion dams (and those
along the riverfront repair their docks). Flows can change appreciably in a
24-hour period.

Besides the Colorado River, this region is also home to one of Arizona's premier bass and crappie fisheries: Alamo Lake, situated along
the Bill Williams River. Knowledgeable anglers refer to Alamo as a "pure
fishing lake."

① Parker Strip

The 15 miles of Colorado River stretching from Parker Dam to the Headgate Rock Dam adjacent to Parker is a popular water-recreation playground known for its water-skiing, fast boats, and great parties during the warmer months.

The Parker Strip also offers fairly good fishing during the cooler months. This stretch of river, also known as Lake Moovalya, receives intense recreational boating pressure from spring through summer. The best time to fish the strip is from October through early March, when boating congestion is reduced and the weather is more temperate.

Private and commercial shoreline development is extensive, making shoreline access difficult for anglers who are just visiting. Most fishing by visitors is done via boat or from shore at one of the public parks or private resorts.

The stretch of river immediately below Parker Dam is known for its good smallmouth-bass fishing. The downstream sections of river provide angling opportunities for catfish, largemouth bass, striped bass, and large redear sunfish.

The stretch of river below Parker Dam is a terrific smallmouth-bass fishery.

Fishing Tips: You'll discover pretty good smallmouth-bass fishing in the strong current just below the Parker Dam. Some anglers drift and fish, but more effective while working the rocky shoreline is using the motor to counter the boat's drift.

➤ For smallmouth bass, try in-line spinners such as Mepps, Rooster Tails, and Blue Foxes, or crankbaits. Jigs, especially curly-tailed grubs, can work well along rocky strata. Shad colors can work, but crayfish colors bring better results.

➤ The Parker Strip is also home to some really impressive, dinner-plate-sized redear sunfish weighing 2 pounds or more. Try night crawlers or mealworms fished under a bobber, especially in areas with little or no current, such as backwaters or inlets. Redears don't readily hit lures.

Drifting the current and fishing for bass.

➤ Channel and flathead catfish fishing is always a fair bet in this section of the Colorado River. For channels, try anchovies, hot dogs, corn, live minnows/shiners, or stink bait. For flatheads, try live bluegills.

➤ Below the dam, striper fishing should also be decent using live shad, anchovies, shadlike crankbaits, or spoons. Cut the anchovies into thirds and use little or no weight.

➤ Largemouth bass are abundant, especially in the downstream portions of the Parker Strip. Try working the edges of the abundant bulrushes with weedless rigs. Soft plastics, such as artificial worms, lizards, and crayfish, can work well. In summer, topwater frogs can provide exciting action.

Special Notes: Visit www.usbr.gov/lc/riverops.html for the latest information on flows. This website also offers boating guides for some areas of the lower Colorado River.

Invasive Species Note: This section of the Colorado River is home to invasive quagga mussels. Please *clean, drain, and dry* your boat and trailer before leaving. Also, wait five days before launching your watercraft someplace else.

A renowned water-recreation playground, the Parker Strip is less famous for its excellent fishing.

RIVER ACCESS LOCATIONS/AMENITIES

(2) Buckskin Mountain State Park:
GPS — 34°15'16.81"N; 114°9'40.84"W

Located 12 miles north of Parker, this park provides good angling access. The 1,677-acre park has a campground, cabana sites, a beach, hiking trails, restrooms, showers, a boat ramp, a picnic area, a basketball and volleyball court, a playground, a restaurant, a camp store, an arcade, a gas dock, and a ranger station. Reservations can be made for certain campsites online at www.azstateparks.com or by calling 928-667-3231.

(3) River Island State Park: GPS — 34°15'12.7"N; 114°8'18.4"W

River Island State Park is located about 1 mile north of Buckskin Mountain State Park. It offers 37 campsites, a ramada with a campfire ring, a sandy beach, a cove, and a boat-launch area.

(4) La Paz County Park: GPS — 34°13'20.89"N; 114°11'47.78"W

Amenities include 114 RV sites with water, power, cable TV, and boat-launching. There are also dry camping areas with 35 shade ramadas and 12 restrooms, four with indoor showers. The 18-hole Emerald Canyon Golf Course is directly across the highway.

5 Colorado River (between Palo Verde Diversion Dam and Walter's Camp)

This segment of the Colorado River near Blythe, California, and Ehrenberg, Arizona, is a little more laid back than the more popular areas upstream. It offers some interesting angling adventures, especially for canoeists, kayakers, and those with flat-bottomed boats.

You can fish for striped bass, largemouth bass, channel catfish, flathead catfish, bluegills, and redear sunfish. Some of the more rocky stretches of river are home to smallmouth bass.

You will find some shore angling, especially for bottom-feeding catfish, along inlets and backwaters, but most fishing here is from a boat. Expect to encounter strong currents except in backwaters, inlets, or side channels.

As the river rambles southward, access becomes more limited, but the sense of adventure and feeling of solitude increase appreciably — as do the side channels and backwaters.

This area abounds with wildlife-watching opportunities. The Cibola National Wildlife Refuge is 28 driving miles south of Blythe (take Neighbors Boulevard), and the Imperial National Wildlife Refuge borders Cibola downstream.

Fishing Tips: This area can provide decent fishing for both smallmouth bass (in the channel) upriver from the Interstate 10 bridge and largemouth bass (in the backwaters) throughout the entire area.

➤ For bass, work the edges of the vegetation, especially any shady pockets, using Texas-rigged soft plastics, spinnerbaits, crankbaits, or jigs. Some anglers like to use live bait, such as shiners or minnows.

Striper fishing is best in the current of the main channel. Be sure to target entryways to the inlets, coves, and backwaters — areas where you can also find largemouth bass. Frozen anchovies, squid, or sardines can work best for stripers and work well for channel catfish.

➤ Channel and flathead catfishing can be good in this section of the Colorado River. Most flatheads will be in the 2- to 5-pound size range. Occasionally a flathead weighing more than 40 pounds is caught in the main channel or in backwaters. Flathead catfish surveys by the Arizona Game and Fish Department routinely yield a

The Cibola Bridge over the Colorado River south of Blythe, California, provides access to the Cibola National Wildlife Refuge — and a pretty good fishing spot.

handful of fish between 25 and 40 pounds in this section of the river, although most of the fish are much smaller.

Catfish season is late spring and throughout the summer. Generally, when fishing for catfish, the hotter the weather, the better the fishing. But during summer months, the fishing is often best at night.

Special Notes: For boating and river guides, visit www.usbr.gov/lc/riverops.html. These illustrated guides provide maps of the river from Blythe to just below Yuma. If fishing this area, you will want these for reference.

Invasive Species Note: This section of the Colorado River is home to invasive quagga mussels and a plant known as giant salvinia. Please *clean, drain and dry* your boat and trailer before leaving. Also, wait five days before launching your watercraft somewhere else.

Snow geese, Canada geese, and other waterfowl abound along the lower Colorado River, along with flocks of sandhill cranes during winter.

Mayflower County Park, Riverside County, California:
GPS — 33°40'18.86"N; 114°32'2.02"W

This park is 6 miles upstream from the Interstate 10 bridge over the Colorado River between Blythe, California, and Ehrenberg, Arizona. The park is just north of Sixth Avenue and Colorado River Road on the California side. There are grassy campsites, covered picnic ramadas on the river, and a small lagoon. Facilities include picnic tables, showers, swimming lagoons, a launch ramp, 28 tent-camping sites, and 152 RV campsites with electric and water. For more information, call 760-922-4665.

Riviera Blythe Marina Park:
GPS — 33°36'10.98"N; 114°32'3.21"W

Located off I-10 on Riviera Drive in the city of Blythe, the marina has picnic facilities, showers, a heated swimming pool, swimming lagoons, a spa, cable TV, coin laundry, a store with propane, a launch ramp, and 285 RV and tent campsites, many with full hookups. Call 760-922-5350 for more information.

McIntyre Park: GPS — 33°30'57.61"N; 114°33'49.22"W

McIntyre is an 87-acre, concession-operated park 6 miles southeast of Blythe on 26th Avenue and the Colorado River. The park has large, grassy sites with shady trees on a protected riverfront beach area. It has a launch ramp, picnic facilities, showers, a dump station, swimming, a snack bar, a grocery store with supplies/bait/propane, and 140 tent-camping and 160 RV sites. Call 760-922-8205 for more information.

Palo Verde Park: GPS — 33°23'17.20"N; 114°42'42.42"W

This park is located 3 miles south of Palo Verde on California State Route 78 along an oxbow of the Colorado River. It is adjacent to Cibola National Wildlife Refuge. Facilities include a launch ramp, primitive camping, water, flush toilets, and a playground.

Cibola National Wildlife Refuge (Cibola Bridge):
GPS — 33°24'49.38"N; 114°39'25.26"W

The Cibola Farmers Bridge off Neighbors Boulevard, which goes all the way to I-10 in Blythe, California, provides the first vehicle crossing of the river south of Blythe. The wildlife refuge is just a few miles from the bridge, on the Arizona side. For more information, call 928-857-3253 or visit www.fws.gov/southwest/refuges/CibolaNWR.

11 Colorado River (between Walter's Camp and Picacho State Park)

Although it is relatively remote and can only be reached by boat from either end, this section of the Colorado River offers terrific fishing and outstanding wildlife-watching opportunities — especially during winter.

Along the Arizona shoreline, the Cibola National Wildlife Refuge is bordered on the south (past Cibola Lake) by the Imperial National Wildlife Refuge. Both refuges abound with wildlife, especially waterfowl migrating along the Pacific Flyway.

For more information on the Imperial National Wildlife Refuge, visit www.fws.gov/southwest/refuges/arizona/imperial.html or call 928-783-3371. There are some seasonal closures and restrictions you may want to know about if visiting the refuges. However, the closures do not affect boating or fishing on the main river channel.

Fishing Tips: This stretch of river is known for its huge flathead catfish. Fishing can be good to excellent, with some weighing more than 40 pounds. The best time is late spring and into summer — the hotter, the better.

➤ The backwaters along this stretch of river are good for largemouth bass, catfish, and sunfish (bluegills and redears).

➤ Because of all the vegetation, it's best to go weedless, such as Texas rigs, soft-plastic jerkbaits, and even some of the swim baits without readily exposed hooks for the largemouth bass.

➤ Some canoeists and kayakers do well using fly rods to fish for bass.

During warmer months, terrestrial patterns such as cicadas, grasshoppers, and dragonflies can work exceptionally well, as can frog imitations.
➤ Other species available in the main river are smallmouth bass, channel catfish, and striped bass. Frozen anchovies can be good for catfish and stripers. Try soft-plastic baits resembling crayfish for the smallmouth.

Special Notes: For boating and river guides, visit www.usbr.gov/lc/riverops.html. Overnight camping is prohibited within the refuge between Walker Lake and Picacho State Recreation Area — approximately 10 miles of river.

Invasive Species Note: This section of the Colorado River is home to invasive quagga mussels and a plant known as giant salvinia. Please *clean, drain, and dry* your boat and trailer before leaving. Also, wait five days before launching your watercraft somewhere else.

RIVER ACCESS LOCATIONS/AMENITIES

12 **Walter's Camp:** GPS — 33°12'52.68"N; 114°40'38.47"W

This little-known riverfront community lies midway between Martinez Lake and Blythe, California. It has a launch ramp, parking lot, picnic areas, a small store, and restrooms. It is easily accessible from both Interstate 10 and I-8 via California State Route 78, 19 miles from Palo Verde, California.

Picacho State Park (California) is easier to reach via boat than by vehicle. It offers a wonderful place to camp for those exploring what some call "Arizona's Everglades."

(13) Colorado River (between Picacho State Recreation Area and Imperial Dam)

This section of the Colorado River near Yuma offers very popular and diverse fishing opportunities, but there can be boat congestion in the main channel during the warmer months. The Trigo Mountains, which border the Colorado River on the Arizona side between Picacho State Park and Martinez Lake, is a good place to observe bighorn sheep. They can frequently be seen coming down to the river in the evenings and mornings during the warmer months.

Because of the good fishing, this area also attracts large and small fishing tournaments. Those bass anglers used to fishing the Sacramento delta area of California will feel right at home.

Anglers will discover many backwaters and interesting side channels providing ample opportunities to escape the crowds and possibly catch some huge fish. Some of these backwaters are large, shallow, marshlike areas full of bulrushes and cattails, such as Ferguson Lake. Others, such as Martinez Lake, are backwaters with lots of development and some pretty good angling opportunities as well.

The Arizona Channel, located between Imperial Dam and Martinez Lake, is one of the larger and more popular backwater channels. It is approximately 4 miles long and connects about to about 12 backwaters. The entire length is designated as a no-wake zone, so plan on spending several hours if you wish to explore or fish the full length of it.

Some refer to the area as "Arizona's Everglades." Spend a day prowling some of the twisting and turning backwaters and channels, especially during the prime waterfowl season, and you'll quickly understand why.

These waters are renowned for "hawg" largemouth bass, tipping the scales at more than 12 pounds, and monster flathead catfish that have weighed in at about 90 pounds. There are also striped bass, crappie, catfish, carp, tilapia, sunfish, and even bullfrogs. In fact, this could be considered the frog-gigging capital of Arizona.

HISTORICAL NOTE

In 1862, a young prospector from Sonora, Mexico, José María Mendivil, discovered gold in Picacho Park. By 1890, a successful large-scale gold-mining operation was booming. At the turn of the 20th century, steam-powered paddleboats delivered mining supplies and passengers here. Visitors can hike to the ruins of the mill sites near the Lower Dock day-use area.

Fishing Tips: Expect good to excellent fishing for largemouth bass, channel catfish, and flathead catfish. You can also find some fairly good crappie fishing in Martinez and Ferguson lakes.

➤ This area can produce lunker bass, especially in some of the backwaters or side channels, and has the potential for producing a new state-record largemouth.

➤ For bass, try flipping and pitching along the edges of vegetation using Texas-rigged soft plastics, such as lizards and worms. Weedless jigs can also work well. Slow down your presentation in the cooler months by using a trailer.

The smaller, 4-inch soft plastics are often easier to work with along the often dense vegetation, but thick-bodied creature baits can be a good bet as well for breaking through cover.

Largemouth bass will often hold in ambush along shady pockets. Some anglers like to use smaller swim baits. Soft-plastic jerkbaits can work well, especially in the spring and fall. There are also times when drop shots work best, especially after a weather front moves through and the bass hold deep.

Some anglers like to use spinnerbaits, but in the cooler months use a trailer and

Silhouettes and reflections on the lower Colorado. | GEORGE ANDREJKO

slow-roll across the bottom along the edge of the reeds, cattails, bulrushes, and tamarisk trees. Starting in late spring, working topwater frogs through the reeds can produce some exciting action at times.

Some of the best places to fish for stripers are the channels connecting the larger backwaters to the main river channel. Try frozen anchovies, swim baits, or any white-colored crankbait.

➤ Channel catfish in excess of 5 pounds are present. Try live minnows, shiners, stink bait, corn, or hot dogs. There are also some huge carp. Try corn or dough bait.

This section of the river is home to huge flathead catfish as large as 40 pounds, and occasionally much larger. The main river channel will be your best bet for these lunkers. There is possibly a new state record or two lurking in these waters. Use heavy fishing tackle for these monster flats.

A couple of years ago, a flathead catfish weighing nearly 90 pounds was measured during a fish survey by Arizona Game and Fish Department biologists; that monster flathead is probably still out there.

➤ Other sunfish such as bluegill and redears are also present in the various backwaters. You can load up on large sunfish in some areas and easily fill a frying pan.

Special Notes: For boating and river guides, visit www.usbr.gov/lc/riverops.html.

Invasive Species Note: This section of the Colorado River is home to invasive quagga mussels and a plant known as giant salvinia. Please *clean, drain, and dry* your boat and trailer before leaving. Also, wait five days before launching your watercraft somewhere else.

Picacho State Park: GPS — 33°1'34.31"N; 114°37'2.94"W

The Picacho State Recreation Area is about 25 miles north of Yuma. A century ago, Picacho was a gold-mining town. Today it is a California state park popular with boaters, hikers, anglers, and campers.

There is a boat ramp, 54 primitive campsites, a group campground, and two boat-in group sites. The sites have picnic tables and fire rings with drinking water, chemical toilets, and a solar shower. Upriver there are five smaller campgrounds with no drinking water.

Take the 24-mile, mostly unpaved road north from Winterhaven near the Mexican border in California. The road to Picacho from Winterhaven is paved only for the first 6 of 24 miles, but it can be navigated by passenger cars when it is not wet.

For more information, including a brochure with a map of this area, visit www.parks.ca.gov or call 760-996-2963.

 Martinez Lake: GPS — 32°58'30.32"N; 114°27'56.07"W

Although referred to as a lake, Martinez is really a large backwater with quite a bit of development along the Arizona side of the Colorado River just south of the Imperial National Wildlife Refuge. Martinez can often be one of the first waters in Arizona with largemouth bass entering their spawning behavior during early spring — sometimes in late February, most often in early March.

Martinez varies from 300 to 500 surface acres, depending on the time of year and the Colorado River flows. There are areas with stick-ups to work and private docks where bass hide in the shadows.

Martinez Lake Resort (www.martinezlake.com) has a launch ramp, a store selling boat fuel and fishing tackle, a restaurant, boat rentals, charters, RV spaces, a gift shop, and a guide service for fishing and wildlife-watching. There are also vacation homes and seasonal rentals. This resort started in 1955 as a fishing camp and expanded over the years into a year-round resort.

Take U.S. Route 95 either from Interstate 40 or Yuma to Martinez Lake Road, and head west 9 miles to Martinez Lake.

16 **Fishers Landing:** GPS — 32°58'11.96"N; 114°27'50.84"W

This is a commercial resort in a large cove immediately downstream from Martinez Lake. There's a launch ramp, gas dock, full-service boat shop, RV park, campground, a store with fishing supplies, a restaurant, a bar and grill, and fishing-guide service. Many fishing tournaments are staged from Fishers Landing. Call 928-782-7049 or visit www.fisherslandingresort.com for more information.

Take U.S. 95 to Martinez Lake Road (which becomes Fishers Land-ing Road just past Martinez) and drive 12 miles to Fishers Landing.

 Meer's Point (Imperial National Wildlife Refuge):
GPS — 32°59'23.76"N; 114°28'57.12"W

The Meer's Point day-use area has shaded tables, toilets, and a boat launch. The refuge surrounds one of the few remaining "wild" places on the Colorado River, valued by boaters for its remote scenery. For more information, visit www.fws.gov/southwest/refuges/arizona/imperial.index.html or call 928-783-3371.

From Yuma, take U.S. 95 north toward Quartzsite for 17 miles. Turn left onto Martinez Lake Road. Follow the road to Red Cloud Mine Road and turn right. Continue down Red Cloud Mine Road and follow signs for Meer's Point.

 Hidden Shores: GPS — 32°53'12.00"N; 114°27'29.16"W

A Bureau of Land Management concession, Hidden Shores is located on the east side of Imperial Dam and has a marina with a boat-launch ramp (18 miles from Yuma). There are RV hookups, showers, restrooms, a store, and fuel sales. For more information, call 928-539-6700 or visit www.hiddenshores.com.

From Yuma, take U.S. 95 north toward Quartzsite for 14.2 miles. Turn left onto Imperial Dam Road and follow it 6.7 miles to a sign for Hidden Shores and turn right.

 Squaw Lake Area: GPS — 32°54'9.21"N; 114°28.590"W

The campground offers RV and tent camping, a boat launch, and a day-use area on a backwater of the Colorado River directly above Imperial Dam. There are 125 RV sites, numerous dispersed tent sites, four restrooms with flush toilets and outdoor showers, potable water, trash and graywater disposal, an RV dump station nearby at South Mesa, two boat ramps, two buoyed swimming areas, picnic tables and grills, day-use and boat-trailer parking, pay phones, and a hiking trail. Visitors must pay daily fees at self-registration fee pipes located at the site or at the Bureau of Land Management Yuma Field Office, 2555 E. Gila Ridge Road in Yuma. Annual permits are available for purchase at the Yuma Field Office.

From Yuma, take U.S. 95 north toward Quartzsite for 14.2 miles. Turn left onto Imperial Dam Road, follow it to Senator Wash Road, and turn right. Follow the signs for 4.2 miles to Squaw Lake.

20 Mittry Lake

A shallow lake along the Colorado River floodplain between the Imperial and Laguna diversion dams, Mittry has about 450 surface acres of water, with much of its shoreline covered with cattails and bulrush.

The Mittry Lake Wildlife Area, jointly managed by the U.S. Bureau of Land Management, the U.S. Bureau of Reclamation, and the Arizona Game and Fish Department, includes 2,400 acres of marsh or upland. A wide variety of vegetative and wildlife species can be found, with a scenic backdrop of three mountain ranges.

Numerous serpentine waterways connect to the main lake body and make exploring and fishing by boat a unique experience. Mittry Lake is typically turbid and doesn't have a lot of freshwater flow-through. There are a number of fishing jetties on the east side of the lake, but the lake is best fished from a boat.

The average size of bass in Mittry Lake is actually one of the highest in the Southwest region, probably because it is such a stable system without the typical boom-and-bust conditions caused from variable seasonal flows. However, fishing Mittry can be a little hit-or-miss, so don't expect high catch rates. Game and Fish biologists routinely survey bass in the 6- to 8-pound range, but never large numbers of fish.

Channel catfish are numerous, mostly in the smaller size classes, but there are a number of 10-pounders, as well as flatheads up to and exceeding 30 pounds.

Sunfish and crappie are also abundant, but rarely reach large sizes. There are many large bullfrogs to catch.

The lake underwent dredging, revegetation, and fish-habitat improvements, making it a great location for fishing and hunting. It's also a superb area for wildlife-watching, especially in winter.

Cattails and bulrushes along the shoreline at Mittry Lake are ideal for flipping and pitching. | GEORGE ANDREJKO

Fishing Tips

➤ The water is often turbid and the lake is shallow, so spinnerbaits can work well, especially in the spring and fall. Be sure to use heavier fishing line.

➤ A popular fishing method is flipping and pitching the edge of the cattails and bulrushes with jigs or Texas-rigged soft plastics. Some of the small weedless swim baits can be effective here. Soft-plastic jerkbaits can work as well.

➤ Crankbaits can be used in the open channels, but trebles can be trouble in the heavily vegetated areas.

➤ There can also be some decent topwater action during fall months. Try using poppers or other topwater baits in the main open-water channels, especially along the edges of the vegetation. In summer, topwater frogs can provide some exciting action at times. Mittry Lake is good for frog gigging at night, especially during the summer.

➤ Crappie fishing can be OK, but don't expect larger ones very often. Try small jigs, mealworms, live minnows, or shiners.

➤ You will also find some decent-sized channel catfish. Try stink baits in the main channels or along the edges of the vegetation. Like bass, channel catfish will sometimes hold in shady pockets along the edges of the vegetation.

Special Notes: Portions of the Mittry Lake are closed to the public from November 15 to February 15 annually. This lake is closed to water-skiing but open to pleasure- and fishing-boat use. Fishermen must have an Arizona or California fishing license with a Colorado River Stamp.

Invasive Species Note: This section of the Colorado River is home to invasive quagga mussels and a plant known as giant salvinia. Please *clean, drain, and dry* your boat and trailer before leaving. Also, wait five days before launching your watercraft somewhere else.

20 | FISHERY FACTS

LOCATION AND DIRECTIONS: GPS — 32°49'10.64"N; 114°28'23.87"W
Mittry Lake is 18 miles northeast of Yuma, on the east side of the Colorado River between Laguna and Imperial dams. To get here, take U.S. Route 95 east 7 miles from Yuma. Turn north onto Avenue 7E, drive north 9.5 miles to the end of the pavement, and follow the unpaved road to the lake.

AMENITIES: There is a two-lane boat-launching ramp, large paved parking lot, handicapped-accessible parking and an ADA-compliant restroom, a ramada, picnic tables, a barrier-free fishing pier, and fishing jetties.

There are no designated areas for camping, but camping is allowed on a first-come, first-served basis. You need to pack most everything in and out. No fee is required for camping, day use, or boat launching. Camping is limited to 10 days per calendar year.

Call the Bureau of Land Management Yuma Field Office at 928-317-3200 for more information.

(21) Colorado River (between Laguna Dam and Morelos Dam)

Laguna Dam is 12 miles north of Yuma, and Morelos Dam is where the Colorado River meets the border with Mexico. Between the dams, the river is shallow and narrow and offers limited access for boats. The river's accessibility depends on the amount of water being released. Shallow draft boats are usually a must.

There are spots where the fishing for largemouth bass and flathead and channel catfish is fairly good. Bass in excess of 5 pounds are common, and flathead catfish more than 20 pounds are a good bet.

The lower end has undergone dredging work, which may allow a larger boat to get onto the river in that area.

RIVER ACCESS LOCATIONS/AMENITIES

A guide to Yuma-area fishing holes providing locations and a map is available online at www.azgfd.gov/h_f/documents/fishingholesbrochure-new.pdf or at the Yuma office of the Arizona Game and Fish Department, 9140 E. 28th St., or 928-692-7700.

(22) Morelos Dredge Launch: GPS — 32°42'30.48"N; 114°43'31.86"W

From Yuma, take Eighth Street west out of town to where it ends at the main levee road. Turn left (south) on the levee road about a half-mile to where you can cross over the canal. Turn right (north) on the west side of the canal, drive 0.4 miles, and turn left on a dirt access to the river. This site contains a graveled launch and parking area with no other facilities.

(23) Mode II: GPS — 32°43'45.54"N; 114°42'52.20"W

From Yuma, take First Street west. Follow it around a curve where it turns into south Avenue C. Turn right (west) onto Riverside Drive and continue straight ahead. Riverside Drive turns into Strand Avenue at the stop sign. Follow Strand Avenue until it comes to a stop sign near the train tracks. Turn left (west) onto the raised levee road. Travel about 0.8 miles and turn right onto the road that crosses the canal. Take an immediate left after crossing the canal and travel along the canal about 0.5 miles to the Colorado River. This site has a graveled launch and parking area but no other facilities.

Special Notes: Some sections of the river here are within Quechan and Cocopah tribal boundaries, and a tribal permit is required to fish from the bank in those areas. Boundaries are not well marked, so do some research prior to fishing this section. You might want to check with local bait shops or visit the Yuma Game and Fish Office at 9140 E. 28th St. or call 928-692-7700. Fishermen must have an Arizona fishing license or California fishing license with Colorado River Stamp.

Invasive Species Note: This section of the Colorado River is home to invasive quagga mussels and a plant known as giant salvinia. Please *clean, drain, and dry* your boat and trailer before leaving. Also, wait five days before launching your watercraft someplace else.

24 Yuma West Wetlands Park:
GPS — 32°43'52.74"N; 114°38'7.32"W

From Yuma, take First Street west. Turn right (north) onto 12th Avenue and follow the road to the park. This site has a paved boat launch and parking area along with playgrounds, picnic tables, ramadas, and restrooms. A small fishing pond is stocked with channel catfish, largemouth bass, rainbow trout (winter months only), and bluegills.

25 Backwater No. 33 (Colorado River):
GPS — 32°43'38.34"N; 114°34'30.66"W

From Interstate 8 in Yuma, take the Giss Parkway exit. Follow Giss Parkway and turn right on Gila Street, then turn right (north) onto First Street. Continue over the ocean-to-ocean bridge. Once across the bridge, continue about 0.2 miles and turn right (east) onto a dirt road (levee road). Follow this road about 3 miles, turn right (south) onto a dirt road next to orange groves, and travel 0.8 miles to the backwater. There is a graveled launch and parking area at the northwest corner of the backwater but no other facilities.

26 Gila River Confluence: GPS — 32°43'13.50"N; 114°33'29.28"W

From Yuma, take U.S. Route 95 to Avenue 7E (Laguna Dam Road) and turn left (north) for about 1.5 miles. Turn left (west) on a dirt road (high levee) for 3.2 miles. Keep the canal on your left side. The confluence will be on your right. There are no facilities.

YUMA-AREA PONDS

These ponds are periodically stocked with trout in the winter and channel catfish in the summer and provide fishing mostly for bass, channel catfish, trout, and bluegill.

POND ACCESS LOCATIONS/AMENITIES

27 Fortuna Pond: GPS — 32°43′25.44″N; 114°27′4.20″W

Largemouth bass, channel catfish, bluegill, mullet, bullhead, carp, and bullfrogs can be caught here. From Yuma, take U.S. Route 95 to Avenue 7E (Laguna Dam Road) and turn left, heading north for about 1.5 miles until you come to the gravel levee road. Turn right onto the levee (the canal should be on your right side) and follow the levee for about 3.3 miles. Fortuna Pond will be on your left. There are no facilities at this site and boats are restricted to electric motors only.

28 Redondo Pond: GPS — 32°44′34.32″N; 114°28′59.82″W

Try your luck with largemouth bass, channel catfish, sunfish, tilapia, carp, and bullfrogs. From Yuma, take U.S. 95 to Avenue 7E (Laguna Dam Road) and turn left (north). Continue for 3.4 miles to Co. 6 Road. Turn right (east) and follow Co. 6 Road for 1.5 miles. Redondo Pond will be on the right (south) side of the road. There is a primitive dirt boat launch, ADA-compliant parking, and an ADA-compliant fishing pier. Boats are restricted to electric motors only.

29 Yuma West Wetlands Pond:
GPS — 32°43′44.8″N; 114°38′05.8″W

This is a small (1.3 acres) urban pond and no boats are allowed. The park has all the typical amenities — playgrounds, restrooms, ramadas, and picnic tables. It provides good fishing opportunities for families who like the urban comforts. Largemouth bass, channel catfish, bluegill, and trout can be caught here. From the intersection of First Street and 12th Avenue in Yuma, take 12th Avenue north to the park.

Sometimes eyes are better than GPS for locating openings to long, often obscured backwater channels full of large fish.

(30) Alamo Lake

Alamo Lake is a pure fishing spot located well off the beaten track in the Mohave Desert west of Phoenix.

You won't encounter hordes of water recreationists at this secluded 4,500-acre fishery along the Bill Williams River. There is no marina and no boat fuel, only miles upon miles of undisturbed desert all around. The closest gas station is 29 lonely miles away in the small community of Wenden, along U.S. Route 60.

At 1,102 feet in elevation, this large shallow lake is tucked into a broad desert valley framed by mountains on one side and low, rocky bluffs on the other. Its geographic attributes resemble those of a solar cooker. On mild winter days, the action can definitely heat up here. In some years, Alamo has bass on beds as early as February. Crappie have been known to spawn in March.

However, the physical attributes that allow this lake to heat up fast on mild winter days also make it susceptible to blasts of cold air from passing weather fronts. In wet, stormy years, Alamo sheds its early-bird cloak.

Alamo is a favorite with winter visitors seeking to thaw out in warm sunshine while enjoying shirt-sleeve fishing for slab-sided crappie, bass, and catfish. It's just a short drive from the community of Quartzsite, which attracts a million or so winter visitors each year. Alamo also hosts lots of bass-club tournaments, in part because of its excellent campgrounds and associated state park amenities.

This lake is definitely for campers — there are no motels or hotels close by. That's one of its attractions for those seeking an away-from-civilization experience where coyotes howl and wild burros bray in the night.

Alamo is ready-made for group or family gatherings and campouts. You might even be treated to the sight of bald eagles swooping down to catch fish. The Alamo Lake Wildlife Area also boasts lots of waterfowl. In some years, quail abound in the adjoining desert uplands.

The quiet desert seclusion also provides another benefit: stargazing. In March 2011, Alamo was one of

Those who make the trek to isolated Alamo Lake are rewarded with excellent fishing.

the first state parks in the nation granted the "One Star at a Time" award and added to the Global Star Park Network. Take along your telescopes, spotting scopes, or binoculars if staying overnight.

Fishing Tips: During winter, you will often see a parade of boats trolling for crappie over the shallow flats and stick-ups where the Bill Williams River enters the lake. This slowly moving boat parade is often referred to as the "crappie flotilla," and the gathering can be seen readily when ambling down to the Cholla Launch Ramp. Just join the parade.

The 283-foot-high, earth-filled Alamo Dam was constructed in 1968 by the U.S. Army Corps of Engineers, primarily for flood-control purposes along the Bill Williams River, which empties into Lake Havasu downstream.

➤ Bass and crappie anglers at Alamo Lake often discover a whiskered surprise on the end of their lines: voracious channel catfish. The catfish here routinely feed on threadfin shad, so they often hit jigs or crankbaits.

➤ During summer, most anglers switch to night fishing for crappie, bass, and catfish under the starry desert sky. However, those who brave the heat of summer during the daylight hours can sometimes be treated to excellent topwater action for bass-chasing shad at the surface.

➤ By fall each year, the topwater action at Alamo can really heat up, creating lots of smiling bass anglers.

Special Notes: Check fishing regulations: Alamo has been subject to a special slot limit, but that is subject to change.

30 | FISHERY FACTS

LOCATION AND DIRECTIONS: GPS — 34°14'49"N; 113°33'168"W
Alamo Lake is about a three-hour drive from Phoenix (approximately 135 miles). There are two main routes: Drive west on U.S. Route 60 to Wickenburg, and on to Wenden, then north to the lake. Or, drive west on Interstate 10, exiting at Salome Road; drive to U.S. 60 and then back east to Wenden. From either route, when at Wenden, take Alamo Lake Road 38 miles to the lake.

AMENITIES: Alamo Lake State Park has two launch ramps plus 211 campsites, including 19 full-hookup sites for RVs. The park has showers, fish-cleaning stations, restrooms, and a visitors center. There is also a store carrying fishing and camping items, fishing licenses, boating supplies (boating flags, life jackets, boat cushions, ropes, anchors, battery clamps, etc.), and firewood.

SOUTHEAST ARIZONA

Off the beaten path, Arivaca Lake is an unpretentious spot that offers a relaxing fishing experience.

SOUTHEAST ARIZONA

TONTO
NATIONAL FOREST

60

Globe

San Carlos

Point of Pine

60

Superior

77

GILA MOUNTAINS

70

Bylas

177

San Carlos
Lake

Gila River

Fort Thomas

Gila River

Hayden

SAN CARLOS
APACHE INDIAN
RESERVATION

Pima

Saffo

Aravaipa Creek

Klondyke

PINALEÑO

5

R
L

To Phoenix

Mammoth

77

Oracle

GALIURO MTS.

Riggs Flat
Lake

6

FR 803

366

MTS.

10

Marana

Oro Valley

SANTA CATALINA MTS.

Summerhaven

7

Rose Canyon
Lake

Redington

Bonita

266

CORONADO
NATIONAL FOREST

Willcox

186

Tucson

Catalina Highway

Tanque Verde

SAGUARO
NATIONAL PARK

San Pedro River

86

SAN XAVIER
INDIAN
RESERVATION

10

Willcox P

191

10

Benson

Santa Cruz River

10

90

CORONADO
NATIONAL FOREST

19

Arivaca Road

83

Amado

Tombstone

SANTA RITA MTS.

82

Sonoita

80

Tubac

Arivaca

Tumacacori

Patagonia Lake

3

83

Sierra Vista

Arivaca Lake

1

Peña Blanca
Lake

Patagonia

HUACHUCA MTS.

FR 39

Ruby

2

289

82

FR 61

4

Parker Canyon
Lake

Bisbee

92

Nogales

ARIZONA
MEXICO

ARIZONA
MEXICO

This captivating corner of Arizona offers year-round fishing in intimate bodies of water tucked in an intriguing terrain abounding with Western lore, especially from Arizona's Territorial history.

When first visiting the rolling grasslands of Southeast Arizona, where yuccas, oaks, and century plants dot the landscape and jagged mountains or limestone bluffs typically define the horizon, it's easy to conjure up visions of cowboys, cattle, vaqueros, and even conquistadores.

Desert breezes rippling the tall grasses seem to whisper the sagas of 18th century Catholic missionaries who built missions in the area that would stand the test of time. But anglers can also conjure up visions of fishing intriguing and diverse lakes where one can escape the crowds that often flock to the state's larger impoundments.

You can catch trout in the secluded pines atop some of the "sky island" mountains of the region, some of which offer glimpses of remnant prehistoric biological communities.

In fact, the reintroduction of Gila trout to the Peloncillo Mountains holds the promise of being able to fish for five species of trout on the same mountain in the near future: Gila trout, Apache trout, brown trout, rainbow trout, and brook trout. No other mountain in North America is able to boast such a potential angling feat.

When exploring the fishing opportunities of Southeast Arizona, be sure to take along your best optics — this is one of the best birding areas of North America. In fact, Southeast Arizona draws birders from around the globe, especially those desiring see the tropical birds that migrate to Arizona each year to nest. You also might glimpse up to 15 species of hummingbird.

① Arivaca Lake

Arivaca is a remote and primitive desert fishery almost hidden in rolling desert grasslands, limestone bluffs, and jagged mountains near the border with Mexico not far from Nogales.

At an elevation of 3,750 feet, Arivaca is a year-round fishery. With just 80 surface acres and averaging 15 feet deep, it is a largemouth bass fishery, but anglers can also expect to catch channel catfish, redear sunfish, and bluegill.

Arivaca suffered fishkill in 1999 due to oxygen depletion, but has recovered nicely from this event. During the spring and summer months, the shoreline of this small lake can be extremely busy. In winter the crowds are much smaller.

This lake is well off the beaten path, so anyone desiring plenty of amenities should avoid Arivaca. This is not a lake for those in a hurry, but is well suited for those seeking a relaxing fishing experience.

The scenic but somewhat meandering drive to Arivaca through oak-studded rolling hills along a curvy and dippy two-lane country road ambles past portions of the Buenos Aires National Wildlife Refuge. It crosses desert grasslands that have changed little since Father Eusebio

With only a concrete boat ramp and restrooms, Arivaca Lake offers few amenities, but plenty of pure fishing.

Francisco Kino first visited the area in 1692 and founded Mission San Xavier del Bac (the oldest intact European building in Arizona), 56 miles away toward Tucson.

Fishing Tips: Arivaca is well-known for the thick mat of aquatic vegetation and filamentous algae that rings the lake during the warmer months. This vegetation not only makes traditional fishing methods a challenge, it can make boating challenging as well. Because of the aquatic vegetation, lures with trebles can be trouble. Instead, try working weedless lures, such as soft-plastic jerk baits, Texas-rigged soft plastics, or even split-shot rigs. Drop shots can work well here, especially in winter and early spring before the weeds get thick.

➤ This lake can provide a unique fishing experience in Arizona — catching lunkers on topwater frogs and rats worked across the thick mats of weeds. Sometimes big bass will erupt through the weed bed to attack the topwater lure. It's a hoot.

➤ During the summer, you may find alleyways of open water along the shoreline. These openings are also worth working, either from shore or a boat, using soft-plastic jerk baits and the like.

➤ Quite often there will be patches of open water in the main lake. These openings can provide good ambush spots for bass. Try working these with flutter-down plastics, especially whacky rigs (a soft-plastic worm hooked in the middle).

Special Notes: Arivaca Lake is catch-and-release only for largemouth bass. There is a mercury consumption advisory for all fish. Boats are restricted to a single 10-hp gas motor or single electric motor. No live baitfish are allowed.

1 | FISHERY FACTS

LOCATION AND DIRECTIONS: GPS — 31°31′36.02″N; 111°15′12.57″W
Arivaca Lake is 60 miles south of Tucson. Take Interstate 19 south, exit at Arivaca Road, and drive west for 21 miles into the town of Arivaca. In Arivaca, turn south at the T intersection and stay on south Ruby Road for approximately 5 miles to the Arivaca Lake turnoff. Drive about 2.3 miles from the main road.

AMENITIES: There is a paved, single-lane concrete launch ramp and restrooms. There is no garbage collection, so please pack out what you carry in. Camping is allowed, but plan to be self-sufficient (bring plenty of water). There is a dirt parking lot. Groceries and gas are available in Arivaca about 8 miles away.

(2) Peña Blanca Lake

Peña Blanca Lake was once the elegant grande dame of fishing spots in southern Arizona. In a bygone era, this picturesque lake was renowned as a plush resort.

Located near the border with Mexico, Peña Blanca is a year-round fishery, but its 4,000-foot elevation can get quite chilly in winter. This 45-surface acre reservoir is shore-angler friendly with easy-to-access shoreline trails. You don't need a boat to fish it, but it is a good place for float tubes, canoes, kayaks, and other small boats.

The Arizona Game and Fish Department stocks rainbow trout from October through March each year. The lake also supports largemouth bass, channel catfish, and bluegill. It is surrounded by grassy oak- and yucca-dotted hills, some topped with limestone bluffs.

In 2009, Peña Blanca was drained dry so its mercury-contaminated sediment could be removed. The source of the mercury was an old mine in the watershed. Today, the mine is no longer a source of contamination. While the lake was dry, Game and Fish teamed up with the Forest Service to install artificial fish habitat in the lakebed.

Although some expected it would take years to refill the lake during normal rainfall times, a series of torrential storms filled it to overflowing.

HISTORICAL NOTE

Peña Blanca Lake was built by the Arizona Game and Fish Department in 1957.

Despite the mercury issue and the removal of the former posh resort, the popularity of the lake in the surrounding community has not diminished, especially on the weekends. It has matured into a family pleasing fishery.

In more recent times, Peña Blanca has also gained a reputation as a lunker-bass lake where one could reel in a nice 3- or 4-pound bucket-mouth. Thanks in part to the artificial habitat, those times should return.

Fishing Tips: During the winter trout season, the most popular fishing method is using prepared trout baits such as Power Bait. You should also try in-line spinners, such as Mepps and Rooster Tails, or small spoons, such as Z-Rays and Kastmasters. Corn and salmon eggs are other options. The lake is just made for float tubers, especially fly anglers.

Anglers at Peña Blanca have caught some lunker bass using drop shots, Texas rigs, jigs, and crankbaits.

Special Notes: No live baitfish are allowed. Boats are limited to 10-hp-and-under motors.

Peña Blanca Lake is well suited for canoes, kayaks, and small boats.

2 | FISHERY FACTS

LOCATION AND DIRECTIONS: GPS — 31°24′5.66″N; 111°5′16.96″W
Peña Blanca Lake is 68 miles south of Tucson and 17 miles northwest of Nogales
in Peña Blanca Canyon. Turn west off Interstate 19 approximately 8 miles north
of Nogales at the Peña Blanca–Ruby Road (State Route 289) exit. Follow the
road about 9 miles to Peña Blanca Lake Recreation Area. Turn right (north)
onto the paved road that leads to the lake and the boat-launching ramp.

AMENITIES: The lake has picnic areas as well as a launch ramp, dock, and parking area. There is camping close by. Nogales is also a half-hour away, where
you can find lodging, restaurants, and shopping.

3 Patagonia Lake

Patagonia Lake is a place where you can use your full tackle box of superlatives and lures. This state park is a fishing and scenic treat. Located along the lush riparian area of Sonoita Creek, the lake provides a verdant contrast to the adjacent rolling grasslands spotted with oak and yucca.

With 265 surface acres, the 1.5-mile-long lake is by far the largest and most popular Southern Arizona fishery and also boasts the most amenities, from boat rentals to foot bridges. There is even an adjacent natural area for wildlife-watching; Patagonia lies in the heart of one of the most popular birding areas in the nation.

Patagonia is a renowned largemouth bass lake where anglers also catch black crappies, catfish (channel and flathead), and bluegills. The Arizona Game and Fish Department stocks rainbow trout every three weeks from October through March.

Those who enjoy fishing Saguaro Lake will feel right at home here. Patagonia Lake is also lined with tule grass where big bass hide and has some boat-in-only camping as well, just like Saguaro.

For anglers' sake, the east half of the lake is a no-wake area. There is a handicapped-accessible fishing dock at the marina behind the Sonoita Creek Visitor Center, and another one can be found in the marina cove.

Patagonia Lake has another unique attribute: a dramatically arched

A pedestrian bridge arches over an inlet at Patagonia Lake, which is known for its excellent bass fishing.

pedestrian bridge spanning a large inlet leading to the marina. This unique bridge is a favorite with photographers and landscape painters.

Be sure to bring along your binoculars and sense of adventure. The Sonoita Creek State Natural Area is home to 36 species of reptiles and amphibians, 106 species of birds, 49 species of damsel- and dragonflies, 130 butterfly species, and five species of bats. The area is also home to the endangered Gila topminnow.

Hikers can stroll along the trail through the wooded riparian area along the creek bottom to see a variety birds such as the canyon towhee, Inca dove, vermilion flycatcher, black vulture, and several species of hummingbirds. This is also a prime quail area where you might find Gambel's, scaled, and Mearns quail.

Fishing Tips: A popular bass-fishing technique here is flipping and pitching soft-plastic baits into the dense tule grass along the shoreline. Spinnerbaits are also popular here. Drop shots have grown in popularity for catching everything from bass to catfish. Shakey heads rigged weedless can be terrific.

➤ Youngsters enjoy fishing for the plentiful sunfish. Try mealworms or night crawlers under a bobber. Catfish are a summer delight; try stink baits at night.

➤ During the winter, try prepared trout baits, night crawlers, inline spinners such as Mepps and Rooster Tails, corn, and salmon eggs.

HISTORICAL NOTE

Patagonia Lake was constructed in the late 1960s by a group of citizens incorporated as the Lake Patagonia Recreation Association, Inc. This association completed acquisition of the land in 1967. The area became a state park in 1975. The tracks of the old New Mexico/Arizona railroad lie beneath the lake.

Special Notes: No live baitfish are allowed. Because the lake attracts a multitude of water-sports enthusiasts during summer, water-skiing and towing a recreational device are prohibited on weekends and holidays from May 1 through September 31. Personal watercraft are no longer allowed, and all boats must have below-waterline exhaust systems.

3 | FISHERY FACTS

LOCATION AND DIRECTIONS: GPS — 31°29'37.43"N; 110°51'17.54"W
Patagonia Lake State Park is located about 72 miles from Tucson near the community of Patagonia on State Route 82 (East Patagonia Highway). There are two primary routes: From Interstate 10, head south on SR 82 to Sonoita and take SR 82 west to the lake. Or, take I-19 south from Tucson toward Nogales and take Exit 8 to connect with East Patagonia Highway (SR 82).

AMENITIES: There is a swimming beach; picnic area with ramadas, tables, and grills; a creek trail; boat ramps; and a marina. A campground features some sites that include electrical and water hookups. There are primitive boat-in campsites, restrooms, showers, and a dump station. The Lakeside Market offers boat rentals, fishing licenses, bait, ice, and more.

(4) Parker Canyon Lake

Parker Canyon Lake is situated in the rolling grasslands where oak and pine trees meet in a vegetative transition zone along the shoulder of the rugged Huachuca Mountains.

At 5,000 feet in elevation and averaging 15 to 20 feet deep, with a maximum depth of approximately 55 feet, this 132-acre reservoir is both a cold-water and warm-water fishery.

Trout are stocked by the Arizona Game and Fish Department from October through April each year. However, knowledgeable anglers can catch trout year-round at Parker Canyon. The lake also has plentiful bass, sunfish for the junior anglers, and catfish.

HISTORICAL NOTE

The Parker Canyon Dam was built by the Arizona Game and Fish Department in 1962.

Parker Canyon is a midelevation reservoir with the feel of a high-mountain lake but without the snow (except on rare occasions). It can get nippy here in winter, so bring warm jackets and fishing gloves.

Tent camping, a shoreline trail, and plentiful wildlife draw families to Parker Canyon Lake.

This lake is a delight to fish for those with small boats, kayaks, canoes, and float tubes. It is also superb for shore anglers — there is a 5-mile-long trail along the shoreline where you can explore and fish at the same time. This trail is also popular with bird-watchers and nature lovers. Some vantage points even have benches and interpretive signs.

Bring your binoculars. The area abounds with wildlife and is also popular for birders. During the winter, bald eagles and osprey routinely ply the skies above, searching for surface-feeding fish. Coues white-tailed deer are routinely seen in the area. There are also coatimundi, javelinas, roadrunners, squirrels, and chipmunks.

At times you'll spot cardinals, warblers, vermilion flycatchers, and hummingbirds. Elegant trogons with their long, colorful tails are known to frequent the area. In fact, birders from around the globe are attracted to Parker Canyon Lake in spring and summer, when migratory birds from southern tropical climes are nesting nearby.

Fishing Tips: During the winter, all trout-fishing techniques can work, including prepared trout baits, night crawlers, small spinners such as Mepps and Rooster Tails, small spoons such as Kastmasters and Z-Rays, corn, or salmon eggs. Trolling is a popular fishing technique.

➤ Parker Canyon is also a popular lake for catfish. Try night crawlers or stink bait. Youngsters enjoy fishing for sunfish using mealworms, corn, or night crawlers on small hooks beneath bobbers.

➤ You might also catch some nice bass here. Try spinnerbaits, Texas-rigged soft plastics, drop shots, or crankbaits. The prime bass spawn here is typically in the late spring, at the tail end of the trout-fishing season. But as at many Arizona lakes, bass anglers typically switch to night fishing during the summer.

Special Notes: Boat motors are restricted to 10 hp and under. No live baitfish are allowed.

4 | FISHERY FACTS

LOCATION AND DIRECTIONS: GPS — 31°25'37"N; 110°27'19"W
From Tucson, travel east on Interstate 10 to State Route 83 (Exit 281) and turn south 50 miles through Sonoita to Parker Canyon Lake. There is a winding 25-mile drive from Sonoita through the scenic Canelo Hills.

AMENITIES: There is a small country store and marina with boat rentals available, as well as a paved boat ramp, courtesy dock, and fishing pier. There are 65 campsites with tables and fire rings, drinking water, toilets, and garbage bins located in two campgrounds on the hill overlooking the lake. Tents, trailers, and RVs are allowed, but there are no hookups. Some campsites are barrier-free. It's first-come, first-served. For more information, call the Coronado National Forest at 520-388-8300.

The closest accommodations and gas are in Sonoita, which is 25 miles away, or Sierra Vista, 30 miles away.

⑤ Roper Lake

Roper Lake State Park is a family camping and fishing attraction well away from the bustling crowds — there are even camping cabins for rent.

The intimate 32-acre lake is one of those agreeable fishing holes where lots of youngsters catch their first fish. It is very shore-angler friendly and has a handicapped-accessible fishing dock. This is a cozy fishery; it may seem like you can cast all the way from one bank to another, but not really.

At 3,130 feet in elevation and averaging 20 feet deep, Roper offers year-round fishing for largemouth bass, channel catfish, black crappie, redear sunfish, and bluegill. From November through March, it is stocked with rainbow trout by the Arizona Game and Fish Department.

A great blue heron catches a sunfish at Roper Lake.

When you are done fishing, you can take a quick dip in a natural rock hot tub nearby where you can relax and enjoy the stunning views of Mount Graham, especially when it is covered with snow.

Fishing Tips: For youngsters, the most versatile bait here is night crawlers, either fished under a bobber or using a small split shot as weight. The crawlers might catch trout, bass, sunfish, and catfish.

➤ This is a good place to learn casting and retrieving soft plastics. Try a simple 4-inch plastic worm on a No. 2 hook Texas-rigged (weedless) with a small split shot as weight. You can fish this rig on light line, such as the fishing line you might find on a push-button or spinning reel. Bass and trout can go after this type of setup.

Cast it out, let the artificial worm sink to the bottom, and reel up the line to take out the slack while lowering your rod tip to about a 45-degree angle or less. Then simply raise the rod tip up a foot or so to move the worm, then reel in the slack again (to keep contact with the lure). Repeat the process.

Roper Lake was developed in the early 1960s as a private recreation area. The lake and the property were sold to the Arizona Game and Fish Commission in 1969. In 1975, Arizona State Parks negotiated with the Game and Fish Department to operate the lake as part of a newly created state park totaling 338 acres in two units.

Special Notes: Boats are limited to small electric motors. No live baitfish are allowed.

Roper Lake offers year-round action for a variety of sport fish. | GEORGE ANDREJKO

5 | FISHERY FACTS

LOCATION AND DIRECTIONS: GPS — 32°45'21"N; 109°42'17"W
Roper Lake is 6 miles south of Safford on State Route 191. It is 123 miles from
Tucson or 171 miles from Phoenix.

AMENITIES: There is a day-use island with picnic tables, a swimming beach,
and grills. There are also camping cabins and campgrounds; call the park at
928-428-6760 to make reservations. The visitors center houses a gift shop with
clothing, children's toys, flora and fauna guides, fishing equipment, and bait.

6 Riggs Flat Lake

Riggs Flat Lake, a lovely seasonal trout fishery, is set in alpine forest and meadow in the Pinaleño Mountains. Riggs' cold, clear waters are stocked during the summer with rainbow, brown, and brook trout. Some of the small streams in the Pinaleño Mountains also have hybrid native Apache/rainbow trout.

At 11 acres in size and averaging 15 feet deep, this small alpine lake has been pleasing anglers for more than a half-century. It is a shore-fishing special, although there is a launch ramp that can accommodate small boats.

Even in the dog days of summer, this cold, deep lake can remain easily fishable because of its 9,000-foot elevation. Don't forget a jacket — sum-

Riggs Flat Lake at Mount Graham is the only alpine lake in southeastern Arizona. | GEORGE ANDREJKO

mer nights can be quite nippy. Nearby Mount Graham, with its remarkably clear air away from any light pollution, provides a terrific platform for stargazing from 10,720 feet, which is why it is home to the Mount Graham International Observatory.

The Pinaleños are the tallest mountain range in Arizona, reaching skyward 7,000 feet from their base (the San Francisco Peaks are the state's highest in elevation). This isolated Madrean sky island (one of 27 in the U.S.), with its subtropical oak-pine woodlands, is surrounded by the Sonoran and Chihuahuan deserts.

The Pinaleño Mountains also have another interesting distinction: They traverse five ecological communities and contain the greatest diversity of habitats of any mountain range in North America. The only habitat or life zone they lack is arctic tundra.

Fishing Tips: The fishing season is usually from early May to September, depending on snowstorms and snowdrifts. The best baits for the rainbows are corn, cheese, garlic cheese, salmon eggs, and worms. Prepared trout baits are also popular. In-line spinners such as Mepps and Rooster Tails can also work. Casting spoons, such as Z-Rays and Kastmasters, can be effective. Trolling is a popular fishing strategy here; try Super Dupers, Kastmasters, Z-Rays, Rapalas, and spinners.

Special Notes: Riggs Flat Lake is restricted to electric trolling motors only. No drinking water is available. Using live baitfish is prohibited. There is no fish-cleaning station.

6 | FISHERY FACTS

LOCATION AND DIRECTIONS: GPS — 32°42′28″N; 109°57′58″W
Riggs Flat Lake is located in the Pinaleño Mountains 42 miles southwest of Safford and 154 miles from Tucson.

From Safford, drive south 8 miles on U.S. Route 191 to State Route 366. Turn right (southwest) onto SR 366 and drive 29 miles on a winding and narrow mountain road to the Columbine Work Center. Continue along Forest Road 803 and FR 287 about 5 miles to the campground. The last 12 miles of this road are not paved. The lake is accessible from mid-April to early October, depending on snow levels.

AMENITIES: There is a boat ramp that will accommodate small boats only. There are 26 campsites with tables and fire grills, offered on a first-come, first-served basis. For more information, call the Coronado National Forest at 520-388-8300. The closest stores, gas, and accommodations are near Safford, more than an hour's drive away.

⑦ Rose Canyon Lake

Generations of Tucson youths have caught their first trout at this popular mountain fishery. At 7,000 feet in elevation, 7 surface acres, and averaging 20 feet deep, Rose Canyon perches like a small crown hidden behind the brow of the Santa Catalina Mountains, which dominate Tucson's horizon. Anglers and other visitors are often treated to the sight of the stately ponderosa pines and rocky mountain slopes reflected on the mirror-like surface of this mountain jewel.

In the Santa Catalina Mountains above Tucson, Rose Canyon Lake is stocked with rainbow trout from April through October. | GEORGE ANDREJKO

Rose Canyon is typically stocked with rainbow trout from April through mid-October, when the road and campground close for the winter. Brown trout are stocked in the fall. It is the typical put-and-take rainbow trout lake, where most fish are caught within five to seven days of being stocked. Some nice holdovers usually greet anglers when the gates open each spring.

The fishing is not year-round, although some anglers walk in past the seasonally closed gates (October 15-April 15, depending on weather) during milder winters.

There is a good foot trail at the lake, providing angling access to the entire fishery as well as opportunities for photography and bird-watching. The trail along the north side of the lake is paved and provides barrier-free access to the entire northern shoreline. This trail terminates at a barrier-free fishing pier.

A few downed logs close to the water provide good places to sit and enjoy a snack, or maybe to rest your tackle box and fishing pole so you can dig out another offering.

Rose Canyon Lake is just across the mountaintop from the community and ski resort of Summerhaven, 8 miles away.

The lake has been drained and renovated, so it is set to provide smiles to even more generations of Tucsonans and other visitors looking to catch a good time in the Santa Catalinas.

Fishing Tips: The most popular fishing technique is using prepared trout baits, primarily Power Bait. Night crawlers and corn also can work. Also try in-line spinners such as Mepps and Rooster Tails, or casting spoons such as Z-Rays and Kastmasters.

Special Notes: Rose Canyon Lake is closed to boats, float tubes, and swimming. No live baitfish are allowed. Dogs must be on a leash.

7 | FISHERY FACTS

LOCATION AND DIRECTIONS: GPS — 32°23'13"N; 110°42'41"W
Rose Canyon Lake is 32 miles from Tucson, but it takes about an hour to drive there. From Tucson, drive northeast on Tanque Verde Road to the Catalina Highway. Continue 17 miles into the Santa Catalina Mountains to the Rose Canyon Campground turnoff. Follow the access road through the campground to the parking lot at the turnaround.

AMENITIES: There is a nearby picnic area and campground with tables and fire grills, group day-use areas, toilets, and drinking water. For campground reservations, call 877-444-6777 or visit www.recreation.gov. Summerhaven is the closest community with accommodations and shopping.

INDIAN
LANDS

The rolling hills near Many Farms Lake
on the Navajo Indian Reservation echo
the colors of the Painted Desert.

Hawley Lake on the White Mountain Apache Indian
Reservation is surrounded by mountain vistas.

Arizona anglers are fortunate to experience the cultural diversity of the Southwest while fishing on three of the state's largest Indian reservations: the Navajo, White Mountain Apache, and San Carlos Apache.

The Navajo Indian Reservation offers interesting fishing waters, mostly along a vast semiarid segment of the Colorado Plateau. The reservation encompasses 17 million acres spread across Arizona, New Mexico, and Utah. Navajoland offers anglers some nice choices for both cold-water and warm-water fishing.

Angling in its purest form is about refreshing one's spirit while making a connection with nature. The Navajo term for attaining such a harmonious balance between man and nature is *hozhóó*, or the "beauty way."

Anglers can also connect with nature among the high-mountain streams and crystal-clear lakes of the 1.7 million-acre White Mountain Apache Indian Reservation.

The White Mountain Apache Tribe has played a crucial role in the comeback of the Apache trout, which Arizona school children chose as the official state fish. You'll find plenty of opportunities to fish for these yellowish-gold trout on this scenic reservation in the White Mountains.

The 1.8 million-acre San Carlos Apache Indian Reservation is home to the sprawling San Carlos Lake, which is known far and wide for its superb largemouth bass and crappie fishing. For decades, San Carlos had the distinction of being Arizona's largest interior reservoir, when full. Now it is only surpassed in size by a not-too-distant older neighbor, Theodore Roosevelt Lake.

The San Carlos Reservation is also home to an out-of-the-way trout fishery, Point of Pines Lake, as well as hike-in smallmouth bass fishing along the Black River.

Special Notes: To fish Indian reservation waters, you'll need proper tribal fishing or other recreational permits.

WHITE MOUNTAIN APACHE INDIAN RESERVATION

To Payson

Lyman Lake

Show Low

MOGOLLON

RIM

Lakeside

Pinetop

APACHE-SITGREAVES
NATIONAL FORESTS

Carnero Lake

Bootleg Tank 4

McNary

6

Cooley Lake

Big Bear
Lake 2

Little Bear
Lake

14

Bog Tank

3

473

12

Horseshoe
Cienega Lake

1 A-1 Lake

Greer

7

17

Cyclone Lake

Hawley
Lake 11

Sunrise Lake

273

261

10

Earl Park
Lake

WHITE MOUNTAIN
APACHE INDIAN
RESERVATION

To Globe

North Fork White River

WHITE

8

R26

5

Christmas
Tree Lake

Mount Baldy

FR 113

Big L.

R25

Diamond Creek

Reservation
Lake

16

FR 116

FR 68

73

East Fork White River

Hurricane Lake 13

9

Drift Fence
Lake

FR 72

Whiteriver

Y55

Y20

FR 25

Fort Apache

R9

15

Pacheta Lake

White River

Big Bonita Creek

Y70

MOUNTAINS

Black River

SAN CARLOS
APACHE INDIAN
RESERVATION

WHITE MOUNTAIN
APACHE INDIAN
RESERVATION

Black River

1500

1200

Point of Pines

1000

Point of Pines
Lake

Arsenic Tubs

SAN CARLOS
APACHE INDIAN
RESERVATION

To Clifton

WHITE MOUNTAIN APACHE INDIAN RESERVATION

The White Mountain Apache Indian Reservation (also known as the Fort Apache Indian Reservation) encompasses 1.6 million acres of superbly forested land that abounds with terrific fishing lakes and clear mountain trout streams.

Visitors are often drawn back time and again by the natural beauty of these rugged high-mountain landscapes teeming with wildlife. You'll experience vast timberlands that look as wild and untamed as they did in historic times.

Although these picturesque tribal lands and waters are exceptional for a host of reasons, they are of inestimable value to anglers who cherish wild Apache trout. The White Mountain Apache Tribe played a decisive and crucial role in the comeback of the native trout.

If you are looking for extraordinary angling experiences, you can fish unique fishing lakes with special regulations, such as Hurricane Lake and Earl Park Lake. All trout anglers should enjoy wetting their fishing line in sprawling reservoirs such as Hawley, Reservation, and Sunrise lakes. You can also discover more intimate waters such as Big Bear (*Shush Be Tou*), Little Bear (*Shush Be Zahze*), and Pacheta lakes.

There is a profusion of rushing trout streams, yet you can also visit the Salt River, where feisty smallmouth bass and whiskered channel catfish lurk in deep pools.

Although the reservation offers four-season fishing opportunities, most anglers visit during the spring, summer, and fall. During the winter, many of the higher-elevation lakes and streams might not be accessible due to snow and ice. However, some high-elevation mountain waters, such as Sunrise Lake near the famous Sunrise Ski Park, can provide ice-fishing opportunities for winter recreationists.

Keep in mind that White Mountain Apache Reservation permits are required for all fishing, hunting, camping, hiking, river-rafting, sightseeing, picnicking, biking, and cross-country skiing on reservation lands. Fishing and hunting licenses from the State of Arizona are not valid for fishing or hunting on the reservation. To find out what permits are required and for regulations on tribal lands, visit www.wmatoutdoors.org or call 928-338-4385. There are permit dealers in Phoenix and Tucson as well.

① A-1 Lake

Motorists driving along State Route 260 across the White Mountain Apache Indian Reservation about halfway between Pinetop and Springerville are treated to a terrific view of this 22-acre lake at 8,900 feet in elevation, where you can often see reflections of the imposing mass of Mount Baldy.

A-1 is stocked with Apache and rainbow trout in summer, and can be good for winter ice fishing. When autumn is in the air, the colorful aspens bordering the lake make it a natural attraction for shutterbugs — bring your camera.

HISTORICAL NOTE

A-1 Lake was named after White Mountain Apache Chief Alchesay, who was given the name "A-1" by U.S. Army officials who thought Apache names were too difficult to pronounce. Sergeant William Alchesay, who was an Indian scout for the Army, was awarded the Medal of Honor in 1873.

Although the highly visible lake gets lots of fishing pressure, A-1 does not have a lot of amenities. Most anglers fish from shore or use float tubes, kayaks, or canoes.

Fishing Tips: A-1 Lake has plenty of shoreline access, and a boat is unnecessary. The most popular fishing method here is using Power Bait, but other typical trout baits can work as well.

Special Notes: Boats are limited to electric trolling motors only and must have a tribal boat permit.

A-1 Lake in fall.

1 | FISHERY FACTS

LOCATION AND DIRECTIONS: GPS — 34°1'50.41"N; 109°37'21.05"W
A-1 Lake is located 31 miles east of Show Low along State Route 260 and is visible from the highway.

AMENITIES: There is a dirt launch ramp.

At *Shush Be Tou,* try fishing from the shore in deeper water.

(2) Big Bear Lake *(Shush Be Tou)*

A delightful 82-surface-acre lake 15 miles east of Pinetop on State Route 260 (just before the Hawley Lake turnoff), Big Bear Lake is stocked in the summer with Apache and rainbow trout. Fishing is best in deeper water from shore, and especially from boats.

Big Bear sits at 7,850 feet in elevation and can be good for winter ice fishing. There are campsites available, but they can be filled quickly during summer weekends. This lake (and its sister lake, Little Bear) was formed by the damming of Bog Creek.

2 | FISHERY FACTS

LOCATION AND DIRECTIONS: GPS — 34°03′44.32″N; 109°43′52.11″W
Big Bear is located on State Route 260, east of McNary. The turnoff is on the north side of the highway, just west of the turnoff for Hawley Lake.

AMENITIES: There are 50 campsites and vault toilets, but no water. There is a boat launch ramp.

3 Bog Tank

Bog Tank is a popular 12-acre fishing pond just across State Route 260 from Horseshoe Cienega Lake at 8,188 feet in elevation. It is approximately 18 miles east of Pinetop (22 miles west of Springerville) and is stocked in the summer with Apache and rainbow trout. The only amenity is a portable restroom. There is no camping.

Bog Tank is on the edge of a huge meadow adjacent to the forest and is a favorite of chair anglers looking to catch tail-dancing rainbows glistening in the mountain sunshine.

LOCATION AND DIRECTIONS: GPS — 34°2'51.97"N; 109°40'47.07"W

4 Bootleg Lake

This 10-acre lake 3 miles south of Hon-Dah along State Route 73 has sunfish, channel catfish, rainbow trout, and few largemouth bass. The lake sits at 7,800 feet in elevation and is usually fishable, but can ice up in winter.

LOCATION AND DIRECTIONS: GPS — 34°4'29.31"N; 34°4'29.31"N

5 Christmas Tree Lake

At 41 surface acres, the moderate size of this lake belies its significance. Christmas Tree Lake, which sits at 8,221 feet in elevation, is not only a great place to catch native Apache trout, it also has a page in history.

But you might have to stand in line to fish this lake; it's open from May to September, and only 20 anglers per day are allowed. But it's worth the wait.

The pristine beauty and scenic surroundings of Christmas Tree Lake will bring you back year after year. The lake is perched at the junction of Sun and Moon creeks, 5 miles south of Hawley Lake.

HISTORICAL NOTE Scenic Christmas Tree Lake at the junction of Sun and Moon creeks was built in 1965. It is named after the site from which the 1965 White House Christmas tree was given to President Lyndon Johnson by the White Mountain Apache Tribe.

Apache trout is the draw here, with a few browns lurking in the shadows. Leave your bait at home — bring flies and lures only. There are special regulations governing use of this lake, so please consult the White Mountain Apache Game and Fish Department in Whiteriver.

The tribe's Apache trout stocking program at Christmas Tree Lake is an important component of its ongoing fisheries-management efforts on the reservation. Christmas Tree Lake represents the first and most successful attempt to grow this rare fish species, which is found only in the mountains of Arizona.

LOCATION AND DIRECTIONS: GPS — 33°54'40.91"N; 109°44'3.27"W

6 Cooley Lake

Cooley Lake is 1 mile south of Hon-Dah on State Route 73, not far from Bootleg Lake, and it sits at 7,083 feet in elevation.

The small 10-acre lake has rainbow trout, largemouth bass, channel catfish, and green sunfish, providing a variety of fishing experiences throughout the summer. Located south of Pinetop-Lakeside, Cooley Lake is accessed via State Route 260. There are family camping units available, along with safe drinking water and fishing and boating activities. The managed season is April to November. Trailers are accommodated. Stays are limited to 10 days. This is a fee area, and permits are required from the White Mountain Apache Tribe.

LOCATION AND DIRECTIONS: GPS — 34°04'16.03"N; 109°55'01.10"W

7 Cyclone Lake

This 37-acre lake is a rare fishing experience at 8,100 feet in elevation near Hawley Lake in the shadow of Mount Baldy. Cyclone Lake is reserved for family reunions, company picnics and other group outings as part of the tribe's Rent-A-Lake Program; for reservations, call 928-369-7669. There is a flat fee plus a per-person day fee as well.

Anglers will find brown trout, cutthroat trout, and rainbow trout at the picturesque lake. Don't expect amenities; this lake is a wild experience. It is perfect for car toppers, canoes, or float tubes, which can be launched from a concrete boat ramp.

LOCATION AND DIRECTIONS: GPS — 33°58'56.92"N; 109°44'06.72"W

8 Diamond Creek

Diamond Creek provides about 11 miles of fishing ranging from 7,500 to 5,600 feet in elevation. The creek is located between Whiteriver and Hon-Dah just off State Route 73. Turn east on Reservation Route 25, which is a dirt road, and after a few miles it will parallel the creek. The creek has rainbow, brown, and Apache trout. The tribe stocks it with Apache trout. The eastern branch of Diamond, called Little Diamond, may have some small trout, but some of this area is closed to access; obey the signs.

LOCATION AND DIRECTIONS: GPS — No GPS coordinates available.

The surface of small Drift Fence Lake reflects afternoon clouds.

⑨ Drift Fence Lake

A rather remote 15-acre lake at 8,970 feet in elevation, Drift Fence Lake is stocked with rainbow trout in the summer and brook trout in the fall. To reach it, take Forest Road 116, which starts near Big Lake, past Reservation Lake. The turnoff is just past the one for Hurricane Lake. The small impoundment can grow nice-sized trout, but because it is only 22 feet deep, it can suffer from winterkills.

There is a small campground with campsites.

LOCATION AND DIRECTIONS: GPS — 33°49'15.07"N; 109°32'17.15"W

⑩ Earl Park Lake

The 47-surface-acre lake just 4 miles from Hawley Lake sits at 8,248 feet in elevation and is managed for trophy fishing; it is catch-and-release with artificial flies only. No bait is allowed. It is stocked with Apache, brook, brown, and rainbow trout. Special permits are required.

LOCATION AND DIRECTIONS: GPS — 33°58'57.41"N; 109°44'4.61"W

11 Hawley Lake

Hawley, a spectacular 260-acre lake, sits at 8,200 feet in elevation and provides full amenities and a welcome cool respite for anglers looking to escape the desert heat and fill their creels with energetic trout.

Trolling at Hawley Lake.

Even in summer, the high-mountain fishery is known for producing chilly nights down to freezing at times. Fishing is good for rainbow trout, best caught from boats, but also Apache, brook, and brown trout. In fact, this large lake tucked under the imposing shoulder of Mount Baldy is noted for producing large brown trout in the spring and fall.

Hawley is also good for winter ice fishing, but the road to it can become impassable due to snow.

Don't plan on using your gas-powered engine; boats are restricted to electric trolling motors only.

11 | FISHERY FACTS

LOCATION AND DIRECTIONS: GPS — 33°59'26.37"N; 109°45'29.74"W
Take State Route 260 east of Pinetop-Lakeside approximately 13 miles to SR 473, then turn south and travel 11 curving miles — only the first 9 are paved — to Hawley Lake.

AMENITIES: Facilities include camping, RV hookups, a store, and boat rentals in the summer.

12 Horseshoe Cienega Lake

This 121-surface-acre reservoir created in the mid-1960s is the fourth largest lake on the White Mountain Apache Indian Reservation and is located off State Route 260 just 15 miles east of Pinetop. The 8,100-foot-high lake once held the brown trout record for Arizona (16 pounds, 7 ounces), but it also has rainbow and Apache trout.

There is plenty of shoreline access, but this shallow lake is favored by fly anglers in float tubes. It is typically open from May through September, but check before going.

LOCATION AND DIRECTIONS: GPS — 34°01'42.34"N; 109°40'58.60"W

AMENITIES: There is a campground, picnic tables, and restrooms.

13 Hurricane Lake

Sixteen-acre Hurricane Lake is home to the world-record Apache trout of 5 pounds, 15.5 ounces and 24 inches long. At 8,940 feet in elevation, this remote but productive fishery is managed under the Rent-a-Lake Program on the reservation. It can be rented for a flat fee plus a daily fee for each person. Hurricane is typically open from Memorial Day through Labor Day.

The reservoir is 3 miles west of Reservation Lake off Indian Route Y20. Only flies and lures are allowed. For more information, call 928-338-4385.

LOCATION AND DIRECTIONS: GPS — 33°50'18.54"N; 109°33'1.75"W

14 Little Bear Lake *(Shush Be Zahze)*

This small, 18-surface-acre lake sits at 7,850 feet in elevation and is located immediately upstream along from Big Bear Lake (*Shush Be Tou*). In fact, to reach Little Bear Lake you must pass by Big Bear.

In the summer, fishing is good for rainbow trout, best caught from boats, but also contains Apache, brook and brown trout. The lake is noted for producing large brown trout in the spring and fall. Ice fishing is possible in winter, but access can be difficult due to snow.

Anglers are often treated to the site of osprey snatching trout from the water, or resident beaver working up Bog Creek, which feeds the lake. Anglers in the fall routinely hear bull elk bugling.

There is a small campground and the sites are spread out, and there is a spring near the entrance for Little Bear and Big Bear Lake (look for a faucet near the corrals), but you will need to haul the water to your campsite.

LOCATION AND DIRECTIONS: GPS — 34°03'44.32"N; 109°43'52.11"W

15 Pacheta Lake

In an area noted for scenic lakes, this small jewel can take your breath away, but its remote location typically keeps down the admirers. On weekdays you might have this lake all to yourself, even during the height of summer.

However, if you are looking for larger-than-normal trout, the long, bumpy drive down dusty dirt roads might be worth it; anglers routinely haul in 16- to 18-inch rainbows and browns.

But don't bring your bait, and leave your treble hooks in the tackle box. The lake is stocked with brown trout and rainbow trout, but it is catch-and-release-only and no bait or treble hooks are allowed.

The 68-acre lake sits at 8,220 feet in elevation just 6 miles southwest of Reservation Lake on Y20 or Y70. Summer monsoon rains can make the road muddy and challenging at times. In early spring, snowmelt can have the same effect. Four-wheel-drive is recommended.

Pacheta is best fished in spring and fall for the larger trout. In summer it can get weed growth along the shoreline, making it best fished from canoe, kayak, or float tube.

LOCATION AND DIRECTIONS: GPS — 33°46'29.36"N; 109°32'22.92"W

(16) Reservation Lake

One of the larger and more productive fisheries on the White Mountain Apache Indian Reservation, this 240-surface-acre lake sits at 9,040 feet in elevation and is home to the state-record brown trout of 22 pounds, 14.5 ounces and 36 inches long. It is a renowned fishery for huge brown trout, large rainbows, and feisty brook trout, but don't expect crowds.

Although there is plenty of shoreline access, the large, sprawling lake is best fished from a boat, float tube, canoe, or kayak. It is electric trolling motor only, but boats are required to have a reservation boat permit.

While many use prepared trout baits, spinners, Z-rays, Super Dupers, and Rapalas are all effective here.

Anglers routinely see bald eagles and osprey catching fish. The lake is in prime elk country, and in the fall anglers often get to hear bull elk bugling. In the early morning and evening, wild turkey, deer, and other wildlife often come to water. This is also prime bear habitat, so be "bear aware."

Reservation Lake is a large, diverse, and productive trout fishery where anglers can escape the crowds.

16 | FISHERY FACTS

LOCATION AND DIRECTIONS: GPS — 33°50'37.80"N; 109°30'28.73"W
From Pinetop, take State Route 260 east for 24 miles to SR 273; turn right (south) for 20.5 miles. Turn left toward County Road 8 for 3 miles, then a slight right at County 8 for 1 mile to the lake.

AMENITIES: There are 60 camping sites, water, and primitive restrooms, but don't count on the store always being open.

Fly-fishing at Sunrise Lake.

(17) Sunrise Lake

Sunrise Lake sits in a rather elongated bowl stretching across the high-mountain grasslands within sight of the Sunrise Ski Resort. Because it is not sheltered with dense forests along its shoreline like many of the other fishing lakes in the region, it can be challenged with winds. But anglers are willing to brave the winds for a chance to catch 16- to 20-inch trout.

The 900-acre lake sits at 9,138 feet in elevation and is home to the state-record brook trout, at 4 pounds, 15 ounces. The large, shallow lake is stocked with rainbow and Apache trout. Sunrise is the only lake on the reservation where 10 hp-and-under gas boat motors are allowed.

17 | FISHERY FACTS

LOCATION AND DIRECTIONS: GPS — 34°00'46.22"N; 109°32'52.38"W
Sunrise Lake is located 26 miles east of Pinetop via State Route 260 to State Route 273 south and is close to the Sunrise Park Ski Area on the reservation, which you should be able to see from the turnoff.

AMENITIES: The Sunrise Hotel is located adjacent to the lake. There is plenty of camping, and RV hookups are available.

Because it's situated in open grassland rather than forest, Sunrise Lake is exposed to wind.

SAN CARLOS APACHE INDIAN RESERVATION

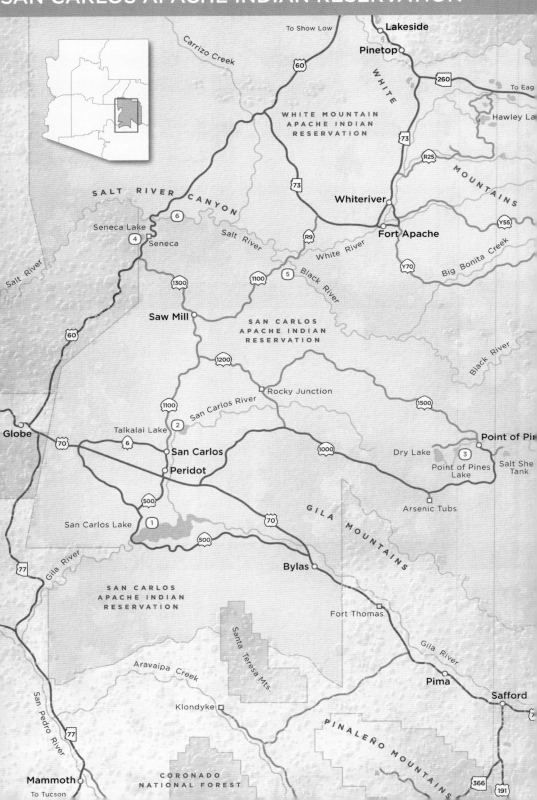

SAN CARLOS APACHE INDIAN RESERVATION

The San Carlos Apache Indian Reservation, near Globe in southeastern Arizona, offers diverse opportunities from year-round warm-water fishing to seasonal cold-water angling, plus other outdoor recreational opportunities — all just a short drive from the Phoenix area.

The fishing is as diverse as the wildlife habitats. The reservation's 1.8 million acres encompass seven biotic communities, ranging from Rocky Mountain montane-conifer forest in the north to Sonoran Desert scrub in the south.

Anglers can choose from four lakes, about 200 small ponds — typically stocked with bass and catfish — and the famous Black River. You can fish for largemouth bass, smallmouth bass, black crappies, rainbow trout, brown trout, flathead catfish, channel catfish, and sunfish; take your pick.

The largest reservoir, San Carlos Lake, is considered one of the premier largemouth bass and crappie fisheries in Arizona. It is renowned for its lunker bass and slab-sided crappies. The largest community on the reservation, San Carlos, is located near San Carlos Lake, a short drive from Globe.

Water-recreation opportunities also are available on the Salt River. U.S. Route 60, between Show Low and Globe, cuts through the Salt River Canyon. Whitewater rafting, kayaking, and canoeing are popular during spring runoff.

Not far upriver, the Black and White rivers join to form the Salt River. The Black River portion of the reservation boundary is renowned for superb smallmouth bass fishing. This is a hike-in fishery where access is limited and the terrain is rugged, but the smallie fishing is terrific. Accessibility varies depending on current weather and runoff levels. Consult the San Carlos Recreation and Wildlife Department at 888-475-2344 for the latest information.

Special Notes: Visitors who want to camp, recreate, fish, or hunt on the San Carlos Reservation must have the appropriate reservation permits. These may be purchased at the Recreation and Wildlife Department headquarters on U.S. Route 70, 20 miles east of Globe, or at any authorized dealer. For more information, visit the San Carlos Tribe's Recreation and Wildlife Department website at www.scatrwd.com or call 888-475-2344.

No live fish, except baitfish, may be transported from the waters from which they are taken. Baitfish may be used only at San Carlos Lake and Talkalai Lake. All freshwater fish possessed and/or transported must have the head, tail, or skin attached so that the species can be identified, numbers counted, and length determined.

Renowned for bass and crappie, San Carlos Lake has varying water levels depending on watershed precipitation and irrigation needs.

① San Carlos Lake

San Carlos Lake near Globe is one of Arizona's premier bass and crappie lakes. At 2,000 feet in elevation, the year-round warm-water fishery offers some of the West's best springtime fishing.

The reservoir is famous for producing trophy largemouth bass, along with record-sized black crappies and flathead catfish. The state-record 4-pound, 10-ounce crappie has graced the record books since 1959. A state-record 71-pound, 10.24-ounce flathead was caught at San Carlos Lake in 2003.

The lake also abounds with fat channel catfish and huge carp. San Carlos attracts bow-hunters in spring, usually in March, to harvest spawning carp in the shallows.

When full, San Carlos Lake covers 19,500 surface acres with 158 miles of fishable shoreline. But, as an irrigation impoundment, it goes through boom-and-bust cycles. The reservoir will reach low ebb, below 10 percent full, then rebound during periods of torrential rains and runoff.

The up-and-down nature of this irrigation lake also helps its productivity. When the water level is low, the fertile lakebed grows vast amounts of vegetation, including prolific salt cedar. When the lake level rises, all the vegetation is flooded, providing added nutrients and cover for fish.

San Carlos is a "top-of-the-line" reservoir, which means that there are no other dams upstream to impede or diminish the direct flow of nutrients from the watershed, which stretches into Southern Arizona and all the way into New Mexico.

There are high-water years when San Carlos can claim the honor of the most productive lake in the state.

Fishing it is a dream. San Carlos is 25 miles long when full and is relatively shallow with few drop-offs. The lake has a maximum depth of 75 feet at the dam. But one of the topographical features that enthuses anglers is its often irregular shoreline with many large and small coves. From the air, the shoreline almost looks serrated.

When it is windy, San Carlos can be difficult to fish.

Fishing Tips: Crappies and largemouth bass become active in spring according to the timing of inflows and water temperatures. During pronounced inflows, the spawns can be delayed. At other times, the fairly shallow lake warms up rapidly and anglers catch bedding fish in March.

➤ **Crappies:** In any given year, the best black crappie fishing starts early in March or April, when water temperatures reach about 60 degrees. Black crappies form large schools that are typically caught in 15 to 20 feet of water adjacent to brushy shorelines during prespawn conditions.

When water temperatures reach the mid-60s, black crappies move closer to shoreline and begin to spawn in and among the submerged points and cover. During the peak of spawning, crappies are caught in 2 to 4 feet of water.

Try a variety of techniques including trolling or drifting crappie jigs, twister tails, or minnows. Still fishing under a bobber can work as well, either with bait or jigs. Slowly trolling small shad-like crankbaits at less than 2 mph can also work, especially when crappies are suspended in open water during winter and summer, or staging just off the mouths of coves before the spring spawn.

During the peak of spawning, you don't even need a boat to catch crappies; they are accessible to shoreline anglers.

➤ **Largemouth Bass:** Springtime largemouth bass fishing typically starts shortly after the crappie spawn when water temperatures reach the mid- to upper 60s. Largemouth bass then begin moving to shallow water adjacent to cover to spawn. They remain near shore until the spawning season is over, during which time fish can be caught using jigs, spinner baits, and plastic worms.

After largemouth bass spawn and early summer approaches, bass can be caught using topwater baits early in the morning and, as the day progresses, crankbaits and plastics worked near main channel points and drop-offs in 10 to 15 feet of water. Texas rigging and other weedless set-ups are advisable. Bring your whole bass-fishing arsenal.

➤ San Carlos can be spinnerbait heaven in the early spring. Until the water warms past the 60-degree mark, it's best to use a trailer and slow-roll the bottom. Flipping and pitching the brushy shoreline can be very productive. Drop-shotting is also very effective here, especially in winter or for postspawn bass. Using jigs and spoons is especially popular in winter and summer.

➤ The fall topwater bite can be glorious in some years. Pick your favorites, from poppers to stick baits. There can be excellent buzzbait-bite in September and October.

HISTORICAL NOTE

Behind Coolidge Dam, San Carlos Lake was built in 1930 as a reservoir to capture flows from the San Carlos and Gila rivers.

1 | FISHERY FACTS

LOCATION AND DIRECTIONS: GPS — 33°11′16.00″N; 110°28′20.00″W
San Carlos Lake is 46 miles east of Phoenix. Take U.S. Route 60 (the Superstition Freeway) east to Globe; go another 25 miles on State Route 70 and then follow the signs, taking Coolidge Dam Road (County Road 3) 11 miles to the launch ramp access road (there are signs), which is located a short distance from the dam.

AMENITIES: There is a boat ramp. The community of San Carlos is not far away; the Apache Gold Casino is operated by the tribe and has the closest lodging and RV park, plus an 18-hole golf course. For more information, visit their website at www.apachegoldcasinoresort.com or call 800-272-2438.

(2) Talkalai Lake

The scenic, 600-acre lake, adjacent to rugged desert highlands and picturesque buttes, offers some fairly good fishing for huge largemouth bass, crappie, sunfish, and channel and flathead catfish.

But don't expect all the angling pressure of its sister lake, San Carlos. Most anglers are drawn to San Carlos and few visit this lake, which was created by damming the Blue and San Carlos rivers.

Fishing Tips: Similar to San Carlos Lake, crappie fishing usually starts in early spring; the fish can be caught on a variety of crappie jigs, twister tails, and minnows in or adjacent to the brush piles.

➤ Fishing for largemouth bass on Talkalai Lake is typical in that crankbaits, plastic worms, and spinner baits work well.

➤ Car toppers, canoes, kayaks, and float tubes are best.

2 | FISHERY FACTS

LOCATION: GPS — 33°23'20.43"N; 110°25'40.37"W
Talkalai Lake is 26 miles from Globe and is located just a few miles north of the community of San Carlos. Take San Carlos Avenue to Pinal Street, turn right, continue onto White Mountain Avenue, turn right onto Road 1100, and follow it for 2 miles to the lake.

AMENITIES: There are none at the lake, but it is only a few miles from the town of San Carlos. There is a dirt launch ramp.

(3) Point of Pines Lake

As its name suggests, this secluded high-mountain lake is surrounded by a ponderosa pine forest. Located at 5,800 feet in elevation, it is truly a mountain jewel, well off the beaten path.

The lake is stocked annually with rainbow and brown trout, which makes it a great family fishery and camping destination.

Wildlife abounds in the area. You might see elk, pronghorn, black bears, Rocky Mountain bighorn sheep, mule deer, white-tailed deer, and javelinas while visiting the relatively remote but easy-to-access lake.

Fishing Tips: You just might catch a limit of trout here using in-line spinners, Z-Rays, Kastmaster spoons, Power Bait, worms, and corn.

➤ Fly-fishing from shore or in a float tube works well for catching rainbow or brown trout.

Although the lake is stocked annually, several larger rainbow and brown trout can be caught as a result of over-summer survival in the higher-elevation lake.

Youngsters like to fish for brown and rainbow trout at Point of Pines Lake.

3 | FISHERY FACTS

LOCATION AND DIRECTIONS: GPS — 33°21'41.97"N; 109°47'48.29"W
Point of Pines Lake is 80 miles from Globe, easily accessible off Indian Route 8, about 50 miles from the junction of State Route 70. Simply follow the signs. The last few miles are on a fairly well-maintained dirt road.

AMENITIES: None. There is only primitive camping at the lake, with no drinking water available. The closest lodging is in nearby San Carlos.

(4) Seneca Lake

The 27-acre lake at 5,300 feet in elevation is managed as both a warm-water and cool-water fishery. Although Seneca Lake has a boat ramp and several fishing piers for access, it is very friendly for shore anglers. You can use small boats, kayaks, and canoes here, and kids love the lake.

Seneca offers fishing for trophy largemouth bass, channel catfish, and redear sunfish during the warmer summer months. Yet you can also fish for rainbow and brown trout during the winter.

Seneca is located in rugged chaparral country dotted with pines. Anglers visiting the area often see mule deer and javelinas.

Fishing Tips: Try using worms or even fly-fishing for sunfish. In fact, night crawlers are good for catching all the fish species here.

➤ For bass, try spinners and assorted plastic worms rigged Texas-style and pitched and flipped into heavy cover.

➤ For trout, try Power Bait, corn, salmon eggs, small spinners (Mepps or Rooster Tails), Z-Rays, Super Dupers, and Rapalas.

4 | FISHERY FACTS

LOCATION AND DIRECTIONS: GPS — 33°45′49.10″N; 110°30′2.04″W
Seneca Lake is 33 miles north of Globe on State Route 60, near picturesque Salt River Canyon. Just watch for the signs.

AMENITIES: The lake has a boat ramp and several fishing piers.

⑤ Black River Recreation Area

⑥ Salt River Recreation Area

These rivers provide a treasure trove of outdoor adventure and fishing on the San Carlos Apache Indian Reservation. Approximately 108 miles long, the rivers comprise the northern border of the reservation.

Many areas of the river are not readily accessible, making it a favorite for those wanting more of a wilderness experience in their outings.

Anglers should concentrate their efforts on the deeper, more secluded pools and back eddies along the river. Artificial baits such as in-line spinners and Power Bait grubs are favorites for local anglers. When fishing the Black River, ultralight fishing tackle is recommended.

5 | 6 | FISHERY FACTS

LOCATION AND DIRECTIONS: Access is very limited to both the Black River and Salt River recreation areas. The easiest access is on U.S. Route 60 as it crosses the Salt River Canyon 40 miles from Globe and 48 miles from Show Low at 33°47′56.57″N; 110°30′0.96″W. Most other access points entail taking dirt roads, and many require hiking into Black River on foot trails. It's a wild and remote area. Check with the San Carlos Tribe for more information.

AMENITIES: None.

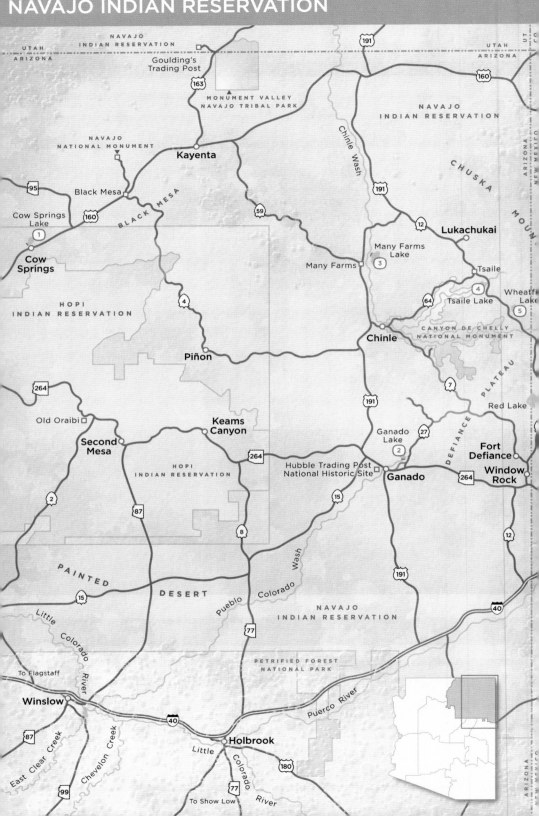

NAVAJO INDIAN RESERVATION

NAVAJO INDIAN RESERVATION

Diné Bikéyah, or Navajoland, is a timeless land of contrasts encompassing more than 17 million acres spread across Arizona, New Mexico, and Utah, where you will find intriguing fishing adventures. With more than 27,000 square miles, the Navajo Indian Reservation is larger than 10 of the 50 states in the United States.

The Arizona portion of Navajoland is spiced with a dozen fishing lakes and ponds where you can walk in beauty and connect with nature. Lake Powell alone caresses 186 miles of Navajoland shoreline. You can also delight in high-country waters full of trout or reel in some excitement along warm-water fisheries where bass and catfish flourish. Some of the most popular fishing lakes are located close to Canyon de Chelly National Monument.

Other outdoor-recreation opportunities are plentiful. You may want to explore more than a dozen national monuments, tribal parks, and historical sites. While wandering Diné Bikéyah, you can step back in time and discover how the ancient ones, the Anasazi, lived thousands of years ago. From the weather-sculpted rock formations gracing Monument Valley to the imposing red sandstone cliffs and refreshing waters of Lake Powell, you can treat your spirit to this mystical land of captivating contrasts, where tradition and geologic time have more significance than wrist watches and nightly news broadcasts.

The Navajo are a spiritual people. To grace your stay, consider the traditional Navajo prayer while facing east to greet the morning:

May it be beautiful before me.
May it be beautiful behind me.
May it be beautiful above me.
May it be beautiful below me.
May I walk in beauty.

Anglers might want to add "*May I fish in beauty,*" especially when greeting the morning sun on a picturesque Navajo Reservation lake.

For complete rules and other information about fishing on this large reservation, contact the Navajo Nation Department of Fish and Wildlife at 928-871-6451 or visit www.nndfw.org. For information on other outdoor-recreation opportunities, contact the Navajo Nation Parks and Recreation Department at 928-871-6647 or P.O. Box 9000, Window Rock, AZ 86515, or visit www.navajonationparks.org.

Special Notes: Any person, Navajo or not, ages 12 and older who fishes for aquatic wildlife in Navajo waters must carry a valid fishing permit. While children under 12 are not required to carry a permit, they are entitled to half the daily bag and possession limits without a permit. Those 12 and under carrying their own permit are entited to the full daily bag and possession limits.

(1) Cow Springs Lake

Cow Springs Lake, a warm-water reservoir with about 240 surface acres when full, contains catfish, bluegill, yellow perch, and largemouth bass. The lake has gone dry in the past, but refilled after a wet winter season. It was restocked with largemouth bass and channel catfish. The interesting, out-of-the-way lake is often unknowingly passed by tourists heading to Monument Valley near Kayenta or by anglers traveling to Halls Crossing or Hite along the upper end of Lake Powell.

Those who stop and wet a line here might have the lake all to themselves. If they happen to have a canoe, kayak, or float tube, the fishing is even better.

Fishing Tips: The long, narrow lake receives minimal fishing pressure due to its remoteness, so fishing tends to be good. Try crankbaits, in-line spinners, or small jigs. Also try Texas-rigged artificial 4-inch worms or lizards. Channel catfish also enjoy corn and hot dogs. The water in the lake can be cloudy in years with good runoff.

1 | FISHERY FACTS

LOCATION AND DIRECTIONS: GPS — 36°23'48.24"N; 110°52'17.59"W
The long and shallow high desert lake is located 30 miles northeast of Tuba City along U.S. Route 160 as it makes its way toward Kayenta. It is not far from Navajo National Monument, which actually has three sites to visit nearby; visit www.nps.gov/nava for more information.

AMENITIES: No facilities are available at the lake. Tonalea is the nearest community with a store. There is no launch ramp. There is camping available at the Navajo National Monument main site, about 30 minutes away. There are motels and popular fast-food restaurants in both Tuba City and Kayenta. The city of Page is about 85 miles away.

(2) Ganado *(Lók aahnteel)* Lake

Ganado has some of the best largemouth bass fishing on the Navajo Reservation and is also loaded with large channel catfish. It is a scenic lake well worth a visit. The dam on the 361-acre lake was recently rebuilt. Prior to the lake being lowered for work on the dam, it was known as a lunker-bass lake.

Ganado is definitely on the comeback trail and will provide you some nice fish on the end of the line. Bring plenty of insect repellent when fishing during the warmer months. The lake sits at an elevation of 6,465 feet.

A dirt road around much of the lake offers pretty good access for shore anglers, canoes, kayaks, and float tubes. The lake draws a fair

Ganado Lake is one of the most productive bass
fisheries on the Navajo Indian Reservation.

amount of waterfowl and apparently is home to a year-round flock of Canada geese.

Fishing Tips: The large lake receives limited fishing pressure, so the fishing is pretty good. In the past, it was an almost secret fishing hole where knowledgeable anglers could catch lunker bass.

➤ Ganado is a fairly shallow lake. Try spinnerbaits worked through the submerged vegetation. During late spring, topwater lures and soft-plastic jerkbaits can be deadly. Also try Texas-rigged lizards. Drop shots are not favored here by the local anglers, but should work well.

➤ Local anglers like to fish for bass wearing hip waders. Float tubes should work well here, and the lake is perfect for fishing from a canoe or kayak. Some of the local anglers say they occasionally catch some aggressive channel catfish on crankbaits while they are fishing for bass.

➤ Fly anglers might want to user streamers for bass — they might even catch a hungry channel catfish.

Special Notes: The temperatures get into the upper 80s or even 90s during the summer and can drop into the teens during the winter. Fall and spring are the most pleasant seasons.

HISTORICAL NOTE

The Hubbell Trading Post National Historic Site is located in nearby Ganado. In 1878, John Lorenzo Hubbell purchased the trading post, 10 years after Navajos were allowed to return to their homeland from their government-enforced exile in Fort Sumner, New Mexico. This ended what is known in Navajo history as The Long Walk.

2 | FISHERY FACTS

LOCATION AND DIRECTIONS: GPS — 35°44'14.11"N; 109°31'3.96"W
Ganado Lake is located 3.5 miles east of Ganado, Arizona, toward Window Rock. Take State Route 264 east 1.4 miles and turn left toward Indian Route 9203 (follow the signs), then turn left on Indian Route 9203 and go 0.4 miles to the lake. From Interstate 40, go north at Chambers on U.S. Route 191.

AMENITIES: No amenities are available at the lake, although the community of Ganado is minutes away, where you can purchase gas or groceries. There is no launch ramp, but you can launch smaller boats from the dirt. Four-wheel-drive is recommended for launching trailered boats.

(3) Many Farms *(Dá ák eh Halání)* Lake

Many Farms Lake is a 1,200-surface-acre impoundment when full and sits at 5,322 feet in elevation. The large yet shallow warm-water lake is stocked with channel catfish and largemouth bass. The water can be cloudy in years with good runoff.

The dam was rebuilt a few years ago and took a while to refill. The lake was restocked with bass and channel catfish. It receives minimal fishing pressure, so it should be a good fishery. Local anglers mostly target the large and abundant channel catfish.

The picturesque rolling hills to the east and the nearby red bluffs give the lake the ambiance of fishing in the Painted Desert.

HISTORICAL NOTE

The dam was built in 1937 to provide irrigation water.

Fishing Tips: Local anglers prefer chicken liver for the abundant channel catfish. Some even fish for the catfish while wearing hip waders because the water can be shallow along the shoreline.

➤ This is a huge lake to work, with decent access mostly on the southern side. There is a lot of submerged vegetation on the northern end of the lake when it is full, making it a great area to run spinnerbaits for bass. In the fall, try using buzzbaits. Texas- or Carolina-rigged lizards can be deadly here, and soft-plastic jerkbaits and the smaller shad-like swim baits can be effective. Topwater action here can be good in the mornings and evenings. Also try poppers.

➤ Gas-powered boats are allowed on the reservoir, but car toppers, inflatables, canoes, and float tubes are best.

3 | FISHERY FACTS

LOCATION AND DIRECTIONS: GPS — 36°21'17.93"N; 109°35'51.64"W
The lake is located just northeast of Many Farms off U.S. Route 191. Many Farms is 80 miles (two hours) from Window Rock and 13 miles north of Chinle (Canyon de Chelly). Take State Route 264 west 34.4 miles and turn right (north) on U.S. Route 191 for 44.3 miles. The large lake is visible just west off the highway. There is a rough, mile-long dirt road leading into the lake.

AMENITIES: There are no facilities and no boat ramps. It is possible to launch a small boat on a trailer, but four-wheel-drive is recommended. The community of Many Farms is just minutes away, where you can purchase gas and groceries. The closet camping is at Canyon de Chelly, which is about 15 miles away. Visit www.nps.gov/cach or call 928-674-5500 for more information.

(4) Tsaile *(Tséhílį)* Lake

Located near the Chuska Mountains, Tsaile Lake is one of the larger impoundments on the reservation, offering 260 acres of fishable water when at full capacity. It is visible from Diné College.

Fish species typically stocked include rainbow trout, cutthroat trout, brown trout, and channel catfish.

This is a scenic area with the Lukachukai Mountains and Tsaile Butte dominating the eastern horizon. At 7,033 feet in elevation, the lake freezes over each winter and is popular for ice fishing. The nearby ponderosa-clad Chuska Mountains are typically the wettest area of the Navajo Reservation and abound with wildlife.

Fishing Tips: Most trout baits and techniques will work well. Try Power Bait, in-line spinners such as Mepps or Rooster Tails, Rapalas, Z-Rays, and Super Dupers. For fly anglers, there is a pretty good midge bite here. During summer, water temperatures can rise and the fishing becomes slow for trout, but it is still good for channel catfish using stink baits.

➤ Car toppers, canoes, kayaks, and float tubes are best.

4 | FISHERY FACTS

LOCATION AND DIRECTIONS: GPS — 36°16'27.41"N; 109°12'15.41"W
The lake is next to the community of Tsaile and is 53 miles (1.5 hours) north of Window Rock on Indian Route 12, only a dozen miles north of Wheatfields Lake.

AMENITIES: There are no facilities or launch ramp. It is possible to launch small boats on trailers from the dirt, but four-wheel-drive is recommended. Diné College is right next door. The community of Tsaile is close by, where you will find a store and gas station. There is camping at nearby Wheatfields Lake.

(5) Wheatfields Lake

This is by far the most popular fishery on the Arizona portion of the Navajo Reservation and offers some of the most diverse trout fishing on the Colorado Plateau.

The sparking trout lake has nearly 250 surface acres of water when at full capacity. Wheatfields sits at 7,295 feet in elevation in a ponderosa-pine habitat at the foot of the Chuska Mountains, just east of the Canyon de Chelly National Monument. It is a lake where you can experience the Navajo way — walk and fish in beauty.

Fish species include rainbow, cutthroat, and brown trout. Fishing and boating are both popular activities. On some weekends, the whole shoreline along Navajo Route 12 can have throngs of anglers connecting with nature and trying to connect with feisty fish.

Just a short drive from Window Rock, Wheatfields Lake offers four-season fishing.

Fishing Tips: This is a renowned trout-fishing lake known for its big browns and mature cutthroat trout. There is plenty of shoreline access, but the lake is best fished from a small boat, canoe, kayak, or float tube.
➤ The trout diversity of the lake means you should bring your full arsenal of trout lures. Spin anglers will want to try spinners, Z-Rays, Super Dupers, and rainbow Rapalas. Power Bait will work at times, especially for rainbows. For those with boats, an effective strategy is trolling Super Dupers, Z-Rays, cowbells, or Ford Fenders. Fly anglers will want to go small in spring, try terrestrials in summer, then do a combination of flies in the fall.

Special Notes: Wheatfields Lake freezes over each winter and is very popular for ice fishing.

5 | FISHERY FACTS

LOCATION AND DIRECTIONS: GPS — 36°12′25.85″N; 109° 5′53.67″W
Wheatfields Lake is 41.5 miles north of Window Rock (45 minutes) along Navajo Route 12. But don't be surprised when the signs say "Entering New Mexico," because Navajo Route 12 leaves and re-enters Arizona between Window Rock and Wheatfields Lake. Tsaile Lake is only a dozen miles north of this trout lake.

AMENITIES: There is a dirt launch ramp. A store is also located at the northwestern shore, between Navajo Route 12 and the lake. The available camping spaces can fill quickly during summer weekends. Campground areas are open year-round. There are picnic tables and fire rings. It is possible to camp along the shoreline, but plan to be self-sufficient.

URBAN FISHING PROGRAM

Urban fishing attracts young and old alike to various waters in and around Phoenix, Payson, and Tucson.

Whether you're a resident or visitor in the Phoenix or Tucson areas, you don't have to travel far to fish — there are 21 Urban Fishing Program waters in Arizona, including those in Phoenix, Chandler, Gilbert, Mesa, Peoria, Scottsdale, and Surprise, plus Tucson, Payson, and Sahuarita. The Arizona Game and Fish Department's award-winning Urban Fishing Program is one of the best in the nation. Visit any of these outdoor oases in our desert cities, and you will readily experience why.

Keep in mind that the cost of an urban fishing license is the same for residents and nonresidents, making it a great value for seasonal visitors.

Urban waters are stocked with rainbow trout from November through March and with channel catfish the rest of the year, except the two hottest months, July and August, when water temperatures preclude stockings. Yet even in summer, these convenient lakes are very fishable.

Each urban lake is stocked at the rates of 75 trout and 50 catfish per acre, providing a quality fishing experience in these often-intimate waters where neighbors, friends, and families gather.

The urban waters are also stocked twice a year with sunfish. Largemouth bass are stocked each year as well. In fact, Papago Ponds near the Phoenix Zoo is a unique blue-ribbon urban bass fishery.

Most urban fisheries are located in city parks where anglers also may participate in a multitude of recreational activities and enjoy a wide range of amenities, including a narrow-gauge railroad, a baseball stadium, dog parks, sports fields, libraries, and multipurpose recreation centers.

One urban lake even has a superb nature preserve that includes an astronomical observatory. Many of the parks also have excellent kid-friendly playgrounds.

PHOENIX-AREA URBAN LAKES

Alvord Lake

With 25 surface acres, Alvord Lake in Cesar Chavez Park is the largest urban fishery, and very popular with residents in the community of Laveen and south Phoenix.

This well-liked fishing lake has a maximum depth of 18 feet and is open daily from 5:30 a.m. to 11 p.m.

For more information, contact the Phoenix Parks and Recreation Department at 602-262-6575 or visit www.phoenix.gov/parks.

Location: GPS — 33°22'39.8"N; 112°8'13.2"W
Cesar Chavez Park, 7858 S. 35th Ave., Phoenix

Amenities: The large park has group ramadas, a playground, sports fields, a library, and a walking trail. The Adobe municipal golf course is next door.

Special Notes: Boating is permitted only between sunrise and sunset. Only canoes, rowboats, and sailboats are allowed (no rafts). No motors are allowed (gas or electric). You must have proper flotation devices on board. Fishing from a boat is prohibited.

Sometimes there's nothing better than fishing in your own backyard.

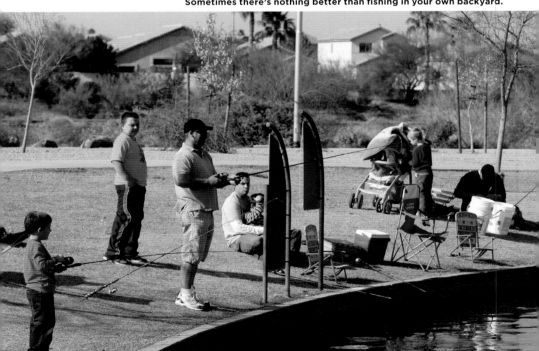

Daily Bag and Possession Limits: Four catfish, four trout, two bass (13-inch minimum), 10 sunfish, and one white amur (30-inch minimum). These urban fishing regulations are subject to change. Statewide limits apply to all other species.

Cortez Lake

Cortez has a maximum depth of 14 feet and is the only urban lake in northern Phoenix (not far from MetroCenter). The 3-acre lake draws a contingent of regular anglers. Park hours are 5:30 a.m. to 11 p.m. For more information, contact the Phoenix Parks and Recreation Department at 602-262-6575 or visit www.phoenix.gov/parks.

Location: GPS — 33°34'12.8"N; 112°7'54.75"W
Cortez Park, 3434 W. Dunlap Ave., Phoenix (just west of Interstate 17)

Amenities: A playground, large shade trees, a wide expanse of grass, and sports fields.

Special Notes: Boating, swimming, wading, glass containers, and littering are prohibited. Alcoholic-beverage permits required.

Daily Bag and Possession Limits: Four catfish, four trout, two bass (13-inch minimum), 10 sunfish, and one white amur (30-inch minimum). These urban fishing regulations are subject to change. Statewide limits apply to all other species.

Encanto Lake

A 222-acre park close to the heart of downtown Phoenix, Encanto has it all — even its own amusement park. The entertaining park has been named a "Phoenix Point of Pride."

Encanto Lake has 7.5 surface acres with a maximum depth of 10 feet. Park hours are 5:30 a.m. to 11 p.m. For more information, contact the Phoenix Parks and Recreation Department at 602-262-6575 or visit www.phoenix.gov/parks.

Location: GPS — 33°28'34.61"N; 112°5'20.99"W
Encanto Park, 260 N. 15th Ave., Phoenix (not far from the Arizona State Fairgrounds)

Amenities: Seasonal paddleboat rentals, a community center, lighted sports courts, exercise course, 18-hole golf course, picnic area, grills, playground, swimming pool, recreation building, and restrooms. The park also is home to Enchanted Island Amusement Park, with rides for children ages 2 to 10.

Special Notes: Swimming, wading, glass containers, and littering are prohibited. Alcoholic-beverage permits required. Private boats not allowed. Fishing prohibited from golf course as posted.

Daily Bag and Possession Limits: Four catfish, four trout, two bass (13-inch minimum), 10 sunfish, and one white amur (30-inch minimum). These urban fishing regulations are subject to change. Statewide limits apply to all other species.

Desert Breeze Park

This family friendly park in Chandler has a 4-acre lake and all the recreational amenities, even a narrow-gauge railroad and a carousel. Kids love it. Park hours are 6 a.m. to 10:30 p.m daily.

Location: GPS — 33°18'48.84"N; 111°55'10.15"W
660 N. Desert Breeze Blvd. in Chandler, between McClintock and Rural roads

Amenities: The railroad and carousel, plus a snack bar, ball fields, tennis courts, picnic ramadas, splash zone, and sand volleyball courts. For more information, call Chandler Community Services at 480-782-2727.

Special Notes: Swimming, wading, glass containers, and littering are prohibited. Alcoholic-beverage permits required. Other rules as posted.

Daily Bag and Possession Limits: Four catfish, four trout, two bass (13-inch minimum), 10 sunfish, and one white amur (30-inch minimum). These urban fishing regulations are subject to change. Statewide limits apply to all other species.

Desert West Park

Neighbors like to meet and eat ice cream, or play sports and catch fish from the 5-acre lake in this residential park on the west side of Phoenix.
The lake has a maximum depth of 15 feet, and the park is open daily from 5:30 a.m. to 11 p.m.
For more information, contact the Phoenix Parks and Recreation Department at 602-262-6575 or visit www.phoenix.gov/parks.

Location: GPS — 33°28'30.19"N; 112°11'47.71"W
Desert West Park and Sports Complex, 6602 W. Encanto Blvd., Phoenix

Amenities: A playground, sports fields, community center, and skate park. This lake is next to the Maryvale police substation.

Special Notes: Boating, swimming, wading, glass containers, and littering are prohibited.

Fishing is a great way for locals to get out and enjoy the outdoors.

Daily Bag and Possession Limits: Four catfish, four trout, two bass (13-inch minimum), 10 sunfish, and one white amur (30-inch minimum). These urban fishing regulations are subject to change. Statewide limits apply to all other species.

Papago Park Ponds

A unique urban blue-ribbon bass fishery, Papago Park Ponds is a well-shaded oasis with three ponds totaling 6 acres situated in the 1,200-acre Papago Park immediately adjacent to the Phoenix Zoo. These productive ponds were part of the Arizona Game and Fish Department's hatchery system about 50 years ago.

Papago Park is home to iconic geologic formations referred to as the Beehives that greet airplanes flying in and out of Sky Harbor Airport. They are also visible from downtown skyscrapers. You can also climb up into a unique sandstone formation called Hole in the Rock, which is a popular vantage point to watch glorious Arizona sunsets.

Park hours are 6 a.m. to 7 p.m. For more information, contact the Phoenix Parks and Recreation Department at 602-262-6575 or visit www.phoenix.gov/parks.

Location: GPS — 33°27'18.05"N; 111°56'53.15"W
Papago Park, 625 N. Galvin Parkway, Phoenix

Amenities: Picnic tables and multipurpose trails. The Phoenix Zoo is located immediately next door, and the famous Desert Botanical Garden is a close neighbor. This fishery is also just minutes away from Tempe Town Lake.

Daily Bag and Possession Limits: Two catfish, two trout, one bass (13-inch minimum), five sunfish, and one white amur (30-inch minimum). These urban fishing regulations are subject to change. Statewide limits apply to all other species.

Children enjoy fishing and operating model boats at Scottsdale's Chaparral Lake.

Chaparral Lake

Skates, bicycles, and fishing poles all fit right in at Chaparral, a 10-acre lake in the heart of Scottsdale.

Chaparral has a maximum depth of 15 feet and is open daily from sunrise to 10:30 p.m. There are waterfowl galore here, from cormorants to Canada geese. It's a popular recreation area for anglers, birders, skaters, joggers, and bicyclists. Whether you are athletic or just want to kick back and relax, Chaparral is a pleaser.

The lake is located in the Indian Bend Wash, an engineering marvel with 7.5 miles of lush, grassy floodplain containing lakes, golf courses, swimming pools, recreational facilities, and an extensive multiuse path system. Indian Bend Wash connects into the Salt River bed. You can fish Chaparral, then ride your bicycle to Tempe Town Lake and fish it as well.

For more information, contact Scottsdale Community Services at 480-312-2353.

Location: GPS — 33°30'38.07"N; 111°54'27.03"W
Chaparral Park, 5401 N. Hayden Road, Scottsdale

Amenities: Boating, large shade trees, group ramadas, a playground, sports fields (north of park), an exercise course, a walking course, and a dog park.

Special Notes: Boating is permitted only between sunrise and sunset and you must have proper flotation devices on board. Electric trolling motors may be used; gas motors are prohibited. Model boats may be operated only in areas that are designated for that purpose. Swimming, wading, glass containers, and littering are prohibited. A permit for beer is required; all other alcoholic beverages prohibited.

Daily Bag and Possession Limits: Four catfish, four trout, two bass (13-inch minimum), 10 sunfish, and one white amur (30-inch minimum). These urban fishing regulations are subject to change. Statewide limits apply to all other species.

Evelyn Hallman Lake

Formerly known as Canal Park, this is a well-loved and well-hidden Tempe neighborhood park just over the canal from Papago Park. It is a rural-like getaway in the midst of the bustling city.

The 3-acre urban lake has a maximum depth of 7 feet and is open from 6 a.m. to 10 p.m. daily. For more information, contact the Tempe Parks and Recreation Department at 480-350-5200.

Location: GPS — 33°26'58.16"N; 111°56'17.33"W
Evelyn Hallman Park, 1900 N. College Ave., Tempe. Located on the east side of the Crosscut Canal (from where it gets its water), it must be reached from the east via 68th Street (aka North College Avenue).

Special Notes: Boating, swimming, wading, glass containers, and littering are prohibited. A permit for beer is required; all other alcoholic beverages prohibited.

Daily Bag and Possession Limits: Two catfish, two trout, one bass (13-inch minimum), five sunfish, and one white amur (30-inch minimum). These urban fishing regulations are subject to change. Statewide limits apply to all other species.

Kiwanis Lake

This fun urban lake in the 125-acre Kiwanis Park is paddleboat heaven. It's a 13-acre lake shaped like an elongated oval, providing lots of lake to paddle and shoreline to fish. If you don't get enough exercise paddling a boat, you can visit the batting cage at this popular park.

Kiwanis Lake has a maximum depth of 8 feet and is open daily from 6 a.m. to midnight. For more information, contact the Tempe Parks and Recreation Department at 480-350-5200.

Location: GPS — 33°22'26.06"N; 111°56'20.44"W
Kiwanis Park, 5500 S. Mill Ave., Tempe (between Baseline and Guadalupe roads)

Amenities: Boating, group ramadas, a playground, sports fields, tennis courts, basketball courts, and baseball fields. There are seasonal paddleboat rentals. The Kiwanis Recreation Center, with an indoor wave pool, is just down the road. There is a Tempe police substation — it's where they keep their horses for the mounted patrols. The Ken McDonald Golf Course is a neighbor.

Memories are made while fishing at urban lakes.

Special Notes: A City of Tempe annual boating permit is required and you must have proper flotation devices on board. Gas and electric motors are prohibited. Boating is permitted between sunrise and sunset. Swimming, wading, glass containers, and littering are prohibited. A permit is required to drink beer; all other alcoholic beverages are prohibited.

Daily Bag and Possession Limits: Four catfish, four trout, two bass (13-inch minimum), 10 sunfish, and one white amur (30-inch minimum). These urban fishing regulations are subject to change. Statewide limits apply to all other species.

Red Mountain Park

This well-appointed, 8-acre park is terrific for bass fishing — try the west side of the lake. There are rabbits everywhere, which is why you can often hear coyotes howling at dusk.

The lake has a maximum depth of 17 feet and is open from sunrise to 10 p.m. For more information, contact Mesa Parks and Recreation at 480-644-5300.

Location: GPS — 33°26'23.87"N; 111°39'31.29"W
7745 E. Brown Road, Mesa

Amenities: Group ramadas, a playground, sports fields, a walking trail, and a multigenerational center. It's also close the Game and Fish Department's Mesa Regional Office.

Special Notes: Boating, swimming, wading, glass containers, and littering are prohibited. No distilled alcoholic beverages permitted. No pets allowed.

Daily Bag and Possession Limits: Four catfish, four trout, two bass (13-inch minimum), 10 sunfish, and one white amur (30-inch minimum). These urban fishing regulations are subject to change. Statewide limits apply to all other species.

Riverview Park

Riverview Park in Mesa is almost across the street from the Bass Pro Shop. The 3-acre lake is a great place to try out your latest fishing-gear purchase.

Riverview has a maximum depth of 16 feet and is open daily from sunrise to 10 p.m. For more information, contact Mesa Parks and Recreation at 480-644-2352.

Location: GPS — 33°25'49.32"N; 111°52'32.09"W
2100 W. Eighth St., Mesa. There is easy access off State Route 202 at Dobson Road.

Amenities: Group ramadas, a playground, and sports fields. There are many nearby restaurants.

Special Notes: Boating, swimming, wading, glass containers, and littering are prohibited. No distilled alcoholic beverages permitted. No pets allowed.

Daily Bag and Possession Limits: Four catfish, four trout, two bass (13-inch minimum), 10 sunfish, and one white amur (30-inch minimum). These urban fishing regulations are subject to change. Statewide limits apply to all other species.

Steele Indian School Park

A veteran-friendly urban lake (the VA Hospital is next door) within sight of the downtown skyscrapers in Phoenix, the lake at Steele Indian School Park has 2.5 acres with a maximum depth of 12 feet and is open from 6 a.m. to 11 p.m. daily.

The 75-acre park occupies the site of the Phoenix Indian School, which opened in 1891 as a boarding school for children of Native American tribes. There is a wide, circular walkway encompassing the three historic buildings remaining on the site.

In the center of the park is a water cistern. Etched into the concrete around the cistern is a poem that explains the Native American design theme of the park. The Circle of Life is 600 feet in diameter and features 24 interpretive columns depicting the history of the Phoenix Indian School.

For more information, contact the Phoenix Parks and Recreation Department at 602-262-6575 or visit www.phoenix.gov/parks.

Location: GPS — 33°34'12.8"N; 112°7'54.75"W
Steele Indian School Park, 300 E. Indian School Road (east of Interstate 17 close to the Central Corridor of Phoenix and accessible via the light-rail system)

Amenities: A playground, group ramadas, a dog park, historic buildings, an amphitheater, and water features. There is an American Indian Veterans Memorial and a memorial hall for events.

Special Notes: Boating, swimming, wading, glass containers, and littering are prohibited. Alcoholic-beverage permits required.

Daily Bag and Possession Limits: Two catfish, two trout, one bass (13-inch minimum), five sunfish, and one white amur (30-inch minimum). These urban fishing regulations are subject to change. Statewide limits apply to all other species.

Surprise Lake

Five-acre Surprise Lake is located in a family friendly neighborhood park made for picnics and good times. Surprise Lake attracts lots of base-ball fans looking to escape the crowds, especially during spring training games (come early and fish while you avoid game-day traffic snarls). The Surprise Stadium close by is the spring training home for the Texas Rangers and the Kansas City Royals. The lake has a maximum depth of 12 feet and is open from sunrise to 10 p.m.

For more information, contact Surprise Community and Recreation Services at 623-222-2000.

Location: GPS — 33°37'47.16"N; 112°22'26.55"W
15930 N. Bullard Ave., Surprise

When lakes are close to home, every member of the family can enjoy the experience.

Amenities: A playground, sports fields, a dog park, a swimming pool, a library, and the baseball stadium.

Special Notes: Boating, swimming, wading, glass containers, and littering are prohibited.

Daily Bag and Possession Limits: Four catfish, four trout, two bass (13-inch minimum), 10 sunfish, and one white amur (30-inch minimum). These urban fishing regulations are subject to change. Statewide limits apply to all other species.

Rio Vista Lake

At 2.7 acres, Rio Vista Lake might be small, but it looms large when it comes to recreational amenities — this is the only urban lake with its own Starbucks. There is a batting cage, skate park, and multipurpose recreation center to help you work off the caffeine.

The lake has a maximum depth of 14 feet and is open daily from 6 a.m. to 10:30 p.m. For more information, contact Peoria Community Services at 623-773-7137.

Location: GPS — 33°36'54.28"N; 112°14'42.82"W
Rio Vista Community Park, 8866-D W. Thunderbird Road, Peoria (just west of State Route 101)

Amenities: Group ramadas, sports fields, a splash park, batting cages, a skate park, Surprise Recreation Center, a playground, and a tot lot.

Special Notes: Boating, swimming, wading, glass containers, and littering are prohibited. Alcoholic-beverage permit required. Leashed dogs are permitted.

Daily Bag and Possession Limits: Two catfish, two trout, one bass (13-inch minimum), five sunfish, and one white amur (30-inch minimum). These urban fishing regulations are subject to change. Statewide limits apply to all other species.

Veterans Oasis Lake

Since it opened in 2008, 5-acre Veterans Oasis Lake has been a hit with south Chandler and Queen Creek residents.

With a maximum depth of 14 feet, it's located near a recharge basin and wetlands loaded with wildlife, especially birds. The park is open daily from 6 a.m. to 10:30 p.m. The Environmental Education Center is a premier attraction here. For more information, contact the Environmental Education Center at 480-782-2890 or eec@chandleraz.gov.

Location: GPS — 33°14'8.05"N; 111°46'14.05"W

Veterans Oasis Park, 4050 E. Chandler Heights Road, Chandler

Amenities: Walking trails, an environmental education center, an open play area, and an equestrian trail. There is excellent bird-watching. A Chandler police precinct is located on the grounds.

Special Notes: Boating is not allowed. No fishing is allowed in the recharge basins. Swimming, wading, glass containers, and littering are prohibited. Alcoholic-beverage permit required. Dogs must remain on leash at all times and are prohibited from lake and recharge basins.

Daily Bag and Possession Limits: Four catfish, four trout, two bass (13-inch minimum), 10 sunfish, and one white amur (30-inch minimum). These urban fishing regulations are subject to change. Statewide limits apply to all other species.

Water Ranch Lake

Part of the Gilbert Riparian Preserve is 5-acre Water Ranch Lake, which has a maximum depth of 15 feet and is open daily from 6 a.m. to 10 p.m. With the adjacent wetland, this is a wildlife-watching and star-watching special. For more information, contact Gilbert Community Services at 480-503-6200 or visit www.riparianinstitute.org.

Location: GPS — 33°21'47.75"N; 111°44'9.8"W
Riparian Preserve at Water Ranch, 2757 E. Guadalupe Road, Gilbert

Amenities: A library, a playground, and a riparian preserve with walking trails and excellent bird-watching. There is also an observatory managed by the East Valley Astronomy Club.

Special Notes: Boating is not allowed. No fishing from bridge. Swimming, wading, glass containers, and littering are all prohibited.

Daily Bag and Possession Limits: Four catfish, four trout, two bass (13-inch minimum), 10 sunfish, and one white amur (30-inch minimum). These urban fishing regulations are subject to change. Statewide limits apply to all other species.

TUCSON-AREA URBAN LAKES

The Tucson area has three popular urban lakes, and not far away there is also an urban lake for the community of Sahuarita. These lakes are stocked with trout in the winter months and catfish in winter. They also have kid-pleasing sunfish.

Silverbell Lake

The 13-acre lake in Christopher Columbus Park gets lots of angling use. With a maximum depth of 7 feet, it has bass, sunfish, and white amur.

Silverbell is stocked in the winter with rainbow trout and receives channel catfish in the spring and fall. Like the other urban lakes, it is not stocked during July and August due to increased water temperatures, but anglers still catch fish in the summer months.

This lake has one unique feature: a model-boat lake, Archer Lake. Silverbell is operated by the Tucson Parks and Recreation Department (www.tucsonaz.gov/parksandrec). Park hours are typically from 6 a.m. to 10:30 p.m.

Location: GPS — 32°17'6"N; 111°2'2"W
4600 N. Silverbell Road, Tucson

Amenities: Boating is allowed. There are large shade trees, group ramadas, a dog park, a playground, a model-airplane area, and even a model-boat lake.

Daily Bag and Possession Limits: Four catfish, four trout, two bass (13-inch minimum), 10 sunfish, and one white amur (30-inch minimum). These urban fishing regulations are subject to change. Statewide limits apply to all other species.

Kennedy Lake

Kennedy Lake affords anglers a good view of the Santa Catalina Mountains, giving it a nonurban feel in a way, but the plentiful amenities in J.F. Kennedy Park can make it seem like the best of both worlds.

The 10-acre lake has a maximum depth of 12 feet and contains bass, sunfish, catfish, trout, and white amur. It is stocked with trout in winter and with catfish during the spring and fall. During the summer months, the lake is not stocked due to high water temperatures. However, fishing is still popular in summer.

Location: GPS — 32°10'52"N; 111°0'29"W
3600 S. La Cholla Blvd., Tucson

Amenities: There is boating, group ramadas, a playground, sports fields, and a swimming pool.

Special Notes: Canoes up to 17 feet and boats up to 14 feet must be properly licensed and have proper flotation devices. Gas motors are prohibited. For more information, visit the Tucson Parks and Recreation Department at www.tucsonaz.gov/parksandrec.

Daily Bag and Possession Limits: Four catfish, four trout, two bass (13-inch minimum), 10 sunfish, and one white amur (30-inch minimum). These urban fishing regulations are subject to change. Statewide limits apply to all other species.

Lakeside Lake

Lakeside is a little larger and deeper than its sister urban lakes in the Tucson area — it has 14 surface acres and its maximum depth is 35 feet.

Despite its depth, this lake can sometimes experience low oxygen levels. An aeration system was installed by the City of Tucson in 2002 to improve lake conditions for fish.

Lakeside is stocked with trout during the winter months and with channel catfish during the spring and fall. It also has largemouth bass and sunfish. For more information, visit www.tucsonaz.gov/parksandrec.

Kennedy Lake in Tucson is especially inviting when the Santa Catalina Mountains are dusted with snow.

Location: GPS — 32°11'10"N; 110°48'59"W
Chuck Ford Lakeside Park, 8300 E. Stella Road, Tucson

Amenities: Boating, a playground, sports fields, and a walking trail.

Special Notes: Swimming, wading, glass containers, and littering are prohibited. No live baitfish allowed. Canoes up to 17 feet and boats 14 feet and under must be properly licensed and permitted and must have proper flotation devices on board. Gas motors are prohibited. Feeding of ducks and geese is prohibited. Other rules as posted.

Daily Bag and Possession Limits: Four catfish, four trout, two bass (13-inch minimum), and 10 sunfish. These urban fishing regulations are subject to change. Statewide limits apply to all other species.

Sahuarita Lake

This urban lake in Rancho Sahuarita Park has the feel of a country lake. Sahuarita Lake encompasses 10 surface acres with a maximum depth of 12 feet.

Like the other urban fishing lakes, Sahuarita is stocked with trout during the winter months and channel catfish in the spring and fall. It also has largemouth bass and sunfish. For more information, contact Sahuarita Parks and Recreation at 520-822-8896.

Location: GPS — 31°58'30"N; 110°58'4"W
Sahuarita Lake Park, 15466 S. Rancho Sahuarita Blvd., Sahuarita

Special Notes: Swimming, wading, glass containers, littering, cleaning of fish on premises, and alcoholic beverages are prohibited. Boating permitted only between sunrise and sunset. Gas motors prohibited. Must have proper flotation devices on board. Animals must be restrained by a leash at all times.

Daily Bag and Possession Limits: Four catfish, four trout, two bass (13-inch minimum), 10 sunfish, and one white amur (30-inch minimum). These urban fishing regulations are subject to change. Statewide limits apply to all other species.

Green Valley Lakes, Payson

These are probably the most unusual urban lakes in Arizona. The shimmering lakes inside the town of Payson sit at 4,800 feet in elevation and are surrounded by ponderosa pines, just like you would expect from a mountain water, yet they also have a fountain and nearby green lawns. There's no other fishery quite like it — the Green Valley lakes will certainly please you.

There are three lakes: a 13-acre main lake, a middle lake of 1 acre, and an upper lake of 2 acres. The maximum depth of the largest lake is 21 feet. They all add up to a lot of fun for anglers.

The Green Valley Lakes are fishable year-round. When most high-country lakes are covered with ice in winter, Green Valley stays ice free and fun to fish. They are stocked with trout much of the year, and are renowned for bass and crappie fishing. Sunfish are also stocked annually. Park hours are 6 a.m. to 10:30 p.m. For more information, contact Payson Parks, Recreation and Tourism at 928-474-5242, ext. 7.

Location: GPS — 34°14'3"N; 111°21'57"W
Green Valley Park, 1000 W. Country Club Drive, Payson

Amenities: Green Valley Park provides three lakes with a total surface area of 13.1 acres, three picnic ramadas, two public restrooms, 3.8 miles of walking paths, boating and fishing facilities, picnic and outdoor cooking facilities, paved parking areas, and a complete irrigation system and pump station for the landscaped areas.

Special Notes: Swimming, wading, glass containers, and littering are prohibited. No live baitfish are allowed. Alcoholic-beverage permits are required. Boating is permitted only between sunrise and sunset; gas motors are prohibited. Must have proper flotation devices on board. Lake receives treated effluent; therefore full body contact is prohibited. All animals must be restrained by a leash. Other rules as posted.

Daily Bag and Possession Limits: Four catfish, four trout, two bass (13-inch minimum), 10 sunfish, and one white amur (30-inch minimum). These urban fishing regulations are subject to change. Statewide limits apply to all other species.

Urban lakes like those in Green Valley also help teach children boating and canoeing skills.

Arizona's Sport Fish

Here are 28 of the most popular sport fish that anglers can fish for in Arizona. Arizona's waterways support many different sport-fish species, most of which are not native to the state. Our native sport fish include the Apache trout, Gila trout, and roundtail chub (also called Verde trout by pioneers). The Gila trout is not pictured because it's a relative newcomer to the list of sport fish in the state.

The Apache trout and roundtail chub illustrations are by Randall D. Babb, and all others are by Mary Hirsch.

Apache Trout

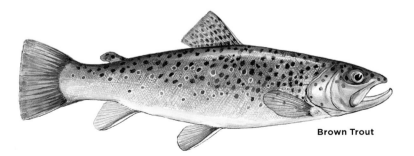

Brown Trout

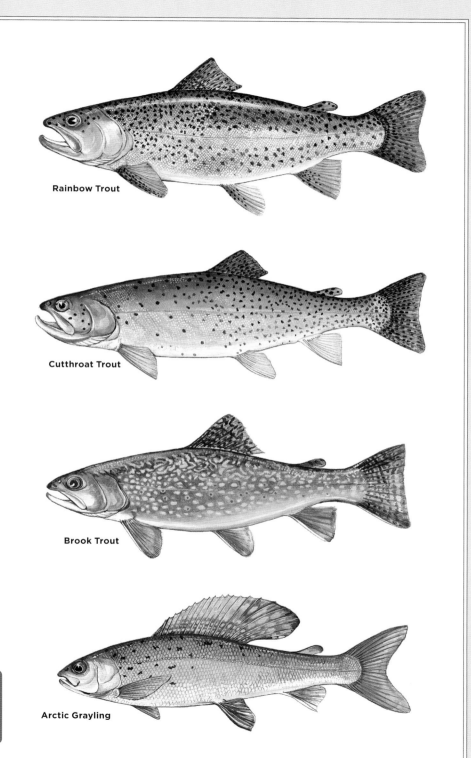

Rainbow Trout

Cutthroat Trout

Brook Trout

Arctic Grayling

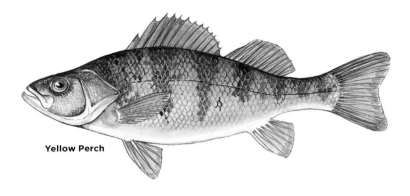

Yellow Perch

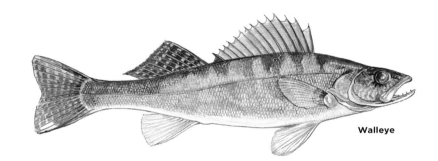

Walleye

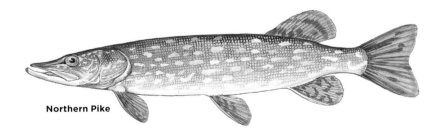

Northern Pike

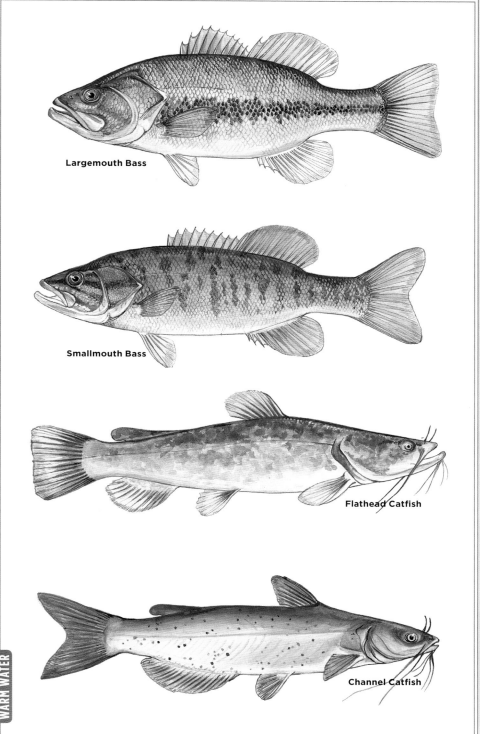

Largemouth Bass

Smallmouth Bass

Flathead Catfish

Channel Catfish

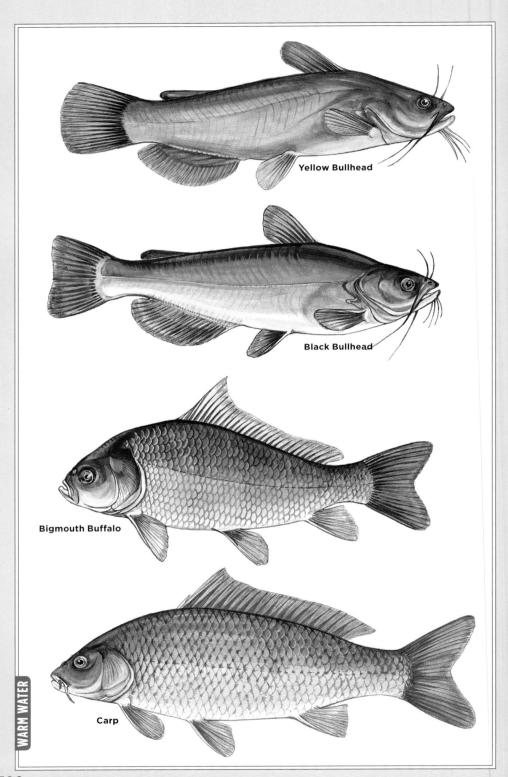

Yellow Bullhead

Black Bullhead

Bigmouth Buffalo

Carp

WARM WATER

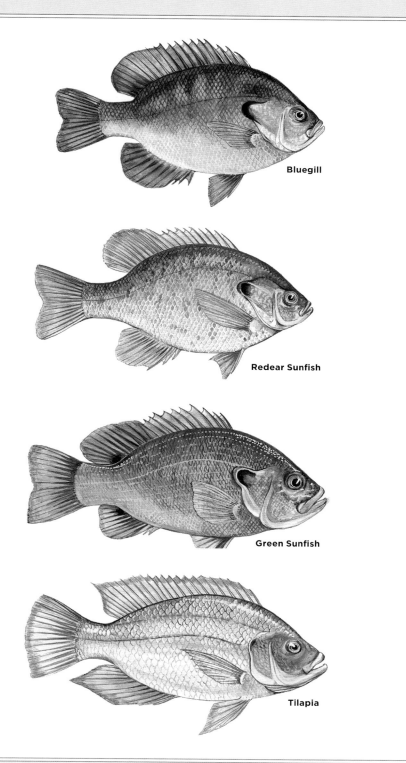

Bluegill

Redear Sunfish

Green Sunfish

Tilapia

White Crappie

Black Crappie

Grass Carp

Roundtail Chub

White Bass

Yellow Bass

Striped Bass

Fishing 101
Basic How-To Guide

Fishing can be simple. While some may have elaborate tackle boxes full of lures of all descriptions, you can also catch fish with a basic setup: a fishing pole, line, hook, and bait. The essence of fishing is simplicity.

In this section we've provided you with some simple how-to basics with a few handy knots and basic rigging setups.

Basic Rigging

Proper rigging of your hooks, weights, and baits is a fundamental part of your fishing success. The following methods have proven to work well for trout, catfish, and bluegill. Use lighter line and smaller hooks and weights for trout and bluegill. Some baits such as worms are effective for all fish; however, most other baits are species-specific.

Catfish
Line: 8 to 12 lb. test
Hook Size: 2 to 6 baitholder
Bait: Worms, stink baits, hot dogs, liver, shrimp

Catfish are best caught using a hook and sinker setup (Fig. 1). Catfish bite best in darker environments. Fish the deepest spots during the daytime and shallower areas after dark.

Trout
Line: 4 to 6 lb. test
Hook Size: 8 to 12 baitholder
Bait: Worms, salmon eggs, Power Bait

When using prepared floating baits, the bottom-fishing setup with an egg sinker is most effective (Fig. 1). When fishing for trout, use the egg sinker setup with 4- or 6-pound line tied below the swivel to the hook. Fishing with a bobber (Fig. 2) can work well for trout when using nonfloating baits such as worms or salmon eggs. In addition to the baits suggested for trout, small in-line spinners such as Panther Martins or Mepps, or spoons such as Kastmasters or Super Dupers, can be effective.

Sunfish/Bluegill
Line: 2 to 6 lb. test
Hook Size: 8 to 12 baitholder
Bait: Worms, mealworms, corn

Sunfish or bluegill can be caught using the bobber setup (Fig. 2). Use a small stick or round bobber and fish along the lake edges in 4 to 8 feet of water. Use enough weight below the bobber so that it can be pulled underwater easily. Try to cover up the hook with the bait.

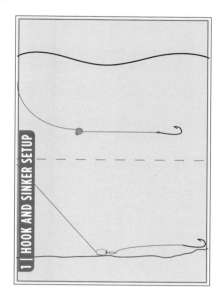

1 | HOOK AND SINKER SETUP

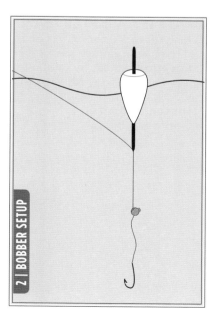

2 | BOBBER SETUP

Tips to Help You Succeed

➤ **Study about fishing and fish habits.**

Fishing is part sport and part biology. Both aspects require study to not only improve your ability to catch fish, but also increase your enjoyment! There are many books and magazines covering basic to highly specialized fishing tips. The Internet is loaded with informative websites and fishing blogs. Attend fishing clinics or seminars, join a fishing club, and seek advice from more experienced anglers.

➤ **Go fishing more often.**

Not only is fishing a great way to relax, but the more often you go, the more your "luck" will improve. Like any sport, fishing takes practice — knowledge and experience will help you consistently succeed. The fastest way to improve is to find a "coach" or experienced angler to take you fishing and show you the basics as well as the many finer points about fishing. Ask around for help.

➤ **Match tackle and techniques to fish.**

Your choice of equipment, lures, and presentation all influence your chances of catching fish. Whether you should fish on the bottom or the surface, the shoreline or the deeper waters varies between types of fish and seasons of the year. Learn to match your techniques to the seasonal habitats and behavior patterns of fish; be adaptable. Pay attention to the methods other anglers are using.

Formula for Fishing Success

F + L + P + A LITTLE LUCK = SUCCESS

F: Fish factor: Understand each fish species' unique habits, and their food and habitat preferences during the year.

L: Location factor: By understanding fish habits, you can fish those spots where fish are likely to be most concentrated or active for that time of day or year.

P: Presentation factor: Match your tackle, bait, technique, and timing to entice fish to bite.

Standard Fishing Knot

**Trilene Knot
(a strong all-purpose knot)**

1. Run the ends of the line through the eye of the hook two times.

2. Loop the line around four or five times, then thread the loose end back between the two loops near the hook, as shown.

3. Pull tight. Trim the loose end.

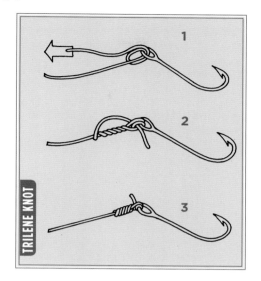

TRILENE KNOT

Get the Kids Involved, Too

Five simple kid-friendly tips will help make your next family fishing trip an enjoyable and memorable experience.

1. Keep it simple and safe.

Forget technique and tactics — kids just want to throw a line in the water and catch something. Choose simple equipment. A push-button spincast reel and a 5- or 6-foot rod are best. Pack only the amount of tackle you need to keep everybody fishing (hooks, bobbers, and weights). Fish with easy-to-use bait secured under a small bobber or on the bottom. Provide your youngster with his or her own small tackle kit. Spend your time teaching and coaching the kids; don't plan to do much fishing yourself.

2. Be prepared.

Have all the things you need to fish beforehand, so when you are ready to go fishing there are no delays. Get lots of worms. They are great universal bait and kids love the dirt, slime, and squirm of worms. Bring drinks and snacks in a small tote — being in the outdoors makes kids hungry. Bring a camera to capture the memories.

3. Make it fun.

Take kids to a place where they can catch a lot of fish, such as bluegill. Help them identify their catch, and teach them how to properly handle the fish they catch.

4. Involve the kids.
Whenever you can, let kids do things themselves — bait the hook, cast their own rods, reel in the fish, and remove the fish from the hook. Give kids a role for the day — choosing where to fish, what to bring for snacks, how long to fish each spot, netting the fish, or counting the birds.

5. Go where the fish are.
If you can't go to the lake or the river, nearby Urban Fishing Program waters are excellent locations to catch all kinds of fish, including bluegill, trout, and catfish. Lakes are stocked every two weeks for 10 months of the year.

Caring for Your Catch

If you're going to eat your catch, you should know how to care for it from the hook to the frying pan.

Responsible anglers catch only what they plan to eat, making sure the fish does not go to waste before it is eaten. Here are some tips to keep your catch fresh and tasty, and avoid having to throw a fish away.

➤ Have a cool, moist place to put your catch. One of the quickest ways a fish can go bad is by being left in a warm area (on land or in the water). A good solution is to bring an ice chest with enough ice for the trip and immediately place the catch on ice. You can also keep the fish on a stringer if the water is cool.

➤ Keep the fish alive until you are ready to leave. The longer you can keep a fish alive and fresh, the better it will taste when you eat it. A wire basket or a stringer is a typical tactic used by most anglers. If using a stringer, thread the stringer through the fishes' lower jaw instead of the gills. This keeps the fish alive a lot longer. Once you are ready to leave the lake, place the fish in a cooler or container. When you leave, remember it is against the law to transport your fish alive in water.

➤ Clean the fish as soon as you get home, and store it properly. The sooner you get home and gut and clean your fish, the better it will taste. Once properly cleaned, the fish will keep for two to three days in the refrigerator sealed in a container. If you need to store it for longer, you can freeze it in water or a resealable plastic bag and it will keep for two to four months.

Proper Release Methods

Fish are a valuable resource, and fishing for them is a fun and exciting recreational experience. Fresh fish are also a great source of nutrition. Keeping only what you plan to eat and releasing the rest is good stewardship of this precious resource. By limiting your harvest and practicing good catch-and-release techniques, you can help preserve the fishery and ensure that fish remain for another day.

Fish can easily die when subjected to excessive handling and poor release techniques. A fish may swim away at first, but likely it will die in a matter of minutes or days if it is: left out of the water too long, covered in dirt, squeezed too hard, or injured from forced removal of a deeply impaled hook. The following catch-and-release tips will greatly improve the fish's chance of survival.

Do's:

➤ Quick hook sets: Avoid letting fish swallow hooks by keeping a taught, well-attended line while fishing.

➤ Quick retrieve: Exhaustion stress can be fatal. The longer you play a fish, the more stress it endures.

➤ Wet hands and a gentle touch: Handling fish with wet hands will help keep their protective slime from coming off.

➤ Keep the fish in the water as much as possible: It is best to unhook the fish while it is still in the water. If you want a picture, have your camera ready to go and limit holding the fish out of the water for too long while you set up the shot.

➤ Carefully remove the hook: Grasp the hook firmly and back it out the same direction it went in. Use pliers or a hook-removal tool, or grasp the hook at the eyelet.

➤ Quick release: Gently place the fish back into the water. If it doesn't swim away, you may need to move the fish forward and back under water so oxygen flows over the gills and it can regain its energy.

Don'ts:

➤ Avoid forcefully removing swallowed hooks: If the hook is embedded down the throat, clip the line as close to the eye of the hook as possible. Hooks will dissolve over time. A fish that has a hook pulled out from its throat has less than a 50% chance of survival. A fish with the hook left in its throat has a 90% chance.

➤ Avoid touching the gills or eyes: Holding a fish by the gills can be lethal; these are extremely sensitive and easily damaged organs.

➤ Avoid letting the fish flop around on the ground: A fish can easily harm itself on land and lose some of its protective slime coating. It is best to minimize the amount of time it spends out of the water.

➤ Avoid a firm grip: Fish are slippery and wiggly. Instinct will lead an angler to tighten the grip on the fish, and potentially crush its internal organs with force.

Other helpful techniques may include using barbless hooks, circle hooks, hook-removal tools, and rubberized nets for handling fish.

Glossary

A.C. Plug brand name of a large, jointed trout-imitating topwater lure made of wood

acidity the degree of sourness of a usually water-soluble substance; measured in pH, with 7 being neutral and 2 being a strong acid

action measure of rod performance, ranging from slow to fast, and describing the elapsed time between when the rod is flexed and when it returns to its straight configuration; also refers to the strength of the rod — light (limber), medium, and heavy (stout rod)

active fish fish that are feeding heavily and striking aggressively

adipose fin on some species, the fatty fin located between the dorsal and tail fins

air bladder gas-filled sac in the upper part of the body cavity of many bony fishes that offsets the weight of the heavier tissue such as bone

algae simple plant organisms, typically a single cell, commonly found in water

alkalinity measure of the amount of acid-neutralizing bases

amur also called white amur or grass carp; a member of the carp family found in China's Amur River stocked to control nuisance weeds and algae; weighing up to 47 pounds

anal fin unpaired fin that lies along the midline of the body beneath the anus, usually on the back half of the fish

anchovy species of 4- to 8-inch baitfish found in the ocean; popularly used as bait for striped bass and catfish

angler person using a fishing pole or rod and reel to catch fish

angleworm any live earthworm placed on a fishing hook

angling usually refers to the recreational catching of fish (sport-fishing) by hook and line

anti-reverse system that prevents reels, typically bait casters, from spinning in reverse and causing tangles

Apache trout one of Arizona's two native trout species, with yellow-gold coloring, dark bold spots on dorsal and tail fin, and sparse body spotting; purebred found in the White Mountains of east-central Arizona; listed as a threatened species under the Endangered Species Act, yet legal to fish for in certain prescribed waters

artificial lures and flies devices intended as visual attractants for fish and not including living or dead organisms or edible parts thereof, natural or prepared foodstuffs, artificial salmon eggs, artificial corn, or artificial marshmallows

attractant liquid, solid, or powder form of scent applied to fishing lures for increased productivity

back casting part of the cast in which the fishing rod — usually a fly rod — and the fishing line are moved from a position in front to one in back of the angler; can have successive back casts as line is played out to increase the distance and accuracy of the cast

backing any type of line used to partially fill a reel before the main fishing line is added; commonly used in fly-fishing or by bass anglers using many of the newer thread-like or polymer lines

backlash overrun of a revolving-spool reel, such as a bait-cast reel, in turn causing the line to billow off the reel and tangle

back trolling method of boat control utilizing a motor and making a series of maneuvers in the presentation of a lure or bait; common to use a front-mounted trolling motor to make the boat move backwards, while dragging or trolling the lure in front of the boat; many methods, including fishing for suspended crappies in winter or summer, involve a slow stop-and-go technique

backwash rough water resulting from boat wakes rebounding off fixed objects such as canyon walls, docks, or anchored boats

backwater shallow area of a river, sometimes isolated and often located behind a sand bar or other obstruction in the river; large isolated backwaters also called oxbows

bag limit restriction in the number of fish an angler may retain, generally on a daily basis

bail metal, semicircular arm of an open-face spinning reel engaging the line after a cast

bait live bait or artificial bait, such as a lure

bait casting fishing with a revolving-spool reel and baitcasting rod, with the reel mounted on the topside of the rod

baitfish small fish, such as threadfin shad, that are often eaten by predatory fish, such as largemouth bass; referring to the fish that predators feed upon, or the kinds of fish placed on a hook to catch a sport fish; use is often regulated

baitwell a special well or livewell in a boat to hold bait

bank fishing method of fishing by casting from an area on a bank of water

bar long, shallow ridge in a body of water

barb a sharp projection on a fishing hook holding a hooked fish

barbless a hook manufactured without a barb, or one made barbless by cutting, filing or flattening the barb, typically with pliers

bass common reference for a number of freshwater and saltwater species sought as game fish; largemouth and smallmouth bass, although commonly referred to as bass, are actually members of the sunfish family; striped bass, white bass, and yellow bass are members of the perch family and often referred to as true bass family

Bass Assassin brand of soft-plastic jerkbait

bass boat a design of shallow-drafting boat developed for modern, competitive bass fishing

bay major indentation in the shoreline of a lake or reservoir

bead-headed midges a type of fly used for fly-fishing

bedding fish during the spawning period

bell sinker a bell-shaped fishing weight

Belly Boat the trademark for a brand of rubber inner tube boats used for fishing in quiet water

benthic occurring at or near the bottom of a body of water

biology the study of living things

biomass the aggregate amount of living matter or a specific species within a specific habitat, or the total number of a specific species in a specific habitat

bite indicator a device activating or signaling when a fish is on the line, such as a bell placed on the line between two fishing pole guides that rings when a fish nibbles at or takes the bait; can be commercially made; often used when bottom-fishing for catfish and carp

black bass common term describing several types of bass of the sunfish family, including the largemouth and smallmouth bass

blind casting casting at no particular target

bluebird skies describing bright, sunny, blue sky conditions, making catching fish difficult

bluegill common species of sunfish; not synonymous with sunfish or panfish

bobber a float attached to the line under which a hook and sometimes a sinker hang, holding the bait or lure at a predetermined depth and also signaling the strike of a fish (strike indicator); variation called a slip-bobber or slip-float, with the line running freely through the bobber and a stop on the line for the predetermined depth

Bomber Long "A" brand name of crankbait

bottom feeder, bottom fish a bottom-feeding fish, such as a catfish or carp, that feeds predominantly on the bottom; not just one that is sometimes caught on the bottom, such as a largemouth bass or trout

bowfishing using a bow and arrow, typically with a reel attached to the bow, to harvest fish

brackish water of intermediate salinity between seawater and freshwater

break a distinct variation in otherwise constant stretches of cover, structure, or bottom type; anything breaking up the underwater terrain

break-off a fish lost when the line breaks, as opposed to losing fish when the hook breaks, straightens, or pulls out

broodfish a large, sexually mature fish capable of breeding; large egg-producing fish in hatcheries

brook trout, brookies species of trout stocked in selected waters in Arizona's high country, not native to the state

brownie a smallmouth bass or brown trout

brown trout non-native species of trout stocked in some of Arizona's high-elevation trout waters; also called German brown

brushline the inside or the outside edge of a stretch of brush

brush pile a mass of small- to medium-sized tree limbs lying in the water; ranging from 1 or 2 feet across to extremely large; visible or submerged, natural or manmade; typically attracting fish and anglers

bubble float a specialty bobber that can be filled with water

bucketmouth a slang term for largemouth bass, also called bigmouth bass

buffalo fish a heavy-bodied carp-like fish weighing up to 39 pounds; found in some of the Salt River lakes

bullet sinker a cone-shaped piece of lead, zinc, or steel of varying weight that slides up and down the line

bumping making a lure hit an object, such as a log, tree, or rock, either intentionally or unintentionally in a controlled manner, getting the attention of a fish and resulting in a strike

buzzbait top-water bait with large, propeller-type blades churning the water during a retrieve; usually composed of a leadhead, a rigid hook and a wire supporting one or more blades; typically has a plastic skirt like a spinnerbait

buzzing retrieving a spinnerbait or buzzbait along the water's surface to create a splash effect resembling a wounded baitfish

caddis fly an aquatic insect of major importance, along with the mayfly and stonefly, for trout fishing; characterized by swept-back wings; completes metamorphosis like a butterfly; the caddis worm is the larva of a caddis fly

California rig method of deep-water fishing in which a plastic worm is placed at the end of a leader trailing behind a sinker

cane pole a pole of natural cane, often made from Calcutta or Tonkin bamboo, used for fishing without a reel by tying the line to the pole; extremely effective for fishing small, narrow streams or creeks

Carolina rig special rig using an exposed or hidden hook with a soft plastic lure placed 2 to 3 feet behind an egg or barrel sinker and swivel; used primarily for deep fishing with heavier weights than a Texas rig; most commonly used with a plastic worm or lizard; can be used with floating crankbaits and other lures; varied by using a lighter, spinning outfit with a split shot placed on the line 12 to 30 inches above the hook, with a small worm or lizard — 4 to 6 inches — rigged Texas style in shallow or deep water especially in the clear, Western reservoirs, or when appropriate to down-size, such as in winter

carp member of the minnow family, introduced to the United States in the late 1800s; typically referring to common carp originally from Europe and not grass carp or amur from Asia

cartop, cartopper boat small enough to be carried on the top of a car and hand-launched, especially at fisheries with limited or no boat launching facilities

casting float a type of tear-shaped bobber than can be cast. Some can be filled with water

catchable for trout in the AZGFD stocking program, this refers to fish 8 inches or longer

catch-and-release catching a fish and immediately releasing it; practiced by anglers as a way to help conserve the resource; required by state fishing regulations in some waters, such as certain small trout streams

catfish any of the many species of catfish, including black, blue, flathead, channel, and yellow species; fishing for catfish also known as catfishing

channel bed of a stream or river; submerged stream or river channel in a reservoir

chugger topwater plug with a dished-out, concave, or cupped head designed to make a splash when pulled sharply; act of systematically working the lure across the surface is known as chugging

chum to throw chum — typically cut-up pieces of baitfish or other bait — overboard to attract fish; chum line refers to the trail of bait or scent in the water attracting game fish

clarity the depth at which one is able to see an object, such as a lure, under the water

clearwater a lake or stream with good visibility

cold front weather condition accompanied by high, clear skies and a sudden drop in temperature

cold-water fishery waters typically in the higher elevations; predominantly trout fisheries

cosmic clock the sun's seasonal effect on water and weather conditions relating to barometric pressure, wind, and cloud cover

cove an indentation along a shoreline; very small indentation a few feet across is known as a pocket cove

cover natural or man-made objects on the bottom of lakes, rivers, or impoundments, especially those influencing fish behavior, including stick-ups, tree lines, stumps, rocks, logs, pilings, docks, and weed patches

cowbell flashing, multi-bladed lure resembling a small school of baitfish; commonly used to troll for trout

crankbait any of a wide number of hard plastic or wooden lures that dive when retrieved by cranking with a reel through the water; also called crank

crappie popular game fish of two species, black and white; white crappies only found in Arizona in Lake Pleasant

crayfish or crawfish a small crustacean found in freshwater, not native to Arizona; also called crawdads

creel limit the daily number of fish an angler can keep in possession as set by state regulations; varies from water to water

Crickhopper brand of plastic lure resembling a grasshopper; commonly used for trout and sometimes for smallmouth bass

culling method of removing and releasing lighter-weight fish from a livewell, retaining the heaviest or tournament limit

Curly Tail trademark for a brand of curved-tail soft plastic lures

curly tailed grub curved-tail soft plastic bait often fitted on a jighead

cutthroat trout or cutthroat species of salmonid characterized by a red or orange slash under the throat; stocked in Big Lake in the White Mountains; not native to Arizona; also called cutts

dabbing working a lure up and down in the same spot a dozen or more times in a bush or beside a tree or other structure

damselfly small member of the dragonfly family

dapping method of fly-fishing allowing the fly to skip or dance on the water while holding the line and leader above the water from a high rod

Dardevle trademark for a brand of spoons typically used for trout and northern pike fishing

deadfall a tree that has fallen into the water

deer-hair bug a floating fly-rodding lure made from hollow deer hair; used principally for bass and panfish

depth finder, depth recorder, or depth sounder a sonar device used for reading the bottom structure, determining depth, and in some cases locating fish; also called a fishfinder

desert sucker a native Arizona fish typically found in rivers and streams, weighing more than 4 pounds

Devle Dog trademark for a brand of fishing lure

die-off having many fish die at the same time, quite often baitfish; also called a fishkill

dillys a type of small earthworm popular for catching sunfish and trout

dink a small bass, usually under 6 to 8 inches long; also called a sub-catch-able

dip bait a smelly, paste-type bait primarily used for catfish

dip net a net with a handle; used to capture baitfish

disgorger a device for removing hooks deeply embedded in the throats of fish

dissolved oxygen the amount of free, usable oxygen in water; usually designated in parts per million

dobsonfly a large aquatic insect, the larva of which is the popular hell-grammite bait

Doll Fly trademark for a brand of chenille-bodied, hackle-wrapped jig

doodlesocking method of cane-pole or long-pole fishing that involves repeatedly dipping and dragging a lure or bait through likely fish struc-tures; used in largemouth bass and crappie fishing; effective when fish are holding tight to cover

dorsal fin the median fin located along the back of a fish; usually sup-ported by rays, which sometimes give the fin a fan- or sail-like appearance; may be two or more

doughball a ball of bait made from bread or specially prepared dough used for bait-fishing; commonly used for carp

drag device on fishing reels allowing the line to pay out under pressure, even though the reel is engaged, ensuring against line breakage when set correctly

drawdown lowering a lake's water level for a specific purpose

drift boating, drift fishing techniques used to fish by drifting with the current, sometimes in a drift boat

drop-off a sudden increase in depth, often created by washes, small creek channels, canyons, pinnacles, and other submerged topographic features

drop shot tackle rigging technique employing a hook tied to the line from 4 inches to 4 feet above the sinker; hook is attached using a Palomar knot with the weight attached to the tag line from the knot then set at a 90-degree angle to the line, typically with the hook point pointing upward toward the pole; typical drop shot-baits are small, usually 4 inches or less

dry fly a fly that floats on the surface of the water by means of hackle (feather) fibers; anglers employing this technique are said to be dry-fly fishing

earthworm common term for any of the many different fishing worms, including night crawlers, garden worms, leaf worms, dillys, and red wigglers

edge border created by a change in the structure or vegetation in a lake, such as edges of tree lines, weed lines, and edges of a drop-off

egg sinker an egg-shaped fishing weight with a hole through the center for the line to pass through

electro-fishing, electro-fish, electro-shocking describing the use of electrical current to temporarily stun fish, typically during fish surveys

eutrophic highly fertile waters characterized by warm, nutrient-rich, shallow basins

eyelets line guides or rings on a fishing rod through which the line is passed

false casting fly-casting line in the air — not touching the water — increasing the length of line and perfecting accuracy to the target

fan casting making a series of casts only a few degrees apart to cover a half circle, more or less; often used to locate actively feeding fish

feeding times certain times of day when fish are most active; often associated with the position of the sun and moon, called solunar tables

filamentous algae a type of algae characterized by long chains of attached cells, giving it a stringy feel and appearance

fillet a method of using a sharp knife to separate the meaty portion of the fish from the bones and skeleton and/or skin for human consumption

finesse fishing angling technique characterized by the use of light tackle — line, rods, reels, and artificial baits; often productive in clear, fairly uncluttered water, like many Western impoundments

fingerling a young fish about a finger long; usually 2 inches or so in length

fishery a lake, river, or stream where people can catch fish, or a particular kind of fish, such as a bass or trout fishery

fishhook a barbed or barbless hook used for catching fish; numerals are used to indicate hook sizes — No. 2, No. 4, etc.

flat a shallow section of water where game fish feed or spawn

flipping method of fishing in which the lure is swung, not cast, to the target or structure, often with as little disturbance of the water as possible; often used for placing baits strategically in thick cover, such as bushes, trees, and stick-ups

flipping stick heavy-action fishing rod; usually a bait-casting rod and reel; 7 to 8 feet long; designed for bass fishing using flipping and/or pitching techniques

floating or float fishing to traverse a river, stream, or lake by some type of watercraft while fishing, most commonly in a tube, raft, canoe, or kayak

float tube special fishing tube in which an inner tube is covered by a casing fitted with a seat to allow an angler to float freely

Florida rig very similar to the Texas rig, except the weight is secured by screwing it into the bait

flutterbait any type of bait that is cast and then allowed to flutter down, resembling a dying bait fish; typically used in bass fishing

fly a natural insect used as food for fish or an imitation of a natural insect used by fly anglers

fly-casting method for a fly angler to cast flies to fish or to spots likely holding fish

fly line line specifically designed to be used with fly-fishing tackle and a fly rod, the act of which is called fly-rodding

forage small baitfish, crayfish, and other creatures that bass or other predator fish eat; also, bass actively looking for food — foraging

Ford Fender a lure with two spinning blades on a leader to attract trout. It was originally fashioned from the reflector from a Model A Ford

foul-hook to hook a fish other than in the mouth, where it should take a bait or lure

free spool reel that allows line to feed freely to the fish or current; method of feeding line without drag or resistance to fish or current

freshwater bodies of water that do not have salt

front weather system causing changes in temperature, cloud cover, precipitation, wind, and barometric pressure

fry immature fish, from the time they hatch to the time they become fingerlings

Gamakatsu brand name of hooks

game fish species of fish caught for sport that fight hard when hooked; including trout of all species, bass of all species, catfish of all species, sunfish of all species, and northern pike, walleye, and yellow perch in Arizona; legal game fish defined in statute; more fish sought for sport than are listed as game fish

gear any tools used to catch fish, such as rod and reel, hook and line, nets, traps, spears, and baits

Gila trout one of Arizona's two native trout species; had been extirpated (eliminated) from Arizona; reintroduced in the mid 1990s; listed as federally endangered under the Endangered Species Act

gill respiratory organ of many aquatic animals, such as fish

gill net commercial (not sport-fishing) net used to harvest fish; named because of the mesh sizes designed to catch the intended species by the gill; commonly used by biologists conducting fish surveys

gill opening opening behind the head that connects the gill chamber to the exterior

Gizit original brand name of tube bait

grayline on a fishfinder, distinguishes between strong and weak echoes;

soft, muddy or weedy bottom returns a weaker symbol, shown with a narrow or no gray line; hard bottom returns a strong signal, causing a wide and dark grayline

grayling northern species of freshwater game fish; member of the trout family; typically found at Lee Valley Lake in the White Mountains in Arizona

grub a short, plastic type of worm, usually rigged with a weighted jig hook

habitat the natural environment where people, animals, and plants live; including water, topography, structure, and cover present in a lake in an aquatic environment

handline a fishing line used without a rod or reel; a line held in the hand

hard bottom a type of bottom that sinks minimally with pressure; consists of clay, gravel, rock, or sand

hawg a slang term describing a large lunker-size or heavyweight bass weighing 4 pounds or more

hellgramite larvae of the dobsonfly, used as bait

holding area a structure habitually attracting and holding bass

holding station place on a lake where inactive fish spend most of their time

honey hole a slang term describing a specific hole, spot, or area containing big fish or many catchable fish

Hopkins spoons brand name of spoon with a hammered appearance

hump an underwater island rising gradually; often holding fish

hydrology the science concerning the distribution, properties, and circulation of water on land, in the soil, and in the atmosphere

ichthyology the science or study of fish

IGFA International Game Fish Association

impoundment artificially created lake where water is collected and stored; also called a reservoir

inactive fish fish that are not in a feeding mood; sometimes referred to as having lockjaw; often occurring following a cold front or during a major weather change causing a sudden rise or fall in the barometer

in-line spinner a spinner with the hook on the same shaft or line, such as a Mepps, Rooster Tail, Panther Martin, or Vibrex spinner

inside bend the inside line of a grass bed or a creek channel

isolated structure a possible holding spot for fish, especially bass, including a single submerged bush or rock pile on a point, a mid-lake hump, or a large tree that has fallen into the water

jerkbait a type of soft plastic or hard plastic bait resembling a baitfish; typically fished in a series of quick jerks or ripped, resembling a darting baitfish

jig a hook with a leadhead; usually dressed with hair, silicone, plastic, or bait

jig-and-pig, jig-n-pig combination of a leadhead jig fitted with a pork trailer; popular for flipping and pitching fish-holding structures, such as submerged bushes and trees

jig fishing using a jig to catch fish

jigging spoon a spoon that is typically jigged or bounced off the bottom with a slight up-and-down motion of the rod or rod tip, resembling a dying shad or other baitfish

johnboat a small flat-bottomed, square-fronted, shallow-draft boat popular with duck hunters and anglers

Kastmaster brand name of a spoon

keeper a fish that is worth taking home to eat or fish of specified lengths that are legal to harvest in lakes with special regulations, including fisheries with slot limits

lake bed the bottom of a lake

lake zones designation including four categories: shallow water, open water, deep water, and basin

largemouth bass member of the black bass family with a green-shaded body, continuous dark stripe along each side, white to yellowish belly, dorsal fin almost completely separated between spiny and soft portion, and lower jaw extending past the gold-colored eye; also called a bucketmouth or bigmouth bass

larva subsurface stage of development of an aquatic insect

leadhead a jig where lead is molded to the hook shaft

ledge a severe drop-off; commonly found in Arizona's deep canyon lakes, including Canyon Lake, Lake Powell, Lake Mead, Blue Ridge Reservoir, and Chevelon Lake

Light Cahill a dry-fly pattern

light intensity the amount of light measurable at certain depths of water, with light projecting farther at greater intensities; recommend use of brightly colored lures in waters with low light intensity

limit-out to catch the daily limit legally allowed for a species of fish

line guides eyelets or rings on a rod through which fishing line is passed

lipless crankbaits artificial baits resembling swimming baitfish that typically vibrate or wobble during the retrieve; some have built-in rattles; typically sink when they are not being retrieved, allowing anglers to fish them deeper than lipped crankbaits; also called swimming baits

lipping method of landing fish, especially bass, by placing a thumb into its mouth to bend the lip down slightly, temporarily paralyzing the fish to get it into the boat or unhook and release it

live baitfish any species of live fish designated by Arizona Game and Fish Commission order as lawful for use in taking aquatic organisms; the act of using live bait is called live-bait fishing

livebox a box or container to designed to keep bait or caught fish alive

livewell compartment in a boat designed to hold water and keep fish alive; typically contains some device for recirculating water

long-lining trolling a bait or lure a long distance behind a boat

loose-action plug a lure with wide, slow movements from side to side; recommended when fish are sluggish in colder water, such as during winter or early spring

lunker a slang term for a very large fish; also called a hawg

marabou jig a weighted jig with light, fluffy feathers attached to the body

marker buoy a small plastic buoy, often fluorescent colored, tossed into the water to mark a fish holding area or a school of fish; popular for schooling sport fish in open water, including crappie, white bass, or striped bass

match the hatch using a fly or lure to mimic the insect that a particular fish is feeding on

mayfly a small aquatic fly; important food for trout

mealworms small beetle larvae often used for catching crappies or sunfish

Mepps spinner a brand name of in-line spinner

mesotrophic lake classification describing middle-aged bodies of water between oligotrophic (young) and eutrophic (old) classifications; body of water with a moderate amount of dissolved nutrients

migration route a path followed by bass or other fish when moving from one area to another

milfoil surface-growing aquatic plants

minijig a small leadhead jig, usually 1/16- or 1/32-ounce; often used for catching crappie or sunfish

mono short for monofilament fishing line

monofilament a single, untwisted, synthetic-filament fishing line

moon times the four phases or quarters of the moon, with bad moon times occurring three days prior and three days after the full moon or new moon and good moon times occurring in the first-quarter and second-quarter periods

nares nostrils of fish

nest spot where fish, such as largemouth bass or bluegill, deposit eggs; with largemouth bass, nests are well defined and females lay eggs while males guard eggs

night crawler a common type of worm used in fishing

night fishing fishing at night

nymph nymphal state of an aquatic insect or imitation for nymph fishing

off-color the color and/or clarity of the water, with normal off-color conditions including brown or mud-stained from runoff, green from algae or algae blooms, and brown from tannic acid

oligotrophic lake classification used to describe young bodies of water; characterized by deep, clear, cold, weedless water supporting fish, such as trout

open-faced reel a typical or standard spinning reel, with the line coming off the fixed spool in loops and no nose cone

organic baits minnows, insects, worms, fish eggs, cut bait, cheese, or similar substances

otolith the ear bone of a fish; can determine age of fish by counting the layers in the otolith, much like the rings of a tree

outside bend the outside line of a creek channel or grass bed; outside line of a submerged wash or arroyo in underwater structures

overcast to cast a lure, fly, or bait beyond the intended target

overfishing fishing pressure beyond which a sustainable population of fish or stocking effort can be maintained

oxbow U-shaped bend in a river or stream; referred to as an oxbow lake when isolated

pan fish any of a variety of species of fish resembling the shape of a frying pan, including sunfish, crappie, perch, and other small fish

Panther Martin brand name of in-line spinner

parr, parr marks small juvenile of the trout or salmon family are characterized by parr marks: pronounced, wide, vertical bars on the sides of the fish until maturity

pattern describing where active fish are holding or what techniques are working to catch fish, especially larger fish; involving use of shallow-running crankbaits on all the major points of a lake or Carolina-rigged worms on all main lake humps

peacock lady a fly used by fly anglers

pectoral fin the fin usually found on each side of the fish body, behind the gill opening

pegging placement of a toothpick in the hole of a bullet or egg sinker to prevent the sinker from sliding along the line; typically done with Texas-rigged bait or other items, including rubber bands slipped through the sinker

pelvic fins pair of juxtaposed fins ventrally on the fish body in front of the anus

Pencil Popper brand name for a topwater lure; long and thin; often used for catching striped bass

PFD personal flotation device or life jacket

pH measurement for liquids to determine acidity or alkalinity; on a scale of 1 to 14, with 7 as neutral, below 7 as acidic, and above 7 as alkaline; factor in the health or activity levels of fish

pick-up the act of a bass or other fish taking a slowly fished lure, such as a plastic worm, crayfish, or lizard; also called a pressure bite

pike common reference to northern pike, a member of the pike family

pitching fishing technique in which worms or jigs are dropped into cover at close range with an underhand pendulum motion using a long bait-casting rod; differs from flipping, as line comes out of the reel during the cast

pocket a small indentation in the shoreline; sometimes referred to as a pocket cove

point a finger of land jutting into the water; can form a peninsula if pronounced; can be submerged and invisible at the surface but detectable in depth finders; often holds fish; good ambush spot for predatory fish

popper topwater plug with a dished-out head designed to make a splash when pulled sharply, imitating a wounded baitfish struggling on the surface

Pop-R brand of popper topwater lure

possession limit the maximum limit or amount of a fish species set by regulation that may be possessed at one time by any one person

post-front period following a cold front characterized by bright, clear atmosphere, strong winds, and a significant drop in temperature; fishing slows during such conditions, especially for bass

post-spawn period immediately following a spawn; recovering, post-spawn fish are often lethargic, becoming hungry and aggressive following recovery

Power Bait, Power Craw, Power Eggs, Power Grubs, Power Worms brand names of commercially prepared scented baits

presentation collective term referring to a combination of choices an angler makes, such as the choice of lure, color, and size; the type of pole and/or tackle used; the structure targeted; the casting technique; the retrieval technique (slow, medium, fast, stop-and-go); and where the bait is worked in the water column (deep, shallow, topwater)

prespawn period of time immediately before the spawn when fish are often feeding more aggressively

pro professional angler; elite angler who makes a living at fishing, typically by fishing tournaments

professional overrun polite term for backlash; also called spaghetti

put-and-take fishery stocking catchable fish, such as trout; caught by anglers in a relatively short period of time; including state's Urban Fishing Program lakes

put-in boat-launching area for the start of a float trip

rainbow trout member of the salmon/trout family; not native to Arizona

ramp launch-retrieve area for a boat; also called a boat ramp or launch ramp

Rapala brand of lure

Rat-L-Trap brand of lipless crankbait

redd individual nest or depression in the gravel excavated by trout and salmon for depositing eggs, with multiple redds making up a bed

reservoir artificially created lake where water is collected and stored; also called an impoundment

restocking the practice of releasing hatchery-reared fish into ponds, streams, rivers, or lakes

riprap man-made stretch of rocks or material of a hard composition; usually extending above and below the shoreline; often found near dams or big impoundments

rollcast type of fly-casting technique in which the line is not cast above the water, but instead rolled over with the line lying on the water

Rooster Tail brand of in-line spinner

saddle thin piece of land extending out from the shoreline and connecting to an island (sometimes underwater), reef, or hump; submerged saddles hold many fish

salmon eggs type of egg bait typically used for trout fishing

San Juan worm type of wet fly designed to look like a small aquatic worm; popularized on the San Juan River in New Mexico; used at Lees Ferry, the Lower Salt River, and other riverine trout fisheries

Sassy Shad brand of soft plastic lure resembling a shad

seine net a rectangular fishing net designed to hang vertically in the water, with the ends drawn together to encircle fish

selective harvest deciding to release or keep fish based on species, size, relative abundance, or culinary plans

shad any of several species of forage fish that have a rather deep body; threadfin shad is most common in Arizona

Shad Rap brand name of crankbait

shiner a small fish often used for bait; gold shiner is most common in Arizona

shoal submerged ridge, bank, or bar

shore fishing fishing from the shore, as opposed to fishing from a boat or wading

short strike occurring when a fish hits at a lure and misses it

sight casting, sight fishing technique of casting and fishing when the fish are spotted first

size limit legal length a fish must be if in possession (kept); slot limits enforced in some fisheries, limiting possession of fish in specified slot size range

skipping method of casting small lures hard and at a low angle to the water, making them skip like a flat stone

slack line loose line from the tip of the rod to the lure; can be a slight bow in the line to an excess of line lying on the water; the opposite is fishing with a tight line, including using a drop-shot outfit

slip float float rigged with a tin stop or bead on the line to make it stop at a predetermined depth

slip sinker lead, zinc, or steel weight with a hole through the center allowing it to freely slide up and down the fishing line, providing the weight for casting, yet allowing the bait to move freely

slot fishing size limit allowing the angler to keep fish shorter than a minimum length but longer than an upper length limit; must by regulation practice catch-and-release on the fish in the slot; special regulations used on specific bodies of water

slough long, narrow stretch of water, such as a small stream or feeder tributary off a lake or river

slow roll spinnerbait presentation in which the lure is retrieved slowly through and over cover and objects, with trailer bait often on the hook

Slug-Go brand of soft plastic jerkbait

slush bait a topwater plug with a flat or pointed head

smallmouth bass black bass, primarily bronze in color, whose jaw does not extend beyond the eye; found in clear rivers and lakes; also called bronzebacks, brown bass, river bass, or smallies

snagging a method of catching fish by jerking an unbaited hook through the water; illegal except for carp in Arizona

soft bottom river or lake bottoms composed of soft material, such as silt, mud, or muck

sonar acronym derived from the expression "sound navigation and ranging"; referring to the method or equipment for determining, using underwater sound techniques, the presence, location, or nature of objects in the water; used by fishfinders

spider jig a type of leadhead jig with a skirt, much like the one on a spinnerbait

spider trolling trolling with several rods at once

spincaster a push-button, closed-faced spinning reel or baitcasting rod, with the reel mounted topside on the rod

spin-casting using a fixed spool enclosed in a nose cone so the line leaving the reel's nose cone comes out straight; also called American spinning or closed-face spinning

spinnerbait an artificial bait consisting of a leadhead and one or two rotating blades with a straight or a safety-pin-style shaft dressed with material, often called a skirt

spinning a manner of fishing employing an open-face or closed-face spinning reel and spinning rod, with the reel and rod guides mounted on the underside of the rod

spinning reel a fixed-spool reel, generally referring to open-face spinning

split shot, split-shotting a style of finesse fishing employing a split shot weight up the line, typically 6 to 18 inches above a small artificial worm, lizard, crawfish, or grub; usually rigged Texas-style, with the hook concealed in the bait

spook alarming a fish by making too much noise or movement, or casting a shadow

spoon a spoon-shaped metal or hard plastic lure that wobbles to attract fish

stained discoloration of water; usually occurring due to heavy rain, significant runoff, or shoreline erosion from wind and rain action; bass hide and feed in bands of discoloration

starboard the right side of a boat or ship

stick bait a slender plug or topwater lure; activated by the angler manipulating the rod and reel; the back-and-forth motion of the bait, resembling a wounded shad, is referred to as "walking the dog"

stick-ups tips of trees and brush sticking up from the water and providing structure, primarily for bass fishing

still fishing fishing from one spot; primarily referring to shore fishing from a single location

stinger hook an additional hook placed on a lure, spinnerbait, or bait rig; also called a trailer hook

stink bait bait, such as chicken liver, releasing odor into the water; typically for catfishing

stocking the practice of releasing hatchery-raised fish into ponds, reservoirs, streams, or rivers; often necessary in waters where fishing pressure exceeds natural fish reproductive capabilities

stragglers bass that remain behind following a general migration

strain a group of related individuals created through selective breeding;

genetically different from other strains of the same species

striped bass member of the true bass family, along with white bass and yellow bass; in Arizona, found in the Colorado River chain of lakes, including Powell, Mead, Mohave, and Havasu, as well as in Lake Pleasant

structure changes in the shape of the bottom of lakes, rivers, or impoundments, especially those influencing fish behavior; including flooded roadbeds, washes, arroyos, humps, ledges, and drop-offs

sub-catchable for trout in the AZGFD stocking program, this refers to 4- to 6-inch fish

sunfish any of dozens of members of the sunfish family, including large-mouth bass, bluegill, redear, and crappie

Super Duper brand of lure typically used for trout fishing; can be cast but is often trolled

suspended fish fish at mid-level depths

swim bladder gas-filled sac found in the upper part of the body cavity of many bony fish

swimming lures sinking-type artificial baits designed to resemble a swimming baitfish; can vibrate or wobble during retrieve; some have built-in rattles; also called lipless crankbaits

tagging marking or attaching a tag to an individual or group of fish for identification on recapture; used by biologists to study the movement, migration, population size, or activity patterns of fish

tail spinners compact, lead-bodied lures with one or two spinner blades attached to the tail and a treble hook suspending from the body

take-out the point where boats are taken out of the water at the end of a float trip

terminal tackle angling equipment, excluding artificial baits, attached to the end of a fishing line; including hooks, snaps, swivels, snap-swivels, sinkers, floats, and plastic beads

Texas rigging the method of securing a hook to a soft plastic bait, such as a worm, lizard, or crawfish, to make the hook weedless (non-protruding); slip sinker — often a bullet sinker — threaded onto the line; hook — often an offset hook — tied to the end of the fish line, inserted into the head of the soft plastic bait about one-quarter of an inch, brought through until eye is embedded in bait, then rotated and embedded slightly into the body of the soft plastic worm without coming out the opposite side; it's important to ensure the bait stays straight when Texas-rigged

thermocline a distinct layer of water where rising warm and sinking cold water meet but do not mix, with temperature changes at least one-half a degree per foot of depth; often developing in spring and breaking down in fall in desert bass lakes; colder layer of water often lacking in oxygen, forcing most baitfish and sport fish to upper layer of water; dense and appearing on sonar as a thick, impenetrable line

threadfin shad most common baitfish in Arizona's warm-water lakes

tight-action plug a lure with short, rapid side-to-side movement; typically used when fish are more active in spring, summer, and fall

tiptop line guide at the tip end of a fishing rod

topwater the technique of using topwater lures for catching fish, especially bass, at the water's surface; topwater lures refer to floating hard baits or plugs creating a degree of surface disturbance during the retrieve, typically mimicking struggling or wounded baitfish on the surface

trailer hook extra hook or cheater hook added to a single-hook lure, including a spinnerbait or weedless spoon; also called a stinger hook

transducer a device converting electrical energy to sound energy, or the reverse; typically associated with depth finders or fishfinders

transition occurring when one type of bottom material or structure changes to another, such as a rock pile to solid rock or sand to gravel; fish are typically located in transition zones, such as mud lines where a river enters a lake

treble hook hook with a single or bundled shaft and three points

triggering using a lure-retrieval technique causing a sport fish to react and strike, such as quickly speeding up a retrieve and then stopping; also referred to as causing a reaction bite

trolling towing a lure or several lures behind a boat; catching a fish on the trolled lure typically stops the boat and fish is reeled in

trolling motor a small electric fishing motor, typically mounted on the bow, used as secondary means of propulsion for positioning or maneuvering a boat quietly in fishing areas

tubing floating down a river or stream or using a float tube in a lake while fishing

turnover occurs in fall in Arizona's warm-water lakes; associated with thermoclines, with the warmer layer of surface water cooling down and becoming colder than or as cold as the distinct layer of cold water below, resulting in the mixing of the two layers of water, the elimination of thermocline, the creation of a fairly uniform water temperature, and perhaps introduction of oxygen to the lower levels of the lake; possibly resulting in stirring of bottom sediments and nutrients due to water movement, sometimes stimulating algal growth; signaling the transition to winter fishing conditions

ultralight lighter than standard fishing rod and/or tackle

ventral fin the paired fin located on the front of a fish's abdomen

Vibrex brand name of in-line spinner

warm-water fish habitat or fish that are warm-water species, such as largemouth bass, sunfish, and catfish, as opposed to cold-water species such as trout, grayling, and salmon, or cool-water species such as northern pike and walleye

water column vertical section of the lake

water dog any of several large salamanders in the larval or aquatic stage; popular as live bait

weedguard a protective device on fishing hooks to prevent picking up weeds

weedless a lure designed to be fished in heavy cover with a minimum amount of snagging

weed line abrupt edge of an aquatic weed bed caused by a change in depth, bottom type, or other factor

weigh-in weighing of fish caught at a tournament

Westy Worm brand name of plastic worm with a leadhead and two exposed hooks already rigged

wet fly a fly that is fished underwater

white bass type of true bass; only found at Lake Pleasant in Arizona; related to striped bass and yellow bass; not native to Arizona

wooly worm, wooly bugger popular type of wet fly often used by fly anglers fishing lakes

worm fishing using worms, either natural or man-made, to catch fish; typically referring to the use of artificial worms

year class fish of a given species all spawned in the same year or at the same time

yellow bass specific species in the true bass family; in Arizona, found in Apache, Canyon, and Saguaro lakes along the Salt River

yellow cat flathead catfish

young of the year fish in their first year of life; often referring to immature fish

Zara Puppy, Zara Spook, Zara Pooch brand names of topwater lures

zooplankton animals — mostly microscopic — drifting freely in the water column

Z-Ray brand name of heavy spoon typically used in trout fishing

Zug Bug a type of wet fly or fly pattern commonly used by fly fishers in lakes

Arizona Game and Fish Department Contact Information

Main Office
5000 W. Carefree Highway
Phoenix, AZ 85086
602-942-3000
www.azgfd.gov

Regional Offices

Region I
2878 E. White Mountain Blvd.
Pinetop, AZ 85935
928-367-4281

Region II
3500 S. Lake Mary Road
Flagstaff, AZ 86001
928-774-5045

Region III
5325 N. Stockton Hill Road
Kingman, AZ 86409
928-692-7700

Region IV
9140 E. 28th St.
Yuma, AZ 85365
928-342-0091

Region V
555 N. Greasewood Road
Tucson, AZ 85745
520-628-5376

Region VI
7200 E. University Drive
Mesa, AZ 85207
480-981-9400

To Report a Game or Fish Violation: 800-352-0700
To Report Vandalism or Livestock Depredation: 800-VANDALS (826-3257)

Other Fishing Resources

- Anglers' Legacy (includes how-to information): www.takemefishing.org/fishing/overview
- Apache Lake Marina: 928-467-2511 or www.apachelake.com
- AZ Bass Zone (fishing reports and discussion forums): www.azbasszone.com
- Bartlett Lake Marina: 602-316-3378, www.bartlettlake.com, or e-mail info@barlettlake.com
- Big Lake Marina and Store (not open in winter): 928-521-1387, www.biglakeaz.com, or e-mail biglakeaz@hotmail.com
- Camping information: www.camparizona.com or www.fishinaz.com
- Canyon Lake Marina: 480-288-9233, www.canyonlakemarina.com, or e-mail info@canyonlakemarina.com
- Colorado River Lakes: www.riverlakes.com

- Lake Havasu Marina: www.havasumagazine.com/marina.htm
- Lake Mead National Recreation Area: www.nps.gov/lame
- Lake Pleasant Harbor: www.azmarinas.com/PleasantHarbor/
- Lake Pleasant Regional Park: www.maricopa.gov/parks/lake_pleasant/
- Lake Pleasant Scorpion Bay Marina: www.scorpionbaymarina.com
- Lake Powell and Lees Ferry, Glen Canyon National Recreation Area: www.nps.gov/glca/
- Lees Ferry Fishing Report: www.leesferry.com
- Martinez Lake: 800-876-7004, www.martinezlake.com, or e-mail info@martinezlake.com
- Powell Fishing Report: www.wayneswords.com
- Public Lands Information Center: www.publiclands.org
- Roosevelt Lake Marina: 928-467-2245 or www.rlmaz.com
- Saguaro Lake Marina: 480-986-5546 or www.saguarolakemarina.com
- Willow Beach Marina: 928-767-4747 or www.willowbeachharbor.com

Other Fishing Websites
- www.azflyandtie.com
- www.flytyingforum.com
- www.gameandfishguides.com
- www.midcurrent.com
- www.theweeklyfly.com

National Forests Contact Information
Apache-Sitgreaves National Forests
www.fs.fed.us/r3/asnf
Supervisor's Office, Springerville: 928-339-4301
- Alpine Ranger District: 928-339-5000
- Black Mesa Ranger District, Heber-Overgaard: 928-535-7300
- Clifton Ranger District, Duncan: 928-687-8600
- Lakeside Ranger District: 928-368-2100
- Springerville Ranger District: 928-333-4372

RESOURCES

Coconino National Forest
www.fs.fed.us/r3/coconino
Supervisor's Office, Flagstaff: 928-527-3600
- Peaks Ranger District, Flagstaff: 928-526-0866
- Red Rock Ranger District, Sedona: 928-203-7500

Mogollon Rim Ranger District Offices
- Blue Ridge Office, Happy Jack: 928-477-2255

Coronado National Forest
www.fs.fed.us/r3/coronado
Supervisor's Office, Tucson: 520-388-8300
- Douglas Ranger District: 520-364-3468
- Nogales Ranger District: 520-281-2296
- Safford Ranger District: 520-428-4150
- Santa Catalina Ranger District: 520-749-8700
- Sierra Vista Ranger District: 520-378-0311

Kaibab National Forest
www.fs.fed.us/r3/kai
Supervisor's Office, Williams: 928-635-8200
- North Kaibab Ranger District, Fredonia: 928-643-7395
- Tusayan Ranger District, Grand Canyon: 928-635-5600
- Williams Ranger District: 928-635-8200

Prescott National Forest
www.fs.fed.us/r3/prescott
Supervisor's Office, Prescott: 928-443-8000
- Bradshaw Ranger District, Prescott: 928-443-8000
- Chino Valley Ranger District: 928-777-2200
- Verde Ranger District, Camp Verde: 928-567-4121

Tonto National Forest
www.fs.fed.us/r3/tonto/home.shtml
Supervisor's Office, Phoenix: 602-225-5200
- Cave Creek Ranger District, Scottsdale: 480-595-3300
- Globe Ranger District: 928-402-6200
- Mesa Ranger District: 480-610-3300
- Payson Ranger District: 928-474-7900
- Pleasant Valley Ranger District, Young: 928-462-4300

Parks, Recreation Areas, and Other Contact Information

- Alamo Lake State Park: 928-669-2088 or www.azstateparks.com
- Arizona State Parks State Office: 602-542-4174 or www.azstateparks.com
- Bill Williams River National Wildlife Refuge: 928-667-4144 or www.fws.gov/southwest/refuges/arizona/billwill
- Buckskin Mountain State Park: 928-667-3231 or www.azstateparks.com
- Cattail Cove State Park: 928-855-1223 or www.azstateparks.com
- Dead Horse Ranch State Park: 928-634-5283 or www.azstateparks.com
- Fool Hollow Lake Recreation Area: 928-537-3680 or www.azstateparks.com
- Havasu National Wildlife Refuge: 760-326-3853 or www.fws.gov/southwest/refuges/arizona/havasu
- Imperial National Wildlife Refuge: 928-783-3371 or www.fws.gov/southwest/refuges/arizona/imperial
- Lake Havasu State Park: 928-855-2784 or www.azstateparks.com
- Lake Mead National Recreation Area (Lake Mead, Willow Beach, and Lake Mohave): 702-293-8906 or www.nps.gov/lame
- Lake Pleasant Regional Park (Maricopa County) Contact Station: 928-501-1710, www.maricopa.gov/parks/lake_pleasant, or e-mail lakepleasant@mail.maricopa.gov
- Lyman Lake State Park: 928-337-4441 or www.azstateparks.com
- Patagonia Lake State Park: 520-287-6965 or www.azstateparks.com
- Powell, Glen Canyon National Recreation Area (Lake Powell): 928-608-6200 or www.nps.gov/glca
- Red Rock State Park: 928-282-6907 or www.azstateparks.com
- Roper Lake State Park: 928-428-6760 or www.azstateparks.com
- San Carlos Apache Recreation and Wildlife Department: 928-475-2361 or www.sancarlosapache.com/San_Carlos_Game_and_Fish
- Slide Rock State Park: 928-282-3034 or www.azstateparks.com
- U.S. Bureau of Land Management State Office: 602-417-9200 or www.az.blm.gov
- White Mountain Apache Tribe Wildlife and Outdoor Division: 928-338-4385; White Mountain Apache Hon-Dah Ski and Outdoor Sport Shop: 928-369-7669, www.wmatoutdoors.org, or e-mail gamefish@wmat.us
- Willow Beach National Fish Hatchery: 928-767-3456 or www.fws.gov/southwest/fisheries/willowbeach.html
- Fire restrictions and/or closures on state and federal lands in Arizona or New Mexico: 877-864-6985 or www.gacc.nifc.gov/swcc
- Road conditions on highways in Arizona: 888-411-7623 or www.az511.com

INDEX

A

A-1 Lake 252
Alamo Lake 226, 227
Alvord Lake (Phoenix) 280
Antelope Point Marina 170
Apache Lake 136-139
Arivaca Lake 232, 233
Ashurst Lake 56, 57

B

Backwater No. 33 (Colorado River) 223
Bartlett Lake 152-155
Bear Canyon Lake 94, 95
Beaver Creek 74, 75
Becker Lake 12, 13
Below Davis Dam (Casino Row and Beyond) 192-195
Big Bear Lake (*Shush Be Tou*) 253
Big Bend State Recreation Area 195
Big Lake 14-17
Black Canyon Lake 96, 97
Black River (on the San Carlos Apache Indian Reservation) 269
Black River, East Fork 47, 48
Black River, West Fork 48, 49
Bog Tank 254
Bootleg Tank 254
Boulder Basin 177, 178
Buckskin Mountain State Park 210
Buffalo Crossing 47, 49
Bullfrog Marina 162, 169, 171
Bunch Reservoir 26, 29

C

C.C. Cragin Reservoir 98, 99
Canyon Creek 109, 110
Canyon Lake 140-142
Carnero Lake 18, 19
Cataract Lake 64, 65
Cattail Cove State Park 203
Chaparral Lake (Scottsdale) 284, 285
Chevelon Canyon Lake 100, 101
Christmas Tree Lake 254
Christopher Creek 111, 112
Cibola National Wildlife Refuge 213

Colorado River
    below Davis Dam 192-195
    between Laguna Dam and Morelos Dam 222, 223
    between Palo Verde Diversion Dam and Walter's Camp 211-213
    between Picacho State Recreation Area and Imperial Dam 216-219
    between Walter's Camp and Picacho State Park 214, 215
    Backwater No. 33 223
    Fisherman's Access 195
Concho Lake 20
Cooley Lake 255
Cortez Lake (Phoenix) 281
Cottonwood Cove 191
Cow Springs Lake 272
Crescent Lake 21, 22
Cyclone Lake 255

D

Dangling Rope Marina 171
Davis Camp, Colorado River 195
Dead Horse Ranch State Park 76, 77
Desert Breeze Park (Chandler) 282
Desert West Park (Phoenix) 282, 283
Diamond Creek 255
Dogtown Reservoir 66, 67
Drift Fence Lake 256

E

Earl Park Lake 256
East Verde River 119
Elk Tank 68, 69
Encanto Lake (Phoenix) 281, 282
Evelyn Hallman Lake (Tempe) 285

F

Fain Lake 86
Fisher's Landing 218, 219
Fisherman's Access, Colorado River 195
Fool Hollow Lake 23, 24
Fortuna Pond 224
Fossil Creek 77-79

G

Ganado *(Lók aahnteel)* Lake 272, 273
Gila River Confluence (Colorado River) 223
Goldwater Lake 87, 88
Green Valley Lakes (Payson) 295
Greer Lakes Recreation Area 25-29
Gregg Basin 179, 183

H

Haigler Creek 113, 114
Halls Crossing Marina 170, 171
Hawley Lake 257
Hidden Shores 219
Hite 171
Horseshoe Cienega Lake 257
Horseshoe Lake 152-155
Horton Creek 115
Hurricane Lake 258

J

JD Dam Lake 68, 69

K

Kaibab Lake 70, 71
Katherine's Landing 191
Kennedy Lake (Tucson) 291, 292
Kinnikinick Lake 60, 61
Kiwanis Lake (Tempe) 285, 286
Knoll Lake 102, 103
knot-tying 307

L

La Paz County Park 210
Lake Havasu 198-203
Lake Havasu Springs Resort (Chemehuevi Indian Tribe) 203
Lake Mary, upper and lower 58, 59
Lake Mead 177-183
Lake Mohave 188-191
Lake Pleasant 124-129
Lake Powell 161-171
Lakeside Lake (Tucson) 293, 294
Laughlin Bay 195
Lee Valley Lake 30, 31
Lees Ferry 172-176

Little Bear Lake (*Shush Be Zahze*) 258
Little Colorado River 28, 29
  West Fork 45, 46
Long Lake 62, 63
Lower Lake Mary 58, 59
Lower Salt River 146-148
Luna Lake 32, 33
Lyman Lake 34, 35
Lynx Lake 89

M

Many Farms (*Dá ák eh Halání*) Lake 275
Martinez Lake 218
Mayflower County Park 213
McIntyre Park 213
Meer's Point 219
Middle Tank 68, 69
Mittry Lake 220, 221
Mode II 222
Morelos Dredge Launch 222

N

Nelson Reservoir 36, 37

O

Oak Creek 80, 81
Overton Arm, Lake Mead 181-183

P

Pacheta Lake 258, 259
Palo Verde Park 213
Papago Park Ponds (Phoenix) 283
Parker Canyon Lake 238, 239
Parker Strip 208-210
Patagonia Lake 236, 237
Peña Blanca Lake 234, 235
Perkins Tank 68, 69
Picacho State Park 218
Picacho State Recreation Area 214-218
Point of Pines Lake 267, 268

R

Rainbow Lake 38, 39
Red Mountain Park (Mesa) 286
Redondo Pond 224
Reservation Lake 259
rigging, basic 305

Riggs Flat Lake 242, 243
Rio Vista Lake (Peoria) 289
River Island State Park 210
River Reservoir 28, 29
Riverview Park (Mesa) 287
Riviera Blythe Marina Park 213
Roosevelt Lake, *see* Theodore Roosevelt Lake
Roper Lake 240, 241
Rose Canyon Lake 244, 245

S

Saguaro Lake 143-145
Sahuarita Lake (Sahuarita) 294
Salt River (on the San Carlos Apache Indian Reservation) 269
Salt River, Lower 146-148
San Carlos Lake 265, 266
Scott Reservoir 40, 41
Seneca Lake 268, 269
Sheeps Crossing 45, 46
Show Low Lake 42, 43
Silverbell Lake (Tucson) 291
Silver Creek 50, 51
Silver Creek Hatchery 50, 51
Soldier Lake 63
sport fish, Arizona's 296-303
Squaw Lake Area 219
Steele Indian School Park (Phoenix) 287, 288
Sunrise Lake 260
Surprise Lake (Surprise) 288, 289

T

Talkalai Lake 267
Tempe Town Lake 149-151
Temple Basin, Lake Mead 183
Theodore Roosevelt Lake 130-135
Tonto Creek 116-118
Topock Marina 197
Topock Marsh 196, 197
Tsaile (*Tséhílí*) Lake 276
Tunnel Reservoir 28, 29

U

Upper Lake Mary 58, 59
Urban Fishing Program 278-295

V

Verde River (Verde Valley) 82, 83
Veterans Oasis Lake (Chandler) 289, 290

W

Wahweap Marina, Lake Powell 169, 170
Walter's Camp 215
Water Ranch Lake (Gilbert) 290
West Clear Creek 84, 85
Wheatfields Lake 276, 277
Whitehorse Lake 72, 73
Willow Beach 184-187
Willow Springs Lake 104, 105
Windsor Beach State Park, Lake Havasu 203
Woodland Lake 44
Woods Canyon Lake 106-108

Y

Yuma West Wetlands Park 223
Yuma West Wetlands Pond 224

SEE EYE TO EYE WITH WILDLIFE.

Subscribe to Arizona Wildlife Views magazine today!

WWW.AZGFD.GOV/MAGAZINE

800-777-0015

Arizona **Wildlife Views**

Arizona Game and Fish Department